PACIFIC ALTERNATIVES

First published in 2015
Paperback edition, 2017
Sean Kingston Publishing
www.seankingston.co.uk
Canon Pyon

British Library Cataloguing in Publication Data
A catalogue record for this book is available from the British Library.

The moral rights of the authors have been asserted.

Printed by Lightning Source

ISBN 978-1-907774-87-4

Pacific Alternatives

✴

Cultural politics in contemporary Oceania

Edited by Edvard Hviding and Geoffrey White

PSK
Publishing

Sean Kingston Publishing
www.seankingston.co.uk
Canon Pyon

Foreword

✳

TERENCE WESLEY-SMITH
Director of Pacific Islands Studies, University of Hawai'i at Mānoa

This volume is unusual in recent scholarship about the vast Pacific Islands region, often referred to as Oceania. The use of this term is appropriate here because of its association with one of the great regional visionaries of our times, the late Epeli Hau'ofa, whose body of work stood for local empowerment above all else. He spoke for ordinary grassroots islanders buffeted by powerful global forces for change, and had scant regard for grand economic and political schemes promising much but delivering little. He urged Pacific intellectuals to seize the initiative, to rehabilitate local values and epistemologies, to construct discourses of change that were genuinely of and for the people of Oceania. *Pacific Alternatives* reflects the guiding spirit of Hau'ofa's work largely because it gets beyond the deficiency discourse of much contemporary literature about the region to represent what island societies have rather than what they lack, and to emphasize local innovation over state weakness, failure or collapse.

These essays are among the products of an ambitious research and education initiative spearheaded by Professor Edvard Hviding and the Bergen Pacific Studies Research Group at the University of Bergen, Norway, in collaboration with researchers and public intellectuals from partner institutions in the Pacific Islands, Australia, Europe and the United States. The project owed its success to the vision and leadership of Professor Hviding, and relied heavily on a Bergen-Honolulu axis for additional energy and inspiration. Five key project participants and contributors to this volume are core or affiliate faculty members of the Center for Pacific Islands Studies, University of Hawai`i at Mānoa, and the centre hosted and co-sponsored the project's first major conference in 2009.

The Pacific Alternatives project had its genesis far away from Oceania in a panelled conference room in the Bergen University Museum in October 2006, where a small group of researchers explored complex entanglements between cultural heritage and political innovation, two major themes in Pacific Studies. What eventuated from this wintry gathering was a successful proposal to the Research Council of Norway for a four-year, collaborative research agenda centred on two main propositions: that cultural heritage represents a viable counterforce to the de-localizing challenges of globalization, and that studying the local intersection of cultural heritage and political innovation in Oceania would provide a useful foil to much state-centred academic discourse about development issues in the Global South.

The Pacific Alternatives project set out to privilege local initiatives and agendas rather than external ones, and to avoid the often teleological narratives of the nation-state framing much regional analysis. In addition to being, in effect, bottom up and inside out, this was to be an interdisciplinary alternative to the discipline-centred scholarly mainstream and, by focusing largely on Solomon Islands and Vanuatu, a counterbalance to an overemphasis in regional studies on Papua New Guinea and the island entities of Polynesia. The project brought together a diverse group of scholars who, in addition to their commitment to project goals, were positioned outside the consultancy culture increasingly prominent in Pacific research. In sharp contrast to other funding agencies, the Research Council of Norway imposed no national interest or other prerequisites, simply demanding high-calibre research in return for its generous support.

This is the second major publication to emerge from the Pacific Alternatives project. The first, *Made in Oceania: Social Movements, Cultural Heritage and the State in the Pacific*, edited by Edvard Hviding and Knut M. Rio (Sean Kingston Publishing, 2011), included materials from the founding symposium in Bergen in 2006, and a special session at the conference of the European Society for Oceanists held in Verona in 2008. The chapters in this second volume are drawn from a major international conference held in Honolulu in March 2009 and co-sponsored by the Center for Pacific Islands Studies, University of Hawai`i, as well as the capstone conference 'Power in Oceania' held at the Solstrand Hotel near Bergen in March 2012. Sadly, then, *Pacific Alternatives* represents the end point, the culmination of a truly remarkable project. It is worth noting, however, that many of the guiding principles and much of energy generated during the life of the project have been channelled into new initiatives managed by the European Consortium for Pacific Studies (ECOPAS), with a particular research focus on the implications of climate change in Oceania (www.ecopas.info). ECOPAS will, no doubt, prove to be as productive and innovative as its predecessor.

Acknowledgements

✳

This collection has been developed from a major conference organized in Honolulu in March 2009 by the Center for Pacific Islands Studies, University of Hawai'i at Mānoa, in collaboration with the Bergen Pacific Studies group of the University of Bergen, Norway. It is the final published result of a major programme of research and education funded by the Research Council of Norway for the years 2008–12 (Pacific Alternatives: Cultural Heritage and Political Innovation in Oceania, Grant No. 185646), and forms a distinct companion volume to *Made in Oceania*, edited by Edvard Hviding and Knut M. Rio, published in 2011 also by Sean Kingston Publishing.

For their inspiration and wisdom over several days of truly pan-Pacific dialogue at the Honolulu conference back in March 2009 we are grateful to conference presenters whose contributions are not part of this collection, but whose thoughts have remained with us. They include Kehau Abad, Maenette Kape'ahiokalani Nee-Benham, Cato Berg, Annelin Eriksen, Lawrence Foana'ota, Manuka Henare, Jon Tikivanotau Michael Jonassen, Jon Kamakawivo'ole Osorio, Tina Rehuher, and Ty Kāwika Tengan. Tisha Hickson and Terence Wesley-Smith were masterful conference organizers. Knut M. Rio has been a constant intellectual force in the Pacific Alternatives journey, and deserves special mention.

The Pacific Alternatives research-and-education programme involved scholars at the University of Bergen and the University of Hawai'i at Mānoa with a wide range of colleagues at partner institutions. We express our gratitude to the Research Council of Norway for funding this unprecedented effort of comparative Pacific Studies, to all the participating institutions for their contributions of so many kinds, and our own home institutions in Bergen and Honolulu for financial contributions towards the publication of this book. The University of Bergen also contributed generously to the final conference of the Pacific Alternatives programme held at Solstrand near Bergen in March 2012, during which many of the dialogues and observations contained in this book found their final form.

For dedicated editorial work on all chapters over several intensive periods, we are deeply grateful to Nora Haukali, Tom Mountjoy and Eilin Holtan Torgersen of the Bergen Pacific Studies group. On behalf of all contributors to the book we express our gratitude to three anonymous readers for constructive criticism, and to publisher extraordinaire Sean Kingston for his continuous attention, dedication and professionalism at every stage of the collection's progress towards publication.

Bergen and Honolulu, June 2015
Edvard Hviding and Geoffrey White

Contents

III – Heritage as political discourse

Pacific alternatives in a global context

Dialogues in Oceania

✳

GEOFFREY WHITE AND EDVARD HVIDING

Pacific alternatives

In this book, twelve authors from a variety of disciplines, thematic approaches and geographic locations raise wide-ranging questions about innovative responses to globalization in Oceania. That great region of ocean and islands is home to only a fraction of the world's human population, but has remained a scene of staggering diversity in terms of its peoples' relationships with, responses to, and influences over initiatives from elsewhere, long before the earliest encounters between Pacific Islanders and European navigators (Thomas 2010). For the islanders of the Pacific, with their unique history of human mobility across an ocean that presented opportunities rather than barriers, and in which islands were more likely to be connected than isolated (Hau'ofa 1993), other worlds beyond the horizon (whether over the currents of the ocean or the next mountain) have always provided aspects of both the known and unknown. These diverse and remarkable patterns also characterize the present era of time-space compression. If struggles over the social, economic and political dimensions of globalization are everywhere a struggle over the fate of the local, then understanding globalization requires engagement with culturally specific challenges to the increasingly stale discourses of 'development' and, indeed, the word 'globalization' itself (see, for example, Appadurai 1996; Tsing 2005).

For example, observations from the Western Pacific region of Melanesia pose interesting challenges in terms of understanding a continuous flow of encounter and engagement that one of us, with reference to observational trajectories of long-term fieldwork, has referred to elsewhere as 'compressed globalization' (Hviding 2012). The reference to compression implies events and situations in which 'a diversity of large-scale connections of a global nature are initiated, engaged in, even performed, locally – by very few participants on the ground, and often in unexpected or unpredictable ways' (Hviding 2012:219). In a related vein, Deborah Gewertz and Frederick Errington (1997:127) have commented that Papua New Guinea, specifically, can be seen 'as a place where the global intersects the local in axiomatically condensed form'. This points to some degree of uniqueness for Melanesia, and the Pacific more widely, in engaging locally with forces of the global.

In global terms the nations and state formations of the Pacific have short histories. A closer look at the culturally and linguistically diverse region of western and central Melanesia is instructive to frame a set of arguments on which many of the following chapters are based. Emerging from a heterogeneous repertoire of twentieth-century colonial rule as new independent nations in 1975 (Papua New Guinea), 1978 (Solomon Islands) and 1980 (Vanuatu), the national histories are not only brief, but also troubled. Understanding the diverse pressures in post-colonial Melanesia of state-level governmental processes and nation-level pursuits of historical and cultural affinities has never been an easy task (see Foster 1995), whether for the Melanesian political actors engaged practically in nation-making, or for academic observers or political commentators grappling with the region's conspicuously dense entanglements of high cultural diversity, decentralized natural resource control, contested levels of nation-making, and states seen as by definition weak (see the review by Douglas 2000). In the twenty-first century, the shortcomings of the analyses of the latter and the often seemingly incomprehensible agendas of the former have contributed to a dominant external view – particularly in Australian government and foreign-policy circles – of Melanesia as a notoriously unstable region of 'failed states' (e.g. Reilly 2000; Wainwright 2003).

Although providing much food for thought, and on occasion even legitimizing international intervention, observations of what transpires in the Melanesian capital cities of Port Moresby, Honiara and Port Vila do not supply all the knowledge required to better understand how Melanesians develop national identities and state formations. Most often, the paradigms applied to the analysis of social and political formations of statehood do so by identifying gaps, weaknesses, and failures identified through a logic of 'absence', the absence of (idealized) Western practices and epistemologies. Nor is the local and rural, as a conventional counterpoint to the national and urban, a sufficient source of information. Insights from rural and urban, local and national scenes need to be supplemented by knowledge of what happens in the levels in between, of which there are a great many in the Melanesian countries. This is a region whose peoples demonstrate a social creativity and an enthusiastic dedication to cultural difference perhaps unsurpassed anywhere else in the world (Knauft 1999; LiPuma 2001; Strathern 1988). On the more material level of political economy, a widespread bone of contention relates to inequities in centre-periphery relations, in that rural areas (typically organized by the post-colonial Melanesian state as 'provinces') tend to provide sources of state revenue disproportionate to what is received from the central government in return (see Hviding, this volume). Not unexpectedly, the most frequent complaints against this kind of national redistribution come from resource-rich provinces that provide substantial proportions of government revenue. Hence, these debates, so typical of Melanesia, are about far more than devolution or decentralization of government – concepts that have met with some resistance from development planners who point to what they see as the inherent instability of provincial governments in Melanesia. The region's most well-known case is Papua New Guinea, where tensions arising from financial irregularities and/or poor relations between the national politicians and the provinces have in several cases led to suspensions of provincial governments (see May 2004).

By focusing particularly on the intersections at which local and global meet, and on the events, knowledge and institutions emerging at those intersections, the chapters of this book attempt, collectively and in dialogue, to advance a critical understanding of Pacific Islands 'alternatives' to the dominant models that continue to be advocated by powerful state-centred forces, despite half a century of apparent failure evident in the way the Pacific is conventionally assessed in the prevailing models of states and economies. In a joint effort to explore Pacific-style local alternatives, the authors discover a great variety of practices that are being actively deployed in local communities across Oceania. Our collective focus is on the expanding uses, throughout the Pacific, of locally distinctive cultural repertoires in dealing with those encounters and engagements in which the global interacts with the local. Whereas talk of 'culture' or 'cultural heritage' is always at risk of losing its edge because of overuse or appropriation, the chapters that follow seek to expand perceptions of cultural heritage in Pacific societies through consideration of contemporary social practices and movements that utilize such notions in order to advance local initiatives in response to the challenges of global political economy.

The framework for this collaboration has been supported by a four-year research and educational project aptly named 'Pacific Alternatives', and coordinated by the Bergen Pacific Studies research group at the University of Bergen, Norway, in cooperation with scholars and institutional partners at the University of Hawai'i, the East-West Center, the Solomon Islands National Museum, the Vanuatu Cultural Centre, the British Museum, University

College London, James Cook University, the University of Queensland, New York University and University of Tulsa. Initial work emerging from this project appeared in a volume collecting papers developed from several project workshops and conference sessions (see Hviding and Rio 2011). The present volume has its origins in a major conference convened by the 'Pacific Alternatives' project group in Honolulu in March 2009, and subsequent research pursued by the authors, culminating in a second conference convened in Bergen, Norway, in March 2012. The 2009 *Pacific Alternatives* conference was a milestone event in this collaborative project of research and education, generating wide-ranging discussions that included keynote addresses, paper presentations, panel discussions and formal and informal planning for future work.

The conference in 2009 was intellectually grounded in a shared appreciation of the contributions to Pacific Studies by the late professor Epeli Hau'ofa, a source of endless inspiration for so many in the audience. Hau'ofa's untimely death in 2008 generated a wide sense of loss in our world of Pacific Studies, and as the conference proceeded over the next days, participants were to recall both personal and professional moments of inspiration provided by Hau'ofa's remarkable career. Attention was given to a not-so-often quoted paragraph in Hau'ofa's famous text 'Our Sea of Islands', that paragraph providing something of a punch-line for the conference itself. There, as in so much of his writing and in his work building the University of the South Pacific's Oceania Centre for Arts and Culture, Hau'ofa directed our attention to:

> ordinary people … who, because of the poor flows of benefits from the top, scepticism about stated policies and the like, tend to plan and make decisions about their lives independently, sometimes with surprising and dramatic results that go unnoticed or ignored at the top. Moreover, academic and consultancy experts tend to overlook or misinterpret grassroots activities because they do not fit in with prevailing views about the nature of society and its development.
>
> (Hau'ofa 1993:2)

We follow Hau'ofa here and argue that these are the people who create and develop distinctively Pacific alternatives. These are the people who fuse cultural heritage and political innovation. These are the people we pay respect to in this volume and to whom we dedicated the conference that preceded it. Subsequently, like our friend Epeli Hau'ofa, the authors, projects and ideas discussed in the following chapters are set to traverse the great world of Oceania and beyond in order to establish connections with other regions of the world through the examples and potentials provided by countless Pacific alternatives. The main axis of interest in the following chapters, then, in many different ways, is to explore and seek deeper insight into how creative processes of political innovation emerge in globally connected situations from a grounding in the diverse cultural heritage of the Pacific. We see relevance for such Pacific alternatives in the cultural politics of globalization everywhere. The work presented in this book seeks connections that can inform situations in very different regions, while at the same time working to empower Pacific island communities and their visions.

Oceania's geo-cultural imaginary

To take seriously the local or the 'cultural' in Oceania implies, immediately, the necessity of specifying the locations, institutions and histories to be included in an effort of regional – pan-Pacific – scope such as this volume. Whereas the Pacific Islands area is indeed diverse, spanning one-third of the globe and encompassing the greatest diversity of indigenous languages and cultures anywhere in the world, some sub-regions do share similar ecologies and cultural and political histories. This volume finds its central focus in Island Melanesia (Spriggs 1997), with more than half of the chapters dealing with Solomon Islands and Vanuatu. From this vantage point in the archipelagos of western Oceania beyond mainland New Guinea, the collective scope of the chapters reaches beyond the Melanesian archipelagos to engage comparatively also with materials from Micronesia, Polynesia and Australia.

Before noting some of the convergences in social and political conditions that emerge from the studies in this volume, we need to call attention also to some of the absences or exclusions that follow from the volume's geo-cultural scope. With an initial focus on the Island Melanesian nations of Solomon Islands and Vanuatu, and a wide range of contributions on and perspectives from Micronesia and Polynesia, we wish to highlight perspectives on the Pacific that have tended to be obscured by an over-representation in Pacific Studies of Papua New Guinea, Fiji and the central archipelagos of Polynesia. Nonetheless, the conference from which these papers derive benefited substantially from roundtables organized to highlight the Hawaiian situation and the diversity of perspectives from Micronesia and Polynesia. Topically, those roundtables expanded on the thematics of the conference and conveyed direct insights from practitioners in the politically charged fields of indigenous activism, vernacular education and digital cultural heritage.

Given our concern with practices evident in the conjunctures of rural locales and globalizing states, we would certainly find even more dramatic distinctions if we were to look south to New Caledonia, with its ongoing French colonial status, or east to Fiji, with its military government that emerged from a series of coups beginning in 1987. To reference Fiji immediately points to the fate of narratives of development and democracy that accompanied the emergence of independent nation-states in the South Pacific during the 1970s. Insofar as independent Fiji was held up in 1970 as the very emblem of Western style democracy and multiculturalism in the Pacific, but stands today as the region's only military regime, we are reminded of how rapidly narratives of the post-colonial Pacific have transformed within the span of a few decades.

Having commented on the cases that fall outside the scope of this volume, the geopolitical emphasis given here to Solomon Islands and Vanuatu is worthy of some elaboration. First, we should note that despite the immense diversity of these two archipelagos, as nation-states they have remarkable similarities in geographic, demographic and political configuration. Both Solomon Islands and Vanuatu are resource-rich archipelagos and complex states that have struggled with nation-building throughout their relatively short post-colonial histories, with independence established in 1978 and 1980, respectively. Despite the size and diversity of the contiguous Solomon Islands and Vanuatu, this island region is often overshadowed in both political and scholarly terms by the massive presence of Papua New Guinea to the north and, historically, by the long-standing Western fascination with Polynesia to the east. But ironically, despite a much lower visibility in the Western imagination, rural peoples of Solomon Islands and Vanuatu have a long history of cultural activism, expressed in social movements (sometimes labelled as 'cargo cults') and continuing political innovations. This book takes a close look at some of the distinctive conjunctures of culture and politics emerging in this region and beyond.

Problem(atizing) 'culture'

'Cultural heritage' is a concept with its own particular history, deeply anchored in the historical emergence of nation-states and, today, in United Nations policy, coded specifically in UNESCO's efforts to preserve global cultural products and practices. In recent years, issues of cultural heritage have come to the centre of attention as an important concern worldwide, not only among politicians and policy-makers, but also in a more general trend in society towards valorization of the local in the face of seemingly dwindling nationalism, disempowerment of the state, and the rise of global corporate influences.

From local Pacific perspectives, we argue that cultural heritage has always been a basic anchor or framework that people use to make sense of, and act upon, their world. Inasmuch as social life in the Pacific, particularly in the diverse archipelagos of Melanesia, seems to be predicated on a certain measure of cultural difference that serves to define distinct social groups in some contrast to one another, cultural heritage relates to specific *peoples,* with specific *collective histories*, linked directly to specific *spatial and social practices*. As such, people, places and objects may all stand for these histories, variously indexing, enacting or institutionalizing visions of collective value and shared pasts. As ideas about cultural heritage are externalized in these iconic forms, they inevitably also become foci for public debates about what identities and values merit public recognition and respect in external spheres of increasingly large scale.

One of the distinct varieties of public recognition that concerns this volume is the place of state-sponsored or state-supported discourses of culture; discourse that somehow becomes marked as 'national' culture or culture of national significance. In Melanesia, the region of famously 'weak' and 'failed' states, the 'problem' of culture, evident in this volume, is very often not the problem – of building a symbolic basis for national integration and unity – diagnosed by Western observers. Rather than diagnose these differences a symptom of the 'problem' of unification, the authors here open up perspectives on alternative means of imagining local-national-global relationships that depart from the standard development calculus of strong nation-state = centralized national culture. As others have argued in assessments of nation-building in the region, it is a mistake to confuse the state with the nation, such that weakness of the state does not imply weakness of the nation. The proliferation of rural and local 'centres' of cultural community has been read by some as the problem of nation-building in the Pacific (e.g. Reilly 2000). The various 'alternatives' explored here suggest that that assessment is limited by the strongly state-centred models emanating from Western models of politics and development.

To be sure, cultural heritage in the public sphere is by nature political, a potent idiom capable of engendering social conflict or mobilizing social movements. Analyzing the concept of cultural heritage in the context of political innovation allows us to develop the idea that cultural heritage represents a viable counterforce to external challenges. In our usage, 'political innovation' describes contemporary processes in Melanesia and the wider Pacific region that are only misrepresented and distorted by simplistic tropes such as 'failed states' or 'invention of tradition'. In this volume we critically examine these concepts not just as social and politically motivated change and transformation, but also as indexes of creative practices engaged in experimenting with social forms themselves (cf. Wagner 1981). From this perspective, creativity and innovation grounded in ideas of local cultural heritage are likely to involve continuities more than disjuncture. While not ignoring the kinds of rupture or discontinuity that are famously analyzed in writings on Melanesian Christianity and social movements (e.g. Robbins 2004), a number of cases taken up here show that such disjunctures may themselves be the focus for efforts to retheorize social principles and practices. The continuities we thus seek to examine and explain in this volume may be further illuminated by the words of three strong voices in Pacific anthropology. They are ones that 'appear in and as the mode of cultural change ... [in which] ... innovations follow logically ... from the people's own principles of existence' (Sahlins 1993:19). Their metaphoric nature may in a 'holographic' sense be continuously made relevant in larger referential frames by way of 'transformational expansion through a relational field ... controlled by the exigencies of ... the "generic"' (Wagner 1986:31). Further, as expressed by Marilyn Strathern (1992:245), such continuities see 'forms appear out of other forms' through the creative, but also analytic, efforts of the active agents – Pacific Islanders themselves.

Problem(atizing) states

In the last two decades of the twentieth century, anthropology, history and related fields woke up to the political significance of national and state discourses of cultural tradition. At the very same time that Eric Hobsbawm and Terence Ranger were writing their introduction to *The Invention of Tradition* (1983), calling attention to the appropriation of rhetorics of tradition by states intent on using the language of tradition and the practices of ritual ceremony to legitimize their authority, Roger Keesing and Bob Tonkinson were publishing their special issue of *Mankind* on 'Reinventing Traditional Culture: The Politics of Kastom in Island Melanesia' (1982) examining the new discourses of tradition (or '*kastom*') emerging in insular Melanesia. Early writing on these subjects in the Pacific, it will be noted, coincided with the first decade of independence in which new states invoked ideas about cultural tradition to variously define and direct the social basis for emergent national communities. Although triggered by recognition of the importance of post-colonial discourses of culture and cultural heritage, anthropology and related fields were ill equipped at the time to work with and across institutions of the state, let alone regional and global organizations.

It is significant that the Keesing and Tonkinson collection, in its presentation of excellent ethnographic studies of the revalorization of *kastom* evident in the first years after independence for the new Melanesian states, included little research based on fieldwork in or on agencies and institutions of the state. Anthropology at that time remained centred in rural communities with a still limited horizon regarding the national and global forces linking them to state or corporate offices elsewhere. In this volume, most contributors experiment with a variety of strategies for addressing the 'problem' of the state, at local or national levels. Cultural practices at every level are now recognized to be inflected with the effects of (trans)national policies and politics, just as the practices of state agencies are, in turn, recognized to be responsive to the vicissitudes of global capital and investment.

One of the outcomes of more specific and focused research on the role and effects of state actors has been the recognition, across anthropology, of the importance of non-state actors who operate on a regional and global scale, providing highly influential connections between local communities and humanitarian and religious groups, on the one hand, and multinational corporations on the other. It is a volatile mix, and one that few have been able to analyze with ethnographic methods. In Melanesia in particular, where central government offices often seem a distant reality, a great deal of policy and action-oriented research has focused on the possibilities for local alliances through a variety of associations in this non-state sector.

For a number of the authors contributing to this volume, the presence of the state is an object of ethnographic interest and documentation, much like the presence of any form of political agency that would be of interest to students of local-level social organization. In this respect, Rosita Henry, in her chapter, reminds us of Kapferer's admonishment that, 'The reality of the state is to be grasped ethnographically both in its imaginary and in the concreteness of the practices that have a state relation or reference.' (2005:ix; see also Trouillot 2001:126). Thus, whether it is the operations of federal agencies involved in struggles over the monumental archaeological/tourist site Nan Madol, policies and practices that connect rural communities with national centres (through such places as Vanuatu Cultural Centre or Solomon Islands National Museum), or issues of land and sea litigation, investigations discussed here follow discursive threads that make connections that lend local specificity to national imaginings, as well as national linkages to local movements.

The politics of research

Historically, the gap between existing modalities of ethnographic research and the politics of scholarship in the post-colonial Pacific became more acute nearly a decade after the first 'invention of tradition' volumes, with the simultaneous publication of articles in anthropology and Pacific journals noting the seeming appropriation of 'culture' and 'tradition' in the rhetorical arsenal of indigenous activists and political movements (Hanson 1989; Keesing 1989). The ensuing debate turned out to be much wider and more heated than authors publishing in academic journals expected. The social and political landscape had shifted, marking the advent of new, more vigorous voices of indigenous scholars, who were moving debates about research practices into a wider arena with as yet unknown effects (Diaz and Kauanui 2001; Smith 1999; Trask 1991).

If nothing else, however, the discussions that swirled around the contentious idea of invented tradition (which seem somewhat worn out today) have drawn attention to the relentlessly public and practical nature of research on contemporary issues. One of the most fundamental developments in Pacific studies, increasingly populated by significant numbers of Pacific Islander scholars, is greater attention to the politics of research (e.g. Diaz 2006; Diaz and Kauanui 2001; Smith 1999; Teaiwa 2005; Tengan 2008; Tengan, Ka'ili and Fonoti 2010). How do the knowledge regimes of academic disciplines intersect with the interests and agencies of local communities concerned to sustain (and transform) indigenous modes of knowledge production (see also White and Tengan 2001)? The act of research may variously create its objects, placed under the gaze of experts, or expand local agencies through more dialogic processes. As indigenous critics have noted repeatedly, research practices have had a wide range of effects, from empowerment to marginalization, especially in communities where colonial history is already deeply felt (Smith 1999). The discussions engendered here begin with these recognitions and explore the potential for alternative practices in which research connects more directly and self-consciously with local modes of cultural production.

Importantly, the studies on which the chapters are based emerge from long-running conversations between scholars *in* and *of* the Pacific. Thus the volume aspires to collapse some enduring distinctions and dichotomies between the concerns of Western scholars of the Pacific and indigenous scholars from the Pacific. In ways increasingly characteristic of current directions in anthropology and social sciences generally, the contributors to this volume describe collaborative approaches to research that seek to bridge gaps between academic and action-oriented research, as well as the geopolitical locations of the authors.

Alternative practices?

In 1992, at about the same time that debates about academic analyses of the 'invention of tradition' were filling anthropology journals and classroom discussions of shifting modes of indigenous scholarship, a group of scholars and cultural practitioners working in Melanesia gathered in a small workshop in Honiara, Solomon Islands, to discuss the practical and political challenges facing local and national efforts to strengthen and institutionalize 'traditional' practices in museums, cultural centres and educational policies. It is notable that that meeting, involving representatives from Papua New Guinea, Solomon Islands and Vanuatu (and attended by Cultural Centre staff from Noumea) attracted the largest, most engaged delegation from the smallest of the Melanesian countries (Vanuatu), significant participation from provincial and national institutions in the Solomon Islands, and modest representation from Papua New Guinea. In other words, the scale of interest in the problem of 'cultural policy' seemed inversely related to the size and scale of these new states.

The provocative observations that emerged in that workshop and in the volume of papers and policies that resulted (Lindstrom and White 1994) were minimally taken up in the academic debates of the time. The discussions remained focused on accounts of projects capable of linking local initiatives with transnational actors and resources while still mobilizing community engagement. In his contribution to the volume, however, Roger Keesing (1994) reflected on the 'responsibilities of long-term research', based on his own career of involvement with the Kwaio of Malaita, noting the particular opportunities and obligations that emerge from sustained fieldwork with the same communities. Pointing toward current interests in 'collaborative' models for research (Howell and Talle 2012; Lassiter 2005), his chapter pointed in directions that are taken up today by indigenous scholars for whom 'long-term' usually has a somewhat more personal significance. The contributions collected here follow these leads in the present-day context, with several participants in the earlier workshop contributing to this volume, providing updated assessments of the trajectory for cultural projects and movements discussed two decades ago.

Our focus on a myriad of social practices circumscribing cultural heritage is not looking back to a solidified or frozen past, but ahead to future or present assemblages of social relations, constituting a huge repertoire of 'Pacific alternatives' traversing local, national and regional boundaries. The most acute example of engagement between an activist cultural agenda and national development discourse in this volume is expressed in the Epilogue by Ralph Regenvanu, who in his own career traverses the spaces of cultural work and national political office. As he states, moving into the centres of state power can be a method for challenging the 'development agenda', something now formalized in the 'Vanuatu National Self Reliance Strategy 2020'.

Overview of the chapters

The book is organized into three main sections: 'States and cultural policies', 'The cultural politics of land and sea' and 'Heritage as political discourse'. While these sections are helpful in highlighting convergences of interest, they should not deter anyone from tracing connections that cross-cut these thematic areas.

In the first set of chapters, the authors draw our attention to state formations and practices that occupy themselves with constructions of 'culture' that variously define and direct collective interests on the basis of assertions about shared culture, especially indigenous cultural tradition. In her contribution, Rosita Henry focuses on the highly visible and influential South Pacific Festival of the Arts as an arena of and for 'statecraft'. As one of the most prominent regional contexts of cultural performance, the Festival is one of the few arenas for fashioning national culture for international audiences. As Henry relates, the Festival offers a venue for states to promote dominant forms of identity that tend to occlude internal struggles for recognition. At the same time, however, it has also been a site for contestations over the legitimacy of cultural and political movements, from Kanak identity in New Caledonia to Papuan struggles in Irian Jaya (now West Papua). Henry's fieldwork with an Australian Aboriginal delegation shows us the important role of creativity and spontaneity, as actors and performers use the festival 'stage' to enact versions of culture and identity that depart from dominant state-sponsored visions. In the end, it is the multiple possibilities, or alternatives, of and for cultural performance that make the South Pacific Festivals an arena that both states and performers embrace.

In Micronesia, where the disparities between small atoll communities and the immense power of the United States are sharply drawn, David Hanlon provides an acutely focused case study in the negotiation of rights with regard to culture, land and sea, as they pertain to control over the monumental cultural and archaeological site of Nan Madol on the high island of Pohnpei. His chapter 'Space wars: Nan Madol as cultural and political property' traces the evolution of these negotiations in concert with applications of US historical property regulations and administrative practices. When he notes that 'The 1974 amendment to the 1966 National Historic Preservation Act marks a critical event that made historic preservation an institutional practice that facilitated in seemingly benign ways American control of the Trust Territory.' he reminds us that, in the domain of culture, exertions or extensions of state authority often go unnoticed as such. Hanlon's discussion resonates strongly with Wickler's account (discussed below) of the politics of archaeology and heritage preservation in the Micronesian state of Palau, where United States regulation of heritage sites often runs parallel to indigenous practices.

Geoffrey White's focus on 'the predicament of cultural policy' presents an historical ethnography of cultural policy and festive cultural events in Santa Isabel, Solomon Islands, to remind us that, for the vast majority of Melanesians, the 'problem' of culture is relentlessly rural and local. In doing so, he, like other authors in this volume, notes an enduring disconnection or disjunction between local discourses of culture or *kastom* and the phantom policies and practices that emerge from government offices, whether island-based (provincial) or centralized in the national capital. Citing a related publication on national cultural policy in and around the national museum (Foana'ota and White 2011), he offers a historical perspective on phases of cultural discourse and governmentality in the post-colonial period. Much like Rosita Henry's ethnography of Festival of the Arts performances, White's account of a provincial 'cultural festival' illustrates the importance, at the local level, of performative enactments of culture in fixing dominant ideas about the nature and value of indigenous culture. His analysis shows that even at the most local level, transnational connections through religious and non-governmental organizations as well as international aid projects significantly influence the valorization of traditional culture.

The next set of chapters, grouped under the theme of the cultural politics of land and sea, also pursues questions related to state policies and the definition of tradition, only in these studies applied to the most critical area of economic and material concern: land and sea (often discussed under the rubric of 'ownership', immediately raising questions of ontology and epistemology).

Vilsoni Hereniko's chapter traces histories of land and power in Rotuma that have meaning for him and his family. Given the economy of affect associated with a narrative that has meaning for the author's own social world, Hereniko draws on his skills as playwright and filmmaker to tell stories of the layered social and cultural meaning of struggles over land and power in an atoll society, where every inch of land has long since been divided and determined by intertwined genealogies. In this context, Hereniko reflects on the contradictions of a system in which power resides in the Fiji state, yet, quite literally, cannot be translated to the Rotuma context. He describes a situation in which:

> Rotumans have only two options: either to seek help from a pseudo-Western
> style court ill-equipped to solve land disputes, or continue to resolve land
> disputes in their own way, oblivious to or ignorant of government processes
> and the laws of Fiji that govern land tenure.

He goes on to invoke the wisdom of Epeli Hau'ofa, although in a somewhat different manner than others who cite his influence in this volume. Hereniko, himself a student of clowning and an author, playwright and screenwriter who makes use of humour and irony in his own writing, finds inspiration in Hau'ofa's ability to 'find humour and absurdity in serious endeavours' – in this case the idea of a Chinese-Fijian district officer presiding over Rotuman land cases despite a complete lack of understanding of the Rotuman language, while refusing to make use of an interpreter.

Like Hereniko, Hviding's chapter also addresses the complex and often contradictory relations between political district and nation-state, in his case between the Western Province of Solomon Islands and the Solomon Islands nation-state. Hviding is concerned with the extent to which the middle-level polity (in this case the indigenously defined Western Solomons, a diverse region itself) can emerge as an imagined community capable of focusing the energy and sentiment of a social movement. In pursuing this question, he is as concerned with the symbolic power of land and sea to define people, as with the power of people to control land and sea. As readers knowledgeable of the social and political history of Solomon Islands will know well, the Western Solomons is a region that has struggled more publicly and prominently than most to define itself separately from other regions in the nation-state, translating sentiments of distinction into a 'breakaway' movement following independence and, more recently, aggressive support for constitutional reform authorizing federalism and provincial autonomy. In seeking to understand the basis for these sentiments, Hviding asks how the idea of 'the West' comes to obtain cultural and emotional capital, and reminds us that in this specific part of Melanesia there is a long history of engagement with the sea, explicit in socialities of inter-island relationships, a situation that has made maritime mobility (especially 'the canoe') an iconic representation of distinctive cultural identities (Hviding 1996).

Melanesianizing Hau'ofa's (1993) argument for the importance of the sea and its expansive horizons for Oceanic identity, Hviding inquires into the manner in which this maritime symbolic complex is appropriated and redeployed at the level of provincial governance. In the process, we begin to understand how 'the West' acquires significance precisely as an oppositional identity set in contrast with the national 'centre'. Importantly, however, Hviding's analysis of the semiotics of the sea and iconic war canoes is accompanied by an account of the circulation of actors in and out of state institutions at several levels. In this way, his account, like others in this volume, provides a glimpse of what an ethnography of the state might look like for Melanesian states, where the stakes are often grounded, literally, in land and sea.

Since independence it has been Melanesian governments, at all levels, that have taken up the problem of articulating modern legal systems with traditional land practices (often with the involvement of banks, regional agencies, NGOs or foreign experts). Lissant Bolton describes one such case. In Vanuatu, where the national government generally voices support for the power of custom in determining landowner rights, the Vanuatu Cultural Centre (VCC or VKS) has played an important role in facilitating discussion of the intractable problems that arise at the intersection of tradition and modern law (see also Regenvanu, this volume). The VCC is distinctive in the region for the role it has played in building a network of locally placed 'fieldworkers' charged with facilitating initiatives in local culture and history, discussed in periodic workshops convened by the Centre. As researchers working in

Vanuatu know well, the VCC fieldworker programme has the capacity to engender an unusually rich local level of debate within the larger national context. (See Geismar's chapter on the experience of curating the VCC's travelling exhibit on urban culture(s) of Port Vila.)

Bolton's chapter discusses a 2008 workshop convened to investigate the nature of customary relationships between women and land in ni-Vanuatu societies, utilizing the Centre's women fieldworker programme to do so – a programme with which Bolton has been deeply involved (Bolton 2003). Describing the larger historical context in which women, since independence, have generally been excluded from government and other arenas of state-sponsored decision-making (Jolly 1997; Molisa 1987, 2002), she states that the 'subtext' for the agenda to discuss women and land was to 'discover what "rights", if any, women might have in relation to land'. Bolton begins her discussion with a statement that resonates strongly with the other chapters in this volume that examine the place of indigenous practices for land management in Oceania's modern nation-states:

> The women fieldworker's workshop took place at the interface, so to speak, of two different systems of thought in contemporary Vanuatu. There is a difference between indigenous ni-Vanuatu knowledge and practice, and global economic and development thinking, especially in relation to ideas about land and land tenure.

In particular, she goes on to say, the very premises of state-sponsored fact-finding or policy-oriented research may miss the point of these differences, as in investigations that focus on issues of 'ownership' and hence fail to understand the tenets of indigenous models before they have even begun.

Again, as Hereniko and others note, while there may be two distinct 'systems', they have long been interacting. Bolton describes some of the implications for women in Vanuatu in terms that resonate in many parts of Oceania, where the more informal and less public role of women in political decision-making is further marginalized by the introduction of new rational-bureaucratic practices associated with 'development'. Thus, as Bolton observes, in Vanuatu the Customary Land Tribunal Act 'disadvantages women, by formalizing the processes that take place in men's house meetings, without allowing for the negotiations that often take place with women before those meetings'.

While rational development planners may not wish to concede the point, informed participants in most Melanesian communities will agree with the VCC workshop's recognition that 'disputes about land will go on forever' and that 'no amount of legislation will ever resolve all land disputes'. The chapters in this volume make clear that even if some kind of final, legally inscribed resolution is not possible for land disputes, the *process* of disputing (or rather discussing, debating) land can work to clarify and define important social relations. Bolton's chapter relates a broad range of nuanced discussion about precisely this, the social relations that are implicated and evoked in discourses of and about land. (Thus, she observes, the women fieldworkers repeatedly discussed the importance of marriage as the 'key strategy for ensuring the ongoing connection between a descent group and their land' with the goal of ensuring continuity in relations between people and land.)

The next section of this volume presents a set of chapters concerned broadly with formations of 'heritage' in contemporary Oceania, examining particular sectors where 'culture' is valorized in and by the state and other institutions (churches) that mediate local, national and global relations through the idiom of culture. The first chapter by Haidy Geismar presents a photo essay, a visual portrait, of another project of the Vanuatu Cultural Centre in which she and colleague Eric Wittersheim, like Lissant Bolton, were active participants: the travelling art exhibit Port Vila Mi Lavem Yu, for which they acted as curators and organizers. It was a collaborative work on several levels, through the cooperation of the VCC, through fieldwork undertaken by both in the urban spaces of the Vanuatu capital Port Vila, and through the voices of artists who participated in the exhibit and contributed comments through its labels.

For her essay, Geismar visually highlights an issue that pervades cultural production in the new states of Melanesia, where the formula 'culture' = (pre-European) 'tradition' implies that 'indigenous culture' does not encompass the many transformations and appropriations that have occurred during the region's long colonial history, not least Christianization, and thereby can only be vanishing. While the urban spaces of mostly rural Melanesia may be relatively small in demographic size, to read their significance accordingly is to miss the fact that nearly everyone circulates through urban centres and maintains important social ties with people resident there (Connell and Lea 2002; Goddard 2005; Jourdan 1995; Mitchell 2004). Thus, in their project Geismar and Wittersheim, working with local artists, challenged these limiting views with an alternative vision that is urban and translocal. In this respect, their vision resonates with Tarcisius Kabutaulaka's chapter, discussed below, urging a radical remaking of the 'native' slot in representations of Melanesia that are so often occupied by images of the primitive. In contrast, 'alternatives' seem to rise up and become visible primarily from the region itself.

The chapter by Lamont Lindstrom focuses on one of the most important and obvious faces of 'heritage' – tourism. For this volume's concern with the politics of cultural production in the contemporary Pacific, tourism obviously looms large as an arena of and for the representation of Pacific peoples through the language of 'culture'. Although surrounded by ambivalence in the early years of independence, Pacific states, aided by regional organizations and development planners, were quick to propose models for developing tourism as a major sector in post-colonial economies. Indeed, it is in contexts of tourism that state agencies in particular begin to take interest in the economic potentials of 'culture'.

Lindstrom approaches tourism in Vanuatu through the case of Tanna, a community known beyond its shores for reasons of its well-publicized and often exoticized 'cargo cult', the Jon Frum movement. As he explains, in the context of Vanuatu tourism, Tanna is particularly significant as a destination on the periphery, away from the national capital and its more comfortable tourist accommodations, where difference becomes even more different. Indeed, his chapter describes much of the specifically Melanesian character of the imagined spaces of Vanuatu tourism, where images of women and children fill advertisements that might otherwise be at risk of less favourable images of male warriors stereotypically opposed to the softer feminized images associated with Polynesia (themes taken up in Kabutaulaka's chapter).

As a mode of travel that seeks out otherness to satisfy domestic desires for the exotic or erotic, tourist agencies everywhere have created and marketed images of indigenous people as native others. Where difference is not only valued but commodified, market forces sustain highly essentialized constructions of Pacific peoples – forces that often include the active participation of Pacific peoples. Lindstrom's account of innovations in places like Tanna, however, adds an important perspective to longstanding critiques of tourism as unremittingly exploitative. Certainly tourism illustrates well the power of 'culture' to distract attention from the ravages of globalization, including the distorting effects of commodification of cultural performance (Jolly 1994), the power of global capital to set agendas (Helu-Thaman 1993), and to conceal the exploitative side of colonization (Trask 1993) and militarization (Kahn 2011; Teaiwa 1994). Yet outside the settler states and still colonial domains, strategies and sentiments are evolving, experimenting with new arrangements that seek ways to connect travellers with local entrepreneurs. In Lindstrom's discussion we can see issues that often arise for the rural communities seeking to find ways to connect with flows of capital that tend to concentrate in urban centres.

Whereas official, state-sponsored interest in 'culture' tends to perk up in the context of tourism, where cultural presentation and performance may yield economic benefits, people themselves often see these practices as tangential to their daily concerns in managing more immediate economic activities and the exchange practices that actually work to create and sustain social relations. The next chapter, by Graeme Were, reminds us that there are other institutional forces capable of valorizing 'culture' and 'heritage' in ways that at times connect more directly with these concerns. His discussion of sectarian rivalries in New Ireland is an important reminder of the highly significant place of Christianity in discourses of cultural 'tradition' in Oceania.

The last decade (or two) has seen a surge of anthropological writing on Christianity, ranging from work on the integration (or lack thereof) of Christian practice at the local level (Engelke and Tomlinson 2006; Robbins 2004), to that documenting the rise of transnational networks that have created new religious communities that have both connected and divided island communities in unprecedented ways (Tomlinson and McDougall 2012). These developments in the globalization of Pacific Christianities greatly complicate assessments of the role of contemporary churches in the rural Pacific. Were's chapter for this volume finds that the debates about the relation between (new) Christian practices and indigenous 'heritage' figure prominently in efforts to remake local social relations with new ideological resources. His analysis of the case of Baha'i in New Ireland demonstrates that, unlike so many cases of antagonism between Christianity and tradition during the era of conversion, heritage in this context can be held up as a source of unifying collective identity.

Stephen Wickler's chapter moves in geopolitical and topical focus, to analyze state-sponsored discourses of 'heritage' in Palau, Micronesia, that exemplifies both a strongly rooted local valuation of indigenous culture and identity, as well as the influence of American institutions dedicated to the formalization and legalization of 'culture' similar to the regimes of knowledge discussed by David Hanlon. Wickler's own involvement with archaeological research conducted under the regulation of the US system allows him a close-up view of the predicament faced by Palauans, who, like numerous other communities discussed in this volume, contend with distinct and often incommensurable knowledge systems applied to the representation of culture.

Wickler's chapter discusses the role played by the Bureau of Arts and Culture as the legal authority for heritage management. His discussion notes disparities between the conservation of 'natural' heritage (protection of the environment) and 'cultural' heritage (particularly what UNESCO calls intangible cultural heritage), reflecting local attitudes that Palauan life continues to nurture indigenous practices to the degree that they need not become objects of preservation dependent on external resources, perhaps reflecting the gap between that everyday reality and the legalistic discourse of state initiatives to protect or promote culture. This disconnect between official discourses of cultural preservation and local values is compounded by the general lack of knowledge or understanding among expatriate experts of indigenous modes of thinking – a gap long noted by observers of Palau. Going beyond critique, Wickler's chapter describes local efforts to connect with heritage projects that have had some success in promoting awareness and generating involvement at the local level. In particular, he discusses one project in which 'competent local actors concerned with small-scale development' were successful in developing both cultural and natural resources as a future investment for the community. In the process, and in line with this volume's interest in innovative approaches to research and cultural activism, he describes the effect of his work in Palau on his understanding of his own role as researcher and advocate: 'The importance of gauging attitudes towards cultural heritage *locally* has been brought home to me at a personal level by my experiences in Palau and forced a re-evaluation of my role as an outside "expert".'

In the final chapter in this section, Tarcisius Kabutaulaka presents an overview of Melanesian 'alter-natives' that melds together a sweeping historical reflection of the machinery of European image-production with a critique of the politics of the categories 'Melanesia' and 'Melanesian' that emanates from a career of navigating their cultural terrain. Although writing from an academic position at the University of Hawai'i rather than an elected post in the Vanuatu Parliament, Kabutaulaka, like Regenvanu, has been deeply involved in the political and economic debates of his home country, in his case Solomon Islands, at the same time as he offers analysis and commentary on political transformations in the Solomons and the region as a whole. With more than two decades of experience as a voice of Guadalcanal, spanning the deeply troubled and troubling period of crisis in Solomon Islands known as 'the Tension' during the early years of this century, he has honed his own critical senses for reading representations of the Solomons and, more generally, Melanesia, inside and outside the region. The result is an incisive and at times ironic critique of Melanesia's particular brand of Orientalism (Said 1979) – an imaginary that flows from European visions of 'the savage' generally (Trouillot 1991), as well as the particularities of European exploration of the Pacific (Jolly *et al.* 2009). Today's images of Melanesia, constructed by scholars, journalists and others as the darker and more violent region of the Pacific (in contrast with feminized Polynesia – Thomas 1997) have long roots in the European imagination, organized around oppositional images that have easily transformed into today's images of ethnic warfare (Kabutaulaka 2005; White 2001). It is fitting that this volume includes an essay that artfully connects critical reflections from personal experience with the historical and geopolitical array of constructions of Oceania that have shaped the imagination of scholars, politicians, journalists and travellers from the earliest moments of cultural encounter.

In order to capture some of the vibrant atmosphere of the conference in 2009, the volume closes with a particularly eloquent exposition of the way Pacific alternatives in the field of politics are made and brought to bear on the challenges of the present: The Hon. Ralph Regenvanu's account of his journey toward election in September 2008 as a member of the National Parliament of Vanuatu. Originally presented as an opening keynote to the Pacific Alternatives conference, Regenvanu's talk, 'Imagining the state as a vehicle for cultural survival in Oceania', is presented here in an expanded and elaborated version as an Epilogue that sets the tone for projecting and applying the volume's work into the future.

References

Appadurai, A. 1996. *Modernity at Large: Cultural Dimensions of Globalization.* Minneapolis: University of Minnesota Press.

Bolton, L. 2003. *Unfolding the Moon : Enacting Women's Kastom in Vanuatu.* Honolulu: University of Hawai'i Press.

Connell, J. and J.P. Lea 2002. *Urbanisation in the Island Pacific :Towards Sustainable Development.* London: Routledge.

Diaz, V.M. 2006. Creolization and indigenity. *American Ethnologist,* 33(4):576–78.

Diaz, V. and J.K. Kauanui 2001. Native Pacific cultural studies on the edge. *The Contemporary Pacific* 13(2):315–42.

Douglas, B. 2000. Weak states and other nationalisms: emerging Melanesian paradigms. *SSGM Discussion Paper* 00/3. Canberra: Australian National University.

Engelke, M.E. and M. Tomlinson 2006. *The Limits of Meaning : Case Studies in the Anthropology of Christianity.* New York: Berghahn Books.

Foana'ota, L. and G. White 2011. Solomon Islands cultural policy?: a brief history of practice. In *Made in Oceania: Social Movements, Cultural Heritage and the State in the Pacific,* E. Hviding and K.M. Rio (eds), 273–99. Wantage, Oxon.: Sean Kingston Publishing.

Foster, R. (ed.)1995. *Nation Making: Emergent Identities in Postcolonial Melanesia.* Ann Arbor: University of Michigan Press.

Gewertz, D. and F. Errington 1997. Why we return to Papua New Guinea. *Anthropological Quarterly* 70(3):127–36.

Goddard, M. 2005. *The Unseen City: Anthropological Perspectives on Port Moresby, Papua New Guinea.* Canberra: Pandanus Books.

Hanson, A. 1989. The making of the Maori: culture invention and its logic. *American Anthropologist* 91:890–902.

Hau'ofa, E. 1993. Our sea of islands. In *A New Oceania: Rediscovering Our Sea of Islands,* E. Hau'ofa, E. Waddell and V. Naidu (eds), 2–16. Suva, Fiji: University of the South Pacific.

Helu-Thaman, K. 1993. Beyond hula, hotels, and handicrafts: a Pacific Islander's perspective on tourism development. *The Contemporary Pacific* 5(1):104–11.

Hobsbawm, E. and T. Ranger (eds.) 1983. *The Invention of Tradition.* Cambridge: Cambridge University Press.

Howell, S. and A. Talle (eds) 2012. *Returns to the Field: Multitemporal Research and Contemporary Anthropology.* Bloomington: Indiana University Press.

Hviding, E. 1996. *Guardians of Marovo Lagoon: Practice, Place, and Politics in Maritime Melanesia.* Honolulu: University of Hawai'i Press.

——— 2012. Compressed globalization and expanding desires in Marovo Lagoon, Solomon Islands. In *Returns to the Field: Multitemporal Research and Contemporary Anthropology*, Signe Howell and Aud Talle (eds), 203–29. Bloomington: Indiana University Press.

Hviding, E. and K. Rio (eds) 2011. *Made in Oceania: Social Movements, Cultural Heritage and the State in the Pacific.* Wantage: Sean Kingston Publishing.

Jolly, M. 1994. Kastom as commodity: the land dive as indigenous rite and tourist spectacle in Vanuatu. In *Culture, Kastom, Tradition: Cultural Policy in Melanesia*, L. Lindstrom and G. White (eds), 131–46. Suva: Institute of Pacific Studies.

——— 1997. Woman-nation-state in Vanuatu: discourses on kastom, modernity and Christianity. In *Narratives of Nation in the South Pacific*, T. Otto and N. Thomas (eds), 133–62. Amsterdam: Harwood.

Jolly, M., S. Tcherkézoff and D. Tryon (eds) 2009. *Oceanic Encounters: Exchange, Desire, Violence.* Canberra: ANU EPress.

Jourdan, C. 1995. Stepping stones to national conciousness: the case of the Solomon Islands. In *Nation Making: Emergent Identities in Postcolonial Melanesia*, R. Foster (ed.), 127–50. Ann Arbor: University of Michigan Press.

Kabutaulaka, T.T. 2005. Australian foreign policy and the RAMSI intervention in Solomon Islands. *The Contemporary Pacific* 17(2):283–308.

Kahn, M. 2011. *Tahiti Beyond the Postcard : Power, Place, and Everyday Life.* Seattle: University of Washington Press.

Kapferer, B. 2005. Foreword. In *State Formation: Anthropological Perspectives*, C. Krohn-Hansen and K.G. Nustad (eds), vii–xi. London: Pluto Press.

Keesing, R. 1989. Creating the past: custom and identity in the contemporary Pacific. *The Contemporary Pacific* 1:19–42.

——— 1994. Responsibilities of Long-term Research. In *Culture, Kastom, Tradition: Developing Cultural Policy in Melanesia*, L. Lindstrom and G. White (eds), 187–97. Suva, Fiji: University of the South Pacific.

Keesing, R. and R. Tonkinson (eds.) 1982. Reinventing traditional culture: the politics of kastom in Island Melanesia. *Mankind* (Special Issue) 13(4).

Knauft, B.M. 1999. *From Primitive to Postcolonial in Melanesia and Anthropology.* Ann Arbor: University of Michigan Press.

Lassiter, L.E. 2005. *The Chicago Guide to Collaborative Ethnography*. Chicago: University of Chicago Press.

Lindstrom, L. and G.M. White (eds) 1994. *Culture, Custom, Tradition: Cultural Policy in Melanesia*. Suva: Institute of Pacific Studies.

LiPuma, E. 2001. *Encompassing Others: The Magic of Modernity in Melanesia*. Ann Arbor: University of Michigan Press.

May, R.J. 2004 [2001] *State and Society in Papua New Guinea: The First Twenty-Five Years*. Canberra: ANU E-Press.

Mitchell, J. 2004. Kilem taem (killing time) in a postcolonial town: young people and settlements in Port Vila, Vanuatu. In *Globalization and Culture Change in the Pacific Islands*, V. Lockwood (ed.), 358–76. Upper Saddle Rivers, New Jersey: Prentice Hall.

Molisa, G.M. 1987. *Colonised People: Poems*. Port Vila Vanuatu: Blackstone Publishing.

——— 2002. *Women and Good Governance*. Port Vila, Vanuatu: Blackstone Publishing.

Reilly, B. 2000. The Africanisation of the South Pacific. *Australian Journal of International Affairs* 54(3):261–8.

Robbins, J. 2004. *Becoming Sinners : Christianity and Moral Torment in a Papua New Guinea Society*. Berkeley: University of California Press.

Sahlins, M.D. 1993. Goodbye to tristes tropes: ethnography in the context of modern world history. *The Journal of Modern History* 65(1):1–25.

Said, E.W. 1979. *Orientalism*. New York: Vintage.

Smith, L.T. 1999. *Decolonizing Methodologies: Research and Indigenous Peoples*. London: Zed Books.

Spriggs, M. 1997. *The Island Melanesians*. Oxford: Blackwell.

Strathern, M. 1988 . *The Gender of the Gift: Problems with Women and Problems with Society in Melanesia*. Berkeley: University of California Press.

——— 1992. The decomposition of an event. *Cultural Anthropology* 7:245–54.

Teaiwa, T. 1994. Bikinis and other s/pacific n/oceans. *The Contemporary Pacific* 6:87–109.

——— 2005. Our sea of phosphate: the diaspora of Ocean Island. In *Indigenous Diasporas and Dislocations: Unsettling Western Fixations*, G. Harvey and C.D. Thompson Jr (eds), 169–91. Aldershot: Ashgate.

Tengan, T.P.K. 2008. *Native Men Remade: Gender and Nation in Contemporary Hawai'i*. Durham: Duke University Press.

Tengan, T.P.K., T.O. Ka'ili and R.T. Fonoti 2010. Genealogies: articulating indigenous anthropology in/of Oceania. Special Issue, *Pacific Studies* 33(2/3).

Thomas, N. 1997. Melanesians and Polynesians: typifications inside and outside anthropology. In *In Oceania: Visions, Artefacts, Histories*, 133–55. Durham: Duke University Press.

———— 2010. *Islanders: The Pacific in the Age of Empire*. New Haven: Yale University Press.

Tomlinson, M. and D. McDougall (eds) 2012. *The Politics of Christianity in Oceania*. New York: Berghahn Books.

Trask, H.-K. 1991. Natives and anthropologists: the colonial struggle. *The Contemporary Pacific* 3(1):159–67.

———— 1993. Lovely hula hands:corporate tourism and the prostitution of Hawaiian culture. In *From a Native Daughter: Colonialism and Sovereignty in Hawai'i*, 179–97. Monroe, Me.: Common Courage Press.

Trouillot, M.-R.1991. Anthropology and the savage slot: the poetics and politics of otherness. In *Recapturing Anthropology*, R. Fox (ed.), 17–44. Santa Fe: School of American Research.

———— 2001. The anthropology of the state in the age of globalization: close encounters of the deceptive kind. *Current Anthropology* 42(1):125–38.

Tsing, A.L. 2005. *Friction: An Ethnography of Global Connection*. Princeton: Princeton University Press.

Wagner, R. 1981. *The Invention of Culture*. Chicago: Chicago University Press.

———— 1986. *Symbols that Stand for Themselves*. Chicago: Chicago University Press.

Wainwright, E. 2003. Responding to state failure: the case of Australia and the Solomon Islands. *Australian Journal of International Affairs* 57(3):485–98.

White, G. 2001. Natives and nations: identity formation in postcolonial Melanesia. In *Places and Politics in an Age of Globalization*, R. Prazniak and A. Dirlik (eds), 139–66. Lanham, MD: Rowman & Littlefield.

White, G. and T.K. Tengan 2001. Disappearing worlds: anthropology and cultural studies in Hawai'i and the Pacific. *The Contemporary Pacific*, 13: 381–416.

Geoffrey White is Professor of Anthropology at the University of Hawai'i at Mānoa.

Edvard Hviding is Professor of Social Anthropology at the University of Bergen.

I

STATES AND CULTURAL POLICIES

CHAPTER 1

State effects and festival performances

Indigenous Australian participation

in the Festival of Pacific Arts

✳

Rosita Henry

Introduction: festival alternatives

In order to shed light on the creative ways that the concept of cultural heritage is being employed in response to global processes in the Pacific, this chapter focuses on the Festival of Pacific Arts, initially called the South Pacific Festival of Arts. I specifically focus on the festival as a site of political engagement between local communities and the state. Participants at the Festival of Pacific Arts are supported to attend the event as delegates and representatives of their nation-states. Yet, my research reveals that for at least some delegates, performing at the festival appears to be as much about discounting the state as representing it. Although the festival is clearly a state affair, it also provides fertile ground for grassroots action and a performative engagement with political alternatives. As David Guss (2000:172) concludes in his book *The Festive State*, in which he explores the power of the state to harness festive forms in its own interests: 'To those involved the stakes are high. For, as participants well know, festivals, for all their joy and color, are also battlegrounds where identities are fought over and communities made.'

The Festival of Pacific Arts was inaugurated in 1972 by the South Pacific Commission (now the Secretariat of the Pacific Community) as a means of encouraging the revitalization of traditional art and other expressive cultural practices in the Pacific. The Secretariat of the Pacific Community, through its Human Development Programme (HDP), provides technical assistance to the Council of Pacific Arts, the body which governs the festival. In 2010 the HDP released the results of an evaluation of the festival (Leahy *et al.* 2010). The evaluation project was designed jointly with UNESCO's section on Intangible Heritage, the main objective being to determine the contribution of the Festival of Pacific Arts to 'the safeguarding, preserving, protecting and promoting of intangible cultural heritage regionally and nationally' (Leahy *et al.* 2010:100). The terms of reference and the content of the report exemplify how a global heritage discourse, and particularly the concept of intangible heritage, is increasingly being used by state agents as a strategy for building regional networks of co-operation and international support for social and economic development in the Pacific (see contributions to Hviding and Rio 2011 and van Meijl 2009; for comparative case studies see Bendix *et al.* 2012). However, rather than dwell on the increasingly dominant role played by 'Western Authorized Heritage Discourse' (Smith 2012:389) in statecraft in the Pacific, my main aim here is to explore how grassroots participants deal with this discourse, in practice, at the Festival of Pacific Arts. After first outlining my approach and conceptual framework, I consider the nature of the festival as a state institution before highlighting some grassroots responses to state agendas, drawing on some particularly revealing cases involving Indigenous Australian participation.

Festival research

The first Festival of Pacific Arts was hosted by Fiji in 1972. The festival is held every four years in a different Pacific country, and there have been eleven so far. I have conducted participant observation at the last three: initially at the 2004 festival hosted by the Republic of Palau (see Glowczewski and Henry 2011), then at the 2008 festival hosted by American Samoa, and, finally, at the festival in 2011 hosted by Solomon Islands (see Henry and Foana'ota 2015). At the Palau festival, fieldwork was conducted with a small team of researchers, including French anthropologists Barbara Glowczewski and Jessica De Largy Healy, and indigenous Australian scholar, Joseph Neparrnga Gumbula. We were independent researchers in the sense that we were not officially attached to any particular country's delegation. I subsequently attended the festivals in American Samoa and Solomon Islands as a lone ethnographer, but worked in collaborative association with Lawrence Foana'ota, Katerina Teaiwa (2012) and Geraldine Le Roux (2011), who were pursuing their own research agendas. My research at all three festivals specifically concerned the nature of indigenous Australian participation, but I was also able to conduct informal interviews with, and observe the participation of, delegates from other countries. In addition to the public performances on stage, I attended many of the workshops and symposia organised as part of the festivals. My interpretive analysis in this chapter is also informed by comparative ethnographic research that I have conducted over a period of eighteen years at cultural festivals in Australia (Henry 2000a, 2000b, 2002, 2008, 2011, 2012).

The Festival of Pacific Arts attracts a good number of researchers, and one can be sure to bump into numerous anthropologists, historians, ethnomusicologists, scholars specializing in cultural studies, creative arts, performing arts, and so on, in addition to the usual crush of journalists and other media personnel. Thus, a plethora of material has been written on past festivals (e.g. Carell 1992; Hereniko 1980; Kaeppler 1987; Kempf 2011; Konishi 2006; Lewis-Harris 1994; Moulin 1993, 2003, 2005, 2007; Myers 1989; Simons 1989; Stevenson 1993, 1999, 2011). Much of this body of literature concerns issues of identity politics and addresses now well-debated ideas concerning 'the invention of tradition' and concepts of cultural authenticity (Hobsbawm and Ranger 1983). For example, Kempf (2011:178), in reflecting upon Banaban performances at the first Festival of Pacific Arts, argues that the festival fostered the growth of essentialist politics by seeking 'to regulate and monitor boundaries of articulation in the art of indigenous societies in the South Pacific, thereby preserving the ideal of a pure cultural essence'. In 2006, the Japan Centre for Area Studies, National Museum of Ethnology, published a fine collection of papers written by members of a team of anthropologists and ethnomusicologists from Japan (Yamomoto 2006a). The authors specifically focused on art and identity issues at the level of the nation-state. Yamomoto (2006b), for example, in a study of the political situation in New Caledonia at the time of the eighth festival, argues that each festival has a different flavour depending on the particular country hosting it.

The festival is clearly deeply entwined with the colonial history of the Pacific. The thirty-nine years since its inception have seen dramatic political transformation, with most of the former Pacific Island colonies and trust territories becoming independent nation-states. At the time of the first festival in 1972, only Western Samoa (which was renamed Samoa in 1997), Fiji, and Tonga were independent countries. This raises some fascinating questions. How has the changing political status of Pacific peoples affected their participation in the festival over the years? How might the festival have operated to disseminate and/or reproduce effects that foster state formation in the Pacific? How might the festival work to facilitate political alternatives to the state? Because each festival is hosted by a different country, different local political agendas as well as shifting cross-cutting political ties and 'narratives of nation' come to the fore at each event (Otto and Thomas 1997; Yamamoto 2006a). In this chapter, I begin to tackle some of these questions by focusing mainly on Australian participation in the festival. Of particular interest to me is what such participation reveals about the changing status of Aboriginal and Torres Strait Islander people in Australia and the ways indigenous peoples attempt to resist the influences of the Australian state. While the Festival of Pacific Arts cuts across state boundaries to celebrate pan-Pacific identity – 'the Pacific Way', it is clearly an institution of statecraft. As Jessop (1990:9) argues, national boundaries 'do not constitute a fixed horizon for emergent state projects: there is no more reason to rule out strategies aiming to build multi- and transnational networks and circuits of state power than there is to exclude local or regional projects'. Thus, for the purposes of analysis, I turn to some insights from anthropological literature on the state for what they might tell us about the role of festivals in political innovation in the Pacific.

State effects: the festival as an institution of statecraft

My approach to understanding the relationship between the festival and the state follows the school of thought that sees the state not as a concrete institutional fixity, but as an ideological construct that, nevertheless, assumes phenomenal reality through concrete practices and their effects. As Kapferer (2005:ix) writes: 'The reality of the state is to be grasped ethnographically both in its imaginary and in the concreteness of the practices that have a state relation or reference'.

Trouillot (2001:126) suggests a strategy for the study of the state that enables us to deal with two apparently contradictory contemporary experiences of state power: that state power 'seems more visible and encroaching', as in the experience of indigenous Australians (indeed all Australians); and 'sometimes less effective and less relevant', as perhaps in the case of so-called failed states. Trouillot argues that the state can be recognized in multiples sites via its effects (Krohn-Hansen and Nustad 2005:7). Influenced by Nicos Poulantzas (1968) and Bob Jessop (1990), Trouillot (2001:126) defines state effects as including:

(1) *an isolation effect*, that is the production of atomized individualized
subjects molded and modeled for governance as part of an undifferentiated
but specific 'public'; (2) *an identification effect*, that is, a realignment of
the atomized subjectivities along collective lines within which individuals
recognize themselves as the same; (3) *a legibility effect*, that is, the production
of both a language and a knowledge for governance and of theoretical and
empirical tools that classify and regulate collectivities, and (4) *a spatialization
effect*, that is, the production of boundaries and jurisdiction (italics in original).

Trouillot's (2001:126) proposition that 'state effects never obtain solely through national institutions or in governmental sites' has inspired me to look for such effects in the festival phenomenon (see also Henry 2008). These, I submit, can be found by paying close attention to what people actually do on the ground in the context of the festival, their practices and performances (on and off the stage), and their reflections on, and responses to, events (whether foreseen or unforeseen) as they unfold in the festival context. I argue that while festival performances can be readily interpreted as *displays* of identity, they are more than mere representations. Festival performances constitute *practices* of identification and differentiation that emerge in confrontation with hegemonic post-colonial discourses on culture as heritage that 'inspire in the indigenous subject a desire to identify with a lost indeterminable object – indeed, to be the melancholic subject of traditions' (Povinelli 2002:39). While it is an institution of statecraft, the festival also provides a forum for grassroots interrogation of global discourses concerning cultural authenticity, intellectual property rights and ownership of heritage.

The Festival of Pacific Arts is a public event where many different state agendas are played out (including those of the large states competing in the Pacific – USA, Japan, France, the People's Republic of China, the Republic of China (Taiwan), Indonesia, New Zealand, and Australia). For example, at the festival in Palau in 2004, one could observe in action, what Ron Crocombe (2007:vii) refers to as 'a spectacular transition' in the Pacific Islands: 'For the past 200 years external influences, whether cultural, economic, political or other, have come overwhelmingly from western sources. That is now in the process of shifting to predominantly Asian sources.' At the Palau festival, there were debates about whether an uninvited group from West Papua, flying the Indonesian flag, should be permitted to perform, and whether Taiwan should have the right to participate. Taiwan first sought permission to participate in 1988 at the festival in Townsville, but at that time the Council of Pacific Arts denied its request. Twelve years later, the Council reversed its decision and Taiwan sent a delegation of eighty indigenous performers and artists to the festival in New Caledonia in 2000. In Palau, a Taiwanese representative introduced the performances of the delegation with a speech describing the prehistoric connections between Taiwan and the Pacific. The delegation sought recognition and legitimation as representatives of the ancestral Austronesian stock from which, they argued, Pacific peoples had originated. Although Taiwan participated again at the festival in American Samoa, whether they should have been invited to do so was still a matter of debate (Ragogo 2008). In addition, concerns were raised at this festival about the legitimacy of the participation of a Samoan delegation from the diaspora in San Diego, California. At issue was whether extra-state teams and individual artists, who are not official delegations of the member states of the Council of Pacific Arts, should be allowed to participate.

Although, state identities are highlighted, particularly at the Opening and Closing Ceremonies of the festival, with the prominent use of official state flags, there are other practices that operate to mute nation-state identities. For example, delegations are announced in terms of the concept of island: 'the island of Hawaii', 'the island of Australia' and, diplomatically at the Festival in American Samoa, the 'island of San Diego'. Thus, emphasis is given to the unifying role of the ocean and the idea of a 'sea of islands' (Hau'ofa 1994). While this works well for Torres Strait Islander Australians, it is not as felicitous a model for Aboriginal Australian delegates. As Jilda Simpson, a member of the Aboriginal singing group 'Freshwater', commented in a documentary on the festival in American Samoa:

> We are not kind of an island kind of community. We don't have an island
> flavour in the way that other small islands of the Pacific do. So I was kind of
> worried about how we slot into that scheme of things over here. At the end
> of the day, not fitting into that scheme made it more special because we are
> so different and we are unique and people appreciated that difference.
>
> (*Festival of Pacific Arts, Part 2*, 2008)

The festival celebrates difference at the same time as it is intended to foster unity in the Pacific. Here the concept of 'island' and 'islander' sets Aboriginal Australians apart as different, but the festival also fosters other differentiations and identifications, such as Melanesians versus Polynesians, categorical identities that have grown out of Western colonial imaginings and representations of the Pacific (see also Kabutaulaka, this volume).

At each of the three festivals I attended, indigenous Australian delegates commented to me that they felt they were received with special warmth. This may be partly because, as Jilda Simpson notes, they appear unique among the huge gathering of Polynesian and Melanesian delegates, but also perhaps because there is recognition of their oppressed status as a Fourth World People. According to Chips Macinolty (pers. comm. 2009), who attended the festival when it was hosted by Papua New Guinea in 1980, there was

> ... an enormous amount of 'sympathy', for want of a better word, from
> the Pacific delegations towards the Aboriginal dancers in particular:
> Perhaps 'high regard' is a better word, and based on the knowledge that
> ... Aboriginal Australians lived in a society overwhelmingly dominated by
> European structures.

While delegations are supported to attend the festival in the expectation that they will act as representatives of bounded nation-states, there is tension and ambivalence among participants about this expectation, particularly among representatives of encompassed groups, so called Fourth World Peoples, such as indigenous Australians. For example, in American Samoa in 2008 the delegation from Rapa Nui refused to carry the Chilean flag, much to the chagrin of the state official accompanying the delegation, while a non-indigenous New Caledonian expressed concern about prominence of the Kanak flag over the official national flag, the French tricolour. At the festival opening ceremony in Palau in 2004, the Australian delegation carried three flags of relatively equal size, the Australian national flag, the Aboriginal flag and the Torres Strait Islander flag. However, in American Samoa in 2008, the Aboriginal and Torres Strait Islander flags dominated. At the opening ceremony the delegation was led by only two flag bearers, Aboriginal and Torres Strait Islander representatives, proudly waving their respective flags. The Aboriginal and Torres Strait Islander flags were proclaimed under section 5 of the Flags Act on 14 July 1995 as flags of Australia, confirming their official usage on government buildings and at state-sponsored public events, including the Festival of Pacific Arts. Nevertheless, indigenous Australian delegates at the Festival are expected to carry the Australian national flag alongside their Aboriginal and Torres Strait Islander flags.

Australian soft diplomacy

Aboriginal and Torres Strait Islander delegates are state sponsored, today, through the Aboriginal and Torres Strait Islander Arts Board of the Australia Council for the Arts in partnership with the various state and territory arts agencies. For example, Australia's delegation to the Festival in 2008 was supported by Arts Victoria, Arts New South Wales, Arts Tasmania, Arts South Australia, Arts Queensland, Arts Northern Territory, Western Australia's Department of Culture and the Torres Strait Regional Authority.

The Arts Board is comprised of Aboriginal and Torres Strait Islander people, well versed in Western management systems, who choose the final delegation that will represent Australia after a process of application from performing groups and individual artists from across the country. For the festival in American Samoa in 2008, indigenous performers and artists were called upon to submit expressions of interest in accordance with particular selection criteria. These criteria included experience in international and/or national touring, an understanding of the responsibility of indigenous artists and/or organizations to be ambassadors of indigenous culture, high artistic skills and the ability to produce export-ready material.

Delegates are chosen on the basis of a state project that appropriates and aestheticizes local cultural performances, reclassifying them so that they are fit to represent the nation-state. Only those artists and performers, with overseas performing experience, who could be trusted to behave according to particular standards of social etiquette, were chosen. What Guss (2000:160) refers to as the 'hegemony of the smile' is in evidence here, as delegates are expected to be able to engage in soft diplomacy both on and off stage as cultural ambassadors and agents of state interest.

Thirty-three indigenous Australian artists, including a Torres Strait Dance Group and the Mornington Island Dance Group, were chosen for the festival in 2004 Palau, while the delegation for the 2008 festival in American Samoa was

forty-three strong, comprising individual artists and performers in addition
to a singing group and three dance groups – two Aboriginal (Doonooch and
Taikurtinna) and one Torres Strait Islander group (Ariu Panipan, led by Jeffery
Aniba from Saibai Island). Fifty-four artists participated at the Solomons
festival, including musicians, visual artists, designers, weavers, filmmakers and
three dance groups – the Chooky Dancers from Arnhem Land, the Nunukul
Yuggera Aboriginal Dancers from southern Queensland, and the Arkapa
Dance Company from the Torres Strait. Perhaps diplomatically so, Australia is
by no means dominant at the festival in terms of number, especially relative to
the New Zealand, Papua New Guinea, Fijian and New Caledonian delegations.
According to one of the officials in the Australian delegation, the size of the
Australian delegation was deliberately small, as their mission is to showcase
cultural performances representative of indigenous cultural diversity in
Australia, not to enter into competition with other delegations.

Heritage bearers: representing the nation

Popular discourses today still represent indigenous Australia in terms of
a disappearing world, or as a doomed culture. For example, Australian
journalist Nicolas Rothwell (2008:5) wrote in the *Weekend Australian* that
Aboriginal dancers at the festival in Fiji in 1972 had performed 'the last perfect
dance'. According to Rothwell, the work of master performers such as Peret
Arkwookerum from Aurukun and Djoli Laywanga from Arnhem Land 'is
gone and they have few successors'. Indigenous Australian participation at the
festival both reproduces and resists this state project, which classifies them as
the bearers of national heritage and as embodying a de-temporalized, mythic
past. The following statement by an Aboriginal dancer after he had observed
the performances of Pacific Islanders at the festival in American Samoa reveals
the impact of this discourse on participants in terms of the creation of a sense
of cultural loss:

> I have only just started in the last few years to realize how much my culture
> means to me and I've really just started to get into it and I'm just starting to
> get into my language now. So I feel just like a spring chicken compared to
> everything around me. I feel alienated but excited ... I did kind of felt like
> young compared with the rest of the cultures around here. Even though our
> culture has been around for so many thousands of years, I felt as though
> these fellas have been dancing!
>
> (Shane McEwan in *Festival of Pacific Arts, Part 1,* 2008)

Another example of how the Australian delegates respond to their role
as heritage bearers concerns an incident with one of the other delegations

in American Samoa. Upon their arrival at the Festival Village the Australian delegates discovered that the Aotearoa (New Zealand) delegation had occupied the shelter (*fale*) that had been allocated to them. The Australians moved to a neighbouring *fale*, but there was a domino effect, as that one had been allocated to the Marshall Islands. Some tensions ensued between the New Zealand and Australian delegations as a result of this situation, and due to the embarrassment the Australians felt at being forced to displace another group. Eventually, members of the Australian delegation decided to hold a traditional smoking ceremony in their new *fale* to clear away the resentment they felt. Later, they found out that the New Zealand team had not deliberately occupied the Australian *fale*, but that it was simply a matter of miscommunication. Nevertheless, the way that the Australian delegation chose to deal with the situation and their subsequent sense of confidence in their cultural knowledge, is telling. There was much discussion in the *fale* after the smoking ceremony about how proud and secure in their culture the ceremony had made them feel. Nardi Simpson, a member of the song group Freshwater, commented on this event as follows:

> Time stood still for me because we walked across this field singing our song and sweeping the ground and sweeping the *fale*. And we were asking people to come to be with us and you could feel it, eh? And from that moment, it grounded everyone. It got us in the zone of being artists. Everything here has been for us about how different we are to everyone. That was the first step in us being comfortable with how different we are from all these other mobs ... It was a perfect example of culture in practice because we had this situation, we all felt a certain way, and the automatic thing that we all did was look to our protocols, look to our traditions, bring that in to 2008 in American Samoa and practice it here. And we didn't do it on stage as a show, but that was us proving that connection that even back home, not just overseas, people think is gone, is over, dead, you know, old ways. That came through us, each one of us there that day. It was an automatic show of strength in culture and from that moment on, everything ... everything, you know, rolled on.
>
> (*Festival of Pacific Arts, Part 1*, 2008)

The ritual proved cathartic in that it provided members of the delegation with a means of addressing their sense of not really belonging, of being somewhat out of place in the Pacific. It also gave them a way to cast off the uncertainty they felt about how their performances might be received, in the face of the hurdle to demonstrate that they are authentic bearers of traditional practices handed down since time immemorial from their ancestors. By choreographing and staging this ritual, I suggest that the Australian delegates challenged problematic definitions of cultural heritage in terms of something fixed and unchanging that must be managed and protected at the level of the state and through international heritage conventions. Their creative response to a situation of stress and tension by staging an impromptu ritual worked to undermine the very idea that heritage is the preserve of the state.

While Aboriginal and Torres Strait Islander delegates are expected to be agents of the state diplomacy, it is clear that the festival also provides opportunities for participants to creatively resist state effects, or at the very least to pursue their own ends. At all three festivals I attended, I noted that delegates, particularly from the Torres Strait, spent much time seeking to establish cross-cutting ties through kinship connections. Many Torres Strait Islanders are genealogically related to Pacific Islanders who came to the Strait either as Christian missionaries or as part of the labour force for the pearling industry during the nineteenth and early twentieth centuries. At the Palau festival, a Torres Strait Islander, armed with a photograph of his grandfather who had come to the Torres Strait from the Pacific during the early twentieth century to work in the pearling industry, found a woman from Niue who was able to identify his grandfather. The woman introduced him to kin from his grandfather's village of origin, who were at the festival. Similarly, at the festival in American Samoa, two Torres Strait artists in the delegation discovered a young Samoan man who was related to them through his mother's father. They spent as much time as possible together throughout the festival, and I observed that the young Samoan came to the airport and waited for hours to wave off his new found relations. Again in 2012, at the festival hosted by Solomon Islands, a Torres Strait Islander accompanying the Australian delegation sought to reconnect with kin from Malaita. When it was the Australian delegation's turn to perform on stage at the satellite festival venue at Auki on Malaita, he was invited to sit on stage as guest of honour, in acknowledgement and recognition of his Malaitan roots. These cases reveal that participants use the festival as a fertile ground for establishing cross-cutting ties, employing a notion of kin relatedness that reaches beyond the state-based identities they have reservations about.

During each of the three festivals at which I conducted research, there was noticeable ambivalence among the indigenous Australian delegates with regard to whom or what they are representing. For example, at the festival in American Samoa, the delegates could be heard chanting 'Aussie, Aussie, Aussie! Oi, Oi, Oi!' in the buses transporting them to and from the venues, yet one of the delegates commented that they were not really there to represent Australia. In a report on the festival published online in *Islands Business*, Ragogo (2008) wrote that a member of the Australian delegation claimed: 'We do not call ourselves Australians, we are from Australia but belong to our respective places.'

Figure 1   Joseph Neparrnga Gumbula and Djambawa Marawili in the hardware store in Koror, Palau, 2004. Photograph by Rosita Henry.

Grassroots diplomacy: the case of the lost freight

The reservations that indigenous Australians have about representing Australia came to the fore at the Palau festival in 2004, after the delegation's freight was lost somewhere in transit. Upon arrival in Palau, the delegation had no costumes, musical instruments or materials for their artists (for example, pearl-shells from Broome in Western Australia and a type of grass from New South Wales used for weaving). Importantly, apart from a small carving that one of the delegates had carried in his personal luggage, there were no gifts to present at the opening ceremony. The officials from the Aboriginal and Torres Strait Islander Arts Board, who were leading the delegation, appeared to be at a loss with how to proceed, while the delegates themselves were unsure of what to do except wait and hope for the freight to arrive. Among the delegation, however,

Figure 2   Joseph Neparrnga Gumbula and Djambawa Marawili working on
material from the hardware store, Koror, Palau, 2004. Photograph by
Rosita Henry.

was an artist from Arnhem Land – Djambawa Marawili, a strong Yolngu
leader, and in our research team happened to be one of his countrymen, Joseph
Neparrnga Gumbula, who subsequently became an Indigenous Research
Fellow at the University of Sydney. Frustrated with the lack of action regarding
the freight, the two Yolngu men decided to take matters into their own hands
and asked me to help them find a hardware store. I sought out the Palauan
official who had been assigned to host the Australian team and facilitate their
well-being at the festival. He enthusiastically accompanied us to the hardware
store, where we purchased various materials that would allow Djambawa
and Joe to make their own musical instruments and other material objects –
didgeridoos, clap sticks, spear throwers and spears (Figure 1).

Djambawa and Joe said they did not need to wait for the freight, when
they were capable of producing these things themselves. They decided to take
matters into their own hands, thus not only signifying the strength of their
knowledge to the Australian delegates from other parts of Australia, but also
assuming a leadership role in terms of the art of cultural diplomacy.

Having observed the huge ceremonial gift exchange that was part of the
opening ceremony, and embarrassed by the fact that the Australian delegation
did not have much to give, Djambawa and Joe were determined to buy
materials at the hardware store to make their own gifts (Figures 2 and 3).

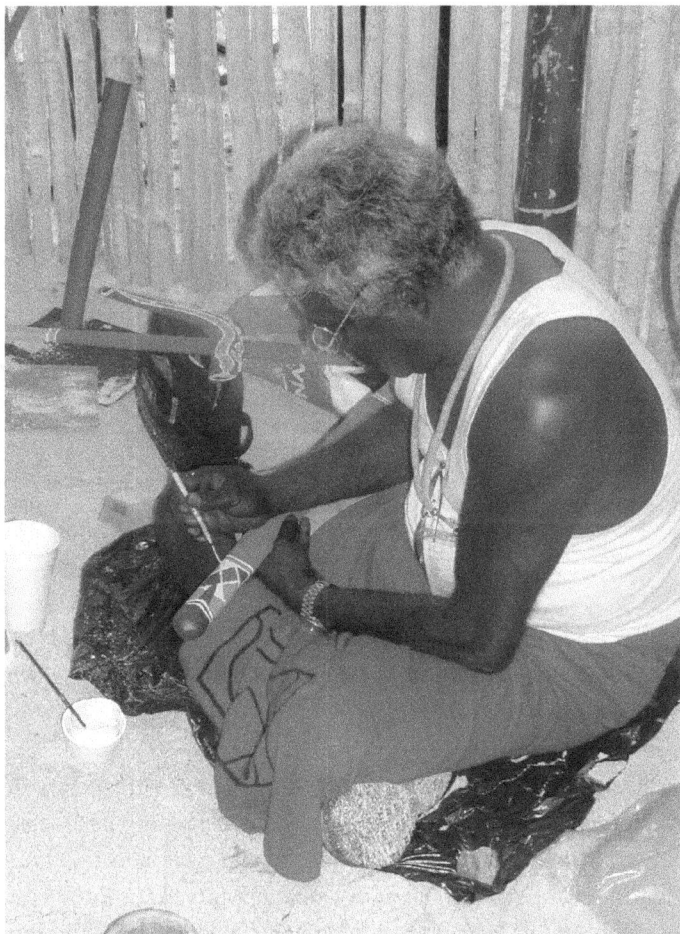

Figure 3   Joseph Neparrnga Gumbula, Koror, Palau, 2004. Photograph by Rosita Henry.

Djambawa was particularly keen to create a painting to present as a gift at the closing ceremony. We bought paints, brushes and a board. The brushes were not of the type or quality to which he was accustomed, so Djambawa asked me to volunteer a piece of my hair, out of which he then made a brush. He finished the painting during the eight days of the festival and did indeed present it at the closing ceremony (Figure 4).

How should one interpret this? Were Joe Neparrnga Gumbula and Djambawa Marawili taking the reins here as complicit agents of state diplomacy, or were they acting as grassroots Yolngu leaders and diplomats on behalf of their own people? Perhaps it was both. In the absolute security of his knowledge and understanding of Yolngu cultural practice, Djambawa felt free to spontaneously and innovatively choreograph a political ritual

*Figure 4   Djambawa Marawili working on the painting that he gifted to the Queen
of Koror at the Festival of Pacific Arts closing ceremony, Palau, 2004.
Photograph by Rosita Henry.*

of gift exchange, independently of the state agents, bureaucrats and arts
administrators accompanying the delegation. The painting itself was a work
of revelation, in which he proposed that Yolngu have a connection to the
Pacific sea of islands that transcends contemporary state formations. This
was confirmed by Joe Neparrnga Gumbula's contribution to the discussion
at a meeting of the International Council of Traditional Music (ICTM) Study
Group on the Music of Oceania held in Palau the day after the festival proper
(for accounts of this workshop, see Flores 2004; Glowczewski and Henry 2011).
Joe reflected upon the ancient connections that Yolngu people have with the
Pacific through the ocean currents that Yolngu perform in 'traditional song
series, the dance and all that' (Glowczewski and Henry 2011:171). Djambawa's
presentation of his painting and the accompanying dance he performed at
the closing ceremony suggested a way of demonstrating relationship and
connection with Pacific peoples via the potency of Yolngu song lines and the
agency of ancestral powers (Figure 5).

Conclusion: grassroots heritage
Ethnographic attention to the Festival of Pacific Arts enables productive
exploration of how heritage discourse is taken up and interpreted in the
Pacific. The festival is a contemporary social institution in which the presence

Figure 5   Djambawa Marawili dancing with his painting at the Festival of Pacific Arts closing ceremony, Palau, 2004. Photograph by Matial Dosdane.

of the state and its effects can be effectively observed and analysed. The practices and performances of participants at the festival reveal how the state becomes 'inscribed in persons and their relations' (Kapferer 2005:ix). Yet, I have argued, while the festival operates as a key site for the state to reproduce its effects, participants embrace it as an opportunity to forge relationships beyond state constraints.

Focusing on indigenous Australian participation in the festival, I have explored some of the ways that delegates respond to demands for them to embody a mythic past as bearers of heritage and representatives of nation-state diplomacy in the Pacific. Delegates assume their official roles as cultural diplomats with reservations. At the same time, they performatively propose alternative forms of social relation that cut across nation-state identities. Djambawa Marawili and Joseph Neparrnga Gumbula turned to ancestral knowledge in an attempt to establish Yolngu links with the Pacific, while Torres Strait Islander delegates at the festival, armed with old photographs and stories passed down to them by their Pacific Island grandparents, pursued kinship ties with long-lost relatives.

The Festival of Pacific Arts works to reproduce a global heritage discourse that valorizes cultural authenticity in performances. This generates anxieties among indigenous Australian delegates, and indeed other participants at the festival, about culture as property and about the loss of culture and tradition. Their anxieties, as Busse (2009:365) argues, 'are concrete, local manifestations of global processes of reification and reconceptualization of traditional knowledge, practices, and objects as property'. However, as I have shown, the festival is a complex social field that also provides fertile ground for participants to work through such anxieties.

Ralph Regenvanu (this volume) raises an important point about cultural heritage and the issue of cultural dynamism that is also pertinent in the context of the festival. On the one hand, indigenous Australians embrace the idea of attending the Festival of Pacific Arts as heritage bearers. After all, cultural heritage provides them a means of gaining state recognition and value as a colonially encompassed people. Yet, the festival generates moments of emergent agency and grassroots empowerment when participants engage in strategic attempts to redefine the heritage concept according to their own terms, that is as dynamic 'culture in practice'.

References

Bendix, R., A. Eggert and A. Peselmann (eds) 2012. *Heritage Regimes and the State* (Göttingen Studies in Cultural Property 6). Göttingen: Universitätsverlag.

Busse, M. 2009. Epilogue: anxieties about culture and tradition – property as reification. *International Journal of Cultural Property* 16:357–70.

Crocombe, R. 2007. *Asia in the Pacific Islands*. Suva: IPS Publications, University of the South Pacific.

Carell, V. 1992. The purpose, origin and future of festivals of Pacific Arts. *Pacific Arts* 5:1–5.

Festival of Pacific Arts, Part 1 2008. Episode on the ABC television show
    Messagestick. Sydney: Australian Broadcasting Commission, 2 November
    2008. www.abc.net.au/tv/messagestick/stories/s2407280.htm

Festival of Pacific Arts, Part 2 2008. Episode on the ABC television show
    Messagestick. Sydney: Australian Broadcasting Commission, 9 November
    2008. www.abc.net.au/tv/messagestick/stories/s2413656.htm

Flores, J. 2004. Report from the ICTM Study Group on the Music of Oceania:
    meeting at Koror, Republic of Belau, August 1–2, 2004. *Bulletin of the
    International Council for Traditional Music* 105.

Glowczewski, B. and R. Henry 2011. Dancing with the flow: political undercurrents at
    the 9th Festival of Pacific Arts, Palau 2004. In *The Challenge of Indigenous
    People: Spectacle or Politics?*, B. Glowczewski and R. Henry (eds), 159–75.
    Oxford: Bardwell.

Guss, D.M. 2000. *The Festive State: Race, Ethnicity, and Nationalism as Cultural
    Performance.* Berkeley: University of California Press.

Hau'ofa, E. 1994. Our sea of islands. *The Contemporary Pacific* 6:148–61.

Henry, R. 2000a. Festivals. In *Oxford Companion to Aboriginal Art and Culture*, S.
    Kleinert and M. Neale (eds), 586–7. Melbourne: Oxford University Press.

——— 2000b. Dancing into being: the Tjapukai Aboriginal Cultural Park and the
    Laura Dance Festival. In *The Politics of Dance*, R. Henry, F. Magowan and
    D. Murray (eds), 322–32. Special Issue, *Australian Journal of Anthropology*
    11(3).

——— 2002. Plesanje v povezanost: Aboriginski plesni in Kulturni Festival v Lauri
    [The Laura Aboriginal Dance and Cultural Festival]. In *Ples življenja, Ples
    Smrti [Dance of Life, Dance of Death]*, B. Telban (ed.), 31–48. Special Issue,
    Poligrafi 7(27–8). Ljubljana, Nova Revija.

——— 2008. Performing tradition: the poetic politics of Indigenous cultural festivals.
    In *The State and the Arts: Articulating Power and Subversion*, J. Kapferer
    (ed.), 52–69. Oxford: Berghahn Books.

——— 2011. Dancing diplomacy: performance and the politics of protocol in
    Australia. In *Made in Oceania: Social Movements, Cultural Heritage and
    the State in the Pacific*, E. Hviding and K.M. Rio (eds), 179–93. Wantage:
    Sean Kingston Publishing.

——— 2012. *Performing Place, Practicing Memory: Indigenous Australians, Hippies
    and the State.* Oxford: Berghahn Books.

Henry, R. and L. Foana'ota. 2015. Heritage transactions at the Festival of Pacific Arts.
    International Journal of Heritage Studies 21(2):133–52.

Hereniko, V. 1980. *Art in the New Pacific.* Suva: Institute of Pacific Studies, University
    of the South Pacific.

Hobsbawm, E. and T.O. Ranger (eds) 1983. *The Invention of Tradition.* Cambridge:
    Cambridge University Press.

Hviding, E. and K.M. Rio (eds) 2011. *Made in Oceania: Social Movements, Cultural Heritage and the State in the Pacific.* Wantage: Sean Kingston Publishing.

Jessop, B. 1990. *State Theory: Putting the Capitalist State in its Place.* Cambridge: Polity Press.

Kapferer, B. 2005. Foreword. In *State Formation: Anthropological Perspectives*, C. Krohn-Hansen and K.G. Nustad (eds), vii–xi. London: Pluto Press.

Kaeppler, A.L. 1987. Pacific festivals and ethnic identity. In *Time Out of Time: Essays on the Festival*, A. Falassi (ed.), 162–70. Albuquerque: University of New Mexico Press.

Kempf, W. 2011. The first South Pacific Festival of Arts revisited: producing authenticity and the Banaban case. In *The Challenge of Indigenous People: Spectacle or Politics?*, B. Glowczewski and R. Henry (eds), 177–86. Oxford: Bardwell.

Konishi, J. 2006. Performance and mediation: a historical view of traditional music and dance presented in the Festivals of Pacific Arts 1972–2000. In *Art and Identity in the Pacific: Festival of Pacific Arts* (JCAS Area Studies Research Report 9), M. Yamamoto (ed.), 111–32. Osaka: Japan Center for Area Studies, National Museum of Ethnology.

Krohn-Hansen, C. and K.G. Nustad 2005. Introduction. In *State Formation: Anthropological Perspectives*, C. Krohn-Hansen and K.G. Nustad (eds), 3–26. London: Pluto Press.

Leahy, J., J. Yeap-Holliday and B. Pennington 2010. *Evaluation of the Festival of Pacific Arts.* Noumea, New Caledonia: Secretariat of the Pacific Community.

Lewis-Harris, J. 1994. The sixth Pacific Arts Festival. *Pacific Arts* 9–10:10–20.

Le Roux, G. 2011. Urban strategies and artistic performances. In *The Challenge of Indigenous Peoples: Spectacle or Politics?*, B. Glowczewski and R. Henry (eds), 123–39. Oxford: Bardwell.

Moulin, J.F. 1993. The VIth Festival of Pacific Arts, Rarotonga, Cook Islands, October 17–27th. *Pacific Arts* 7:69–71.

——— 2003. Words of tomorrow: 'spectacle' and the Festival of Pacific Arts. *Pacific Arts* 25:23–30.

——— 2005. Oltobed a malt (nurture, regenerate, celebrate): the ninth Festival of Pacific Arts in Koror, Palau. *The Contemporary Pacific* 17:512–16.

——— 2007. Untying the knots in the aha tau, the sacred cord of time. In *Oceanic Music Encounters: The Print Resource and the Human Resources* (Research in Linguistics and Anthropology (RAL) Monograph 7), R. Moyle (ed.), 81–96. Auckland: Department of Anthropology, University of Auckland.

Myers, D. 1989. 5th Festival of Pacific Arts. *Australian Aboriginal Studies* 1:59–62.

Otto, T. and Ni. Thomas (eds) 1997. *Narratives of Nation in the South Pacific.* Amsterdam: Harwood Academic Publishers.

Poulantzas, N.A. 1968. *Political Power and Social Classes.* London: New Left Books.

Povinelli, E. 2002. *The Cunning of Recognition: Indigenous Alterities and the Making of Australian Multiculturalism*. Durham: Duke University Press.

Ragogo, M. 2008. Culture: who qualifies for the Pacific Arts Festival? The $Million question now being asked. *Islands Business Online*, November 2008. www.islandsbusiness.com

Rothwell, N. 2008. Rhythm sticks. *The Australian* (25–6 October):4–6.

Simons, S.C. 1989. The 5th Festival of Pacific Arts. *Oceania* 59(4):229–310.

Smith, L. 2012. Discussion. In *Heritage Regimes and the State* (Göttingen Studies in Cultural Property 6), R. Bendix, A. Eggert and A. Peselmann (eds), 389–95. Göttingen: Universitätsverlag.

Stevensen, K. 1993. The 6th Festival of Pacific Arts. *Pacific Studies* 6:67–9.

——— 1999. Festivals, identity, and performance: Tahiti and the 6th Pacific Arts Festival. In *Part and Performance in Oceania*, C. Anderson and B. Craig (eds), 29–36. Honolulu: University of Hawai'i Press.

——— 2012. *The Festival of Pacific Arts Celebrating 40 Years*. Suva, Fiji: Secretariat of the Pacific Community.

Teaiwa, K.M. 2012. Choreographing difference: the (body) politics of Banaban dance. *The Contemporary Pacific* 24(1):65–94.

Trouillot, M.R. 2001. The anthropology of the state in the age of globalization: close encounters of the deceptive kind. *Current Anthropology* 42(1):125–38.

van Meijl, T. (ed.) 2009. *Pacific Discourses about Cultural Heritage and its Protection*. Special Issue *International Journal of Cultural Property* 16(3).

Yamamoto, M. 2006a. *Art and Identity in the Pacific: Festival of Pacific Arts* (JCAS Area Studies Research Report 9). Osaka: National Museum of Ethnology.

——— 2006b. The eighth Festival of Pacific Arts: representation and identity. In *Art and Identity in the Pacific: Festival of Pacific Arts* (JCAS Area Studies Research Report 9), M.Yamamoto (ed.), 5–27. Osaka: National Museum of Ethnology.

Rosita Henry is Professor of Anthropology at James Cook University.

CHAPTER 2

Space wars

Nan Madol as cultural and political property

✳

DAVID HANLON

Prefatory remarks

This essay follows from a chapter on Nan Madol that appeared in an earlier volume emerging from the Pacific Alternatives project (Hanlon 2011). In that chapter, I sought to give some sense of this remarkable, truly impressive megalithic site of 93 human-made islets, linking channels and bordering structures that lies off the south-eastern coast of Pohnpei Island in the Eastern Caroline group of the larger Micronesian geographical area. I surveyed the archaeological work on Nan Madol, now a part of the chiefdom and municipality of Maldolenihmw, and considered the earliest written descriptions of Nan Madol as more than a seemingly innocent collection of travellers' tales, missionary musings, colonialist speculation and inaccurate scientific treatises. I argued for an understanding of these writings as discursive attempts to appropriate Nan Madol as a powerful symbol that worked to justify outlanders' diverse presences and purposes in the area.

Opposed to these writings are local histories of Nan Madol that are partial, often times ambiguous and even conflicting, but are histories nonetheless. These multiple and contested histories speak of the foreign identity of Nan Madol's designers, the system of political and religious rule established there, the assertion of that rule over Pohnpei proper, and the varying responses from different areas of the island, which included a complex mix of acquiescence, adaptation and resistance. In assessing Nan Madol's contemporary significance as a cultural property intimately connected to Pohnpeian identity, I reviewed the changing demographics and landscapes on Pohnpei, and underscored the differing histories of four colonial regimes that need to be factored into any reading of Nan Madol's more recent past, or of its future. The story of Nan Madol's colonization is ongoing.

We need to consider the word 'state' and the myriad of issues surrounding Pohnpei's restlessness as one of the four constituent states of the Federated States of Micronesia (FSM). On the other hand, there is also the relationship of the FSM to the United States of America through the Compact of Free Association. These state relationships have created a host of jurisdictional conflicts, including ones over the maintenance, management and preservation of important historical properties. A programme of historic preservation,[1] begun during the American administration of the Caroline, Mariana and Marshall Islands, known then as the Trust Territory of the Pacific Islands, continues today as specified by the terms of the Compact of Free Association between the United States and the FSM. Funding comes from the US National Park Service and is managed through a regional umbrella organization known as the Micronesian Endowment for Historic Preservation. In what some might consider the ultimate colonial act, Nan Madol is currently registered as a National Historic Landmark on the US National Register of Historic Places.[2] Despite assertions of national sovereignty and autonomy, the historic preservation programme in the FSM remains driven by the definitions, criteria and priorities of its principal, external donor, the United States. Stephen Wickler's contribution to this volume offers a similar assessment of the historic preservation programme in the Republic of Palau, which was once a part of the US-administered Trust Territory of the Pacific Islands.

Nan Madol, however, has not been so easily subdued. Understood by many as the place where the island's current chiefly system originated, Nan Madol has figured prominently in constructions of Pohnpeian identity and history. It can be seen as affecting instances of both overt and subtle forms of resistance to outside domination, ranging from violent conflict and rebellion during the Spanish (1886–99) and German (1899–1914) colonial periods to votes against the Compact of Free Association and persistent talks of secession from the FSM. My intention here is to look at an early and prolonged conflict between Pohnpeians and those who would, for their own purposes and on their own terms, prescribe how Nan Madol was to be preserved and conserved through seemingly benevolent means. I undertake this examination in light of one of this volume's major themes; namely, the connections between expanding perceptions of cultural heritage and the emergence of differing, more localized political forms. But how to approach this conflict in terms that do not continue the reification of old, tired and colonial categories or oppositions, but rather offer other, more insightful grounds on which to critique and understand, and with an eye to an alternative future?

*Figure 1   The exterior west wall of Nan Dauwas, one of Nan Madol's most
prominent structures. (Courtesy of J. Stephen Athens, International
Archaeological Research Institute, Honolulu, Hawai`i.)*

My account of this contestation over Nan Madol begins in 1950, and
then moves both backward and forward in time, with 1979 being the end
date. Throughout this chapter, I employ an ethno-historical approach
that examines Nan Madol in terms of competing epistemologies and
differing historiographies. The advantage in this struggle lay with American
administrators, who used their power and privilege to require that Pohnpeians
make their case in English and through a host of foreign procedures that
included the formation of a special committee, public hearings, legal research
into colonial land policies and the histories of specific claims, and the filing
of a final report. I rely then on a largely discursive analysis of historical
documents in which Pohnpeian perspectives emerge through a decidedly
colonial filter. Some might find it tempting to discredit Pohnpeian arguments
as too colonially affected, and thus distorted. The willingness, however, of
Pohnpeians to engage the issue of Nan Madol through the language, laws
and administrative procedures of their colonizers, is better understood as
evidence of what Lauren Benton (2002) has described as an effective counter-
response to the conditions of colonial domination that, at the same time, risks
the debasement of more indigenous forms of dispute resolution. There must
also be recognition of the essentializing quality of the often-made statement
that Nan Madol stands as the source or origin point for traditional Pohnpeian
culture. Those Pohnpeians who argued publicly for local control did so

because of their immediate and vested interests in the high chiefly titles, clan rankings, political paramountcy and cultural privileges chartered in Nan Madol's histories. Nan Madol's past and future relationship to the larger island is a point of local debate and contestation, the dimensions of which can be seen in the more contemporary space wars considered at the end of this essay.

A different kind of Micronesian archaeology

Barbara Kirshenblatt-Gimblett (1995) has written about the need to rethink disciplinary subjects and practices as a way to theorize heritage more critically. Not only do the meanings of history and culture as they are understood and practised locally need to be examined, the production of the knowledge that sustains work in cultural heritage – or, as it is known in the American-affiliated areas of Oceania, historic preservation – also requires more careful assessment.[3] Part of theorizing heritage in the Micronesian instance involves a critical examination of the local apparatus or programme of 'historic preservation'. The discourses around cultural heritage and historic preservation are both a product of and a response to the processes of empire and its direct descendant, globalization. Put another way, this heterogeneous ensemble of ideas about the past is related to, and indeed a part of, a very long history involving the forces, mechanics, ambiguities and contradictions of colonialism. But there are trajectories of agency, appropriation and mimicry that must be accounted for as well. There is no simple history of the interplay between external forces and local responses to be found. Things are far more complicated than that.

Bhabha's (1987) notion of mimicry is helpful in understanding the contestation over Nan Madol. He writes of the mix of uncertainty, ambivalence, indeterminacy and appropriation that are a part of the local response to colonial impositions. Bhabha (1994) also writes of a third space, in which cultural sites are separated from an indigenous source at the same time that they are covered by colonial inscription. In many ways, this is a particularly apt metaphor for Nan Madol, whose name translates as 'in the space between things'. We might then understand the struggles over Nan Madol as taking place in a third space filled with differing representational practices and historical understandings that have been affected by the asymmetry of power. In short, Bhabha's approach invites an interstitial reflection, or mediation on an interstitial entity.

At the same time, oppositions must not be seen as absolute. James Clifford's (2001) attention to the pragmatic, entangled, contemporary forms of indigenous cultural politics is useful in understanding Pohnpeian articulations around Nan Madol in the period under study and in more contemporary times. Nan Madol is understood and represented by different groups of

Pohnpeians, with varying claims, connections and historical and genealogical linkages to the site. This is a flexible heritage, and one that is about local, varied enunciations in competition with one another at the same time as they seek to address the larger swirl of global forces that would blow them away. Unlike Bhabha, however, I am not willing to concede that Nan Madol now exists as no more than the sum of all of the archaeological investigations, preservation projects and development plans produced about it. Nan Madol's past and the histories concerning that past amount to much more than a constructed authenticity or an archival assemblage of processes, practices and politics. I suggest, then, a selective use of Bhabha's third space as a way to interrogate the contestation over the ownership and control of Nan Madol.

Bhabha's phrases 'constructed authenticity' and 'archival assemblage' direct attention to the historic preservation programme in the Trust Territory of the Pacific Islands. A way of understanding this programme is through an examination of the discursive practices that ultimately allowed for the normalization of Nan Madol as a historic site under the jurisdiction of the US National Parks Service. I am referring here to an archaeological approach that is quite different from the science of archaeology practised on Pacific pasts; an approach inspired by Foucault that is concerned with discursive (archival) and non-discursive (institutional) practices that, if left unchallenged, permit the meaning of things to be altered or transformed to something very different to anything they had ever been before.

If, as Foucault (1977) notes, power works institutionally and through an established set of habits and discursive practices, then we might understand the US-sponsored historic preservation programme as an institutional manifestation of colonial power operating to refashion the history of the peoples called 'Micronesians'. The depth and complexity of islands' pasts are reduced to a single general history. A regime of truth is thus established regarding the islands' common past, the importance of its preservation, and the ways in which that preservation can and should be effected. The result is a discourse that establishes historic preservation as normal, desirable, even essential, and certainly good. There is the assumption too that places like Nan Madol need to be protected and preserved not just from external development projects, but also from the ambitions, neglect and indifference of Micronesians themselves. The issue of 'legibility' comes into play here. James Scott (1998) writes of the ways in which the state seeks to make legible the activities, interests and needs of its residents for purposes of identification and control. These include population registers, cadastral studies, the standardization of language, the invention of freehold land tenure systems, and the creation of law codes. The imposition of a historic preservation programme such as that found in the Trust Territory of the Pacific Islands can be similarly viewed as an effort to make the deeper indigenous past more legible to those who sought to understand, interpret, refashion, and manipulate it.

The 1974 amendment to the 1966 National Historic Preservation Act marks a critical event that made historic preservation a legible and institutional practice that facilitated in seemingly benign ways American control of the Trust Territory. The inclusion of Micronesia under the 1966 National Historic Preservation Act through the 1974 amendment also contributed to the islands' domestication. Historic preservation proved a particular feature of American colonialism in Micronesia that distinguished it from other preceding colonial regimes that were indifferent to or dismissive of local histories. Historic preservation gave a more beneficent face to American colonialism at the same time as it contributed to a hegemonic dominance over the islands' pasts as well as their multiple presents.

The historic preservation programme in Micronesia is linked in both historical and contemporary times to the process of development. I understand development in the Micronesian context as an externally defined, imposed and totalizing discourse that seeks to fundamentally transform peoples' ways of knowing, being and interacting with each other and their physical environment (Hanlon 1998). Development is about being made to become something else and other, and includes not just political and economic aspects, but the cultural, historical, religious and spiritual as well. If programmes of economic development in the Trust Territory were about making people productive workers and responsible consumers, historic preservation might be understood as a remaking of their historical consciousness, and hence their sense of themselves. The continuation of that programme under the terms of the Compact of Free Association between the United States and the FSM belies the use of the term 'post-colonial' when referring to historic preservationist practices in the area.[4]

At the same time, we need to concede that a colonial system is less than totally efficient or effective. It can be possessed of internal contradictions and tensions that dilute its force or make it vulnerable to local machinations. What also tempers or at least adjusts a simply theoretical or largely discursive take on matters of historic preservation in the former Trust Territory of the Pacific Islands is both the existence of local histories and the responses of island peoples themselves, who sought to preserve in their own ways their historical and cultural properties from those who sought to do those things for them.

In examining struggles over Nan Madol, we need then to be mindful of the hegemonic nature of colonial policies in Micronesia, but aware too of the subtle, complex, varied, contradicting and even conflicting ways in which the people called 'Micronesians', in this case Pohnpeians, engaged with the structures, procedures and processes employed by those who claimed the right to govern them and their islands. Ranajit Guha (1983) has written of the ideological tools and constructs of domination that can be used by subordinated or subaltern peoples for counter-hegemonic purposes. Mimicry there may have been, which Bhabha (1987) reminds us was unsettling to colonial officials in its almost but not quite familiar features. Quetzil Castañeda (1996) cautions us against the use of the term 'impact' when referring to development because of its easy elision or slighting of the local. Following Castañeda, I am concerned with more than discourse and the development of hegemonic practices and beliefs affecting history and historic preservation. I look also to the local engagements with these discursive and institutional practices that marked the struggles for control of Nan Madol. As Lynn Meskell (2012) has observed, debates over cultural heritage reflect the tense, contentious, complex and always fraught interplay between the pressing realities of the present and the fluid memories of the past.

Nan Madol as contested terrain[5]

My account of the struggles or space wars over Nan Madol begins in 1950, six years after the United States' forceful seizure of the Caroline, Mariana and Marshall Islands from Japan, and three years after the United Nations' awarding of a strategic trusteeship to the United States over the three island groups. In the absence of a still-to-be-established law code for the Trust Territory of the Pacific Islands, Civil Administrator J.R. Bass, with the prior approval of the high commissioner, issued on 15 December 1950 a proclamation regarding historical monuments on Pohnpei, or Ponape as it was then called, and elsewhere in the Trust Territory.[6] Nan Madol received explicit mention in the proclamation. Ownership of these historical monuments rested with all of the people of the Trust Territory through their government; responsibility for the preservation and protection of these properties, including Nan Madol, was given to the district or island administration and the local municipality in which they were found.[7] Any private interests granted by previous colonial regimes were revoked.

While the first Trust Territory Law Code was promulgated in 1952, it would not be until the issuance of the revised 1970 code that there would be specific provisions dealing with historic properties. Chapter 11, Sections 251 through 256, established policies and administrative procedures for historic sites and antiques, and charged the Trust Territory deputy director for resources and development with administrative powers and responsibilities. The Historic Sites Commission, an eleven-member advisory board created by the Congress of Micronesia in 1967, was recognized. The congress was itself a recently constituted entity, authorized in 1965 by the United States government to provide more representative government for Micronesians.

Members of the board could be 'citizens of the United States or Micronesia or both'; were expected to be competent in history, archaeology, architecture and human geography; and served at the pleasure of the high commissioner.[8] These provisions remained unchanged in all future issuances of the Trust Territory Code.

The claims to ownership and control of Nan Madol by the Trust Territory government did not go uncontested. At the urging of Pohnpeian traditional leaders through their elected representatives, the newly formed Congress of Micronesia passed House Resolution No. 34 during its third regular session in 1967; the resolution requested the high commissioner to appoint a special committee to investigate the legal status of Nan Madol. Selected by then Ponape District Administrator Boyd Mackenzie at the request of the high commissioner, members were officially charged by Deputy High Commissioner Martin P. Mangan, in a memo dated 11 March 1968, with reviewing the rights of ownership, use, possession and custodianship of Nan Madol.[9] The Special Committee was also tasked with a consideration of any prior agreements affecting Nan Madol, and with making recommendations on the general maintenance and preservation of the site in light of community and governmental interests.

The committee members were all Pohnpeians and were drawn from the district legislature, Madolenihmw municipality and its municipal government. Samuel Hadley, the *nahnmwarki* or paramount chief of Madolenihmw, and thus the most senior and ritually prominent of all the island's chiefs, sat on the committee, as did two local historians or 'cultural experts'. Mackenzie had requested that the advisory committee serve beyond the remit of its commission as an advisory body for the maintenance of all archaeological and historic properties in the district. Mangan declined, however, to expand the responsibilities of the Special Committee, noting that there now existed the Historic Sites Commission to serve that very function on a Trust Territory-wide basis.[10]

The Special Committee on Nan Madol filed its report in English on 2 August 1968 after a series of public meetings at which numerous people testified.[11] The committee also consulted records from previous colonial administrations housed at the District Land Management Office. The committee prefaced its findings with a history of Nan Madol from the time of its construction under the Saudeleurs to their overthrow by the local Pohnpeian hero Isohkelekel. Isohekelekel's victory established a precedent, the report argued, that placed ownership of Nan Madol with his immediate heirs, the holders of the ruling title of *nahnmwarki* of Madolenihmw.

The report also dealt with a long-standing controversy over a land-use agreement at Nan Madol.[12] The committee noted that during the German administration of the island, then Nahnmwarki Paul gave a man named Alexander and his descendants the right to harvest tree crops at Nan Madol, with the profits divided between the *nahnmwarki* and Alexander and his family. At the time of this agreement, Alexander held the title of *nahlaimw*, a high-ranking title in a second or junior line of chiefs that traditionally assisted with the governance of a chiefdom. In 1912, German Governor Hermann Kersting endorsed the *nahnmwarki's* grant by issuing a deed of trust naming Alexander as trustee, and giving him and his heirs perfect use rights to Nan Madol. In the committee's collective opinion, this was a valid and still operative land-use agreement. The committee's report noted that the agreement was never disputed during German times and that the *nahnmwarki's* ownership of Nan Madol had never been questioned. An English-language translation of the trust deed was appended to the report.

Upon Alexander's death, his use rights to Nan Madol passed to his eldest natural son, Salvador Alexander. During Japanese times (1914–44), a Japanese school teacher identified as Kiriyama organized a group of young men from Madolenihmw, and forcefully prevented Salvador Alexander from exercising his access rights to Nan Madol. A subcommittee report included an English-language translation of a 1937 quitclaim document, signed by Salvador Alexander, various Japanese officials, and their local Pohnpeian representative, that formalized Alexander's abrogation of any use rights to Nan Madol.[13] The full committee noted in its report that this quitclaim was coerced; Salvador Alexander did not speak or read Japanese, and was thus unaware of the rights he was relinquishing. Moreover, the then reigning *nahnmwarki* of Madolenihmw, Moses Hadley, was not consulted and certainly did not give his approval. The report also noted that Salvador Alexander had unsuccessfully sought reaffirmation of his harvesting privileges with regard to Nan Madol in the early years of the American administration, and was continuing to wait for the restoration of his use rights.

The body of the report closed with a reference to *luhwen wei*, a term referring to land unoccupied but belonging to the *wei* or chiefdom in which it was located. The report argued that the disposition of any lands considered *luhwen wei* could only be made by the *nahnmwarki* 'who owns such lands and (in) whose jurisdiction the land is located'.[14] *Luhwen wei* was not to be equated with what the Trust Territory administration called 'public land', land that was considered unoccupied, unused and unclaimed. Moreover, Nan Madol's historical significance could not be overestimated because it 'is where the Ponapean customs originated from'.[15] The committee's report asserted that Nan Madol was *luhwen wei*; that the *nahnmwarki* of Madolenihmw in whose chiefdom Nan Madol was located had responsibility to see that all *luhwen wei* be used and maintained for the benefit of the entire municipality; and that the

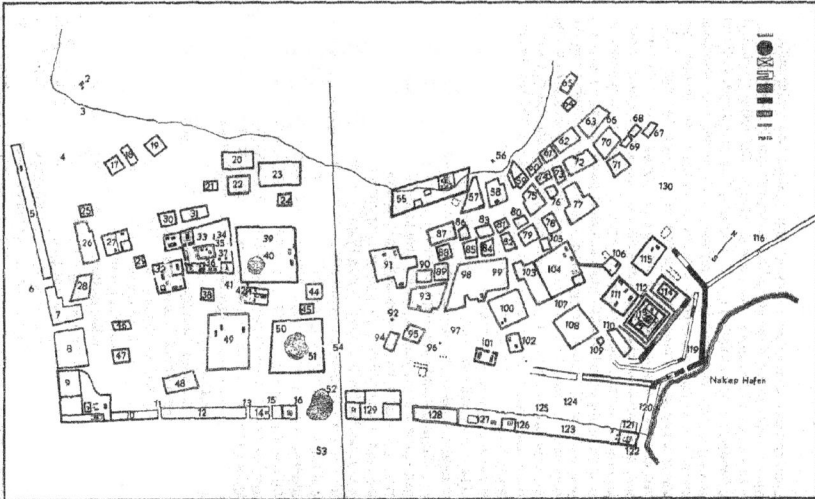

Figure 2   A site map of Nan Madol that appeared in volume three of Paul Hambruch's Ergebnisse der Südsee Expedition, 1908–1910, Ponape, *edited by Georg Thilenius and published in Hamburg by Friederichsen and De Guyter, 1936.*

nahnmwarki of Madolenihmw was thus the owner of Nan Madol.[16] The report also took strong exception to Civil Administrator Bass's earlier declaration that Nan Madol was the property of the Trust Territory government, arguing that this was done without the approval of the *nahnmwarki* and contrary to individual rights and freedoms as specified in Trust Territory Law Code's Bill of Rights. Pohnpeians' defence of their lands and traditions did not preclude supporting reference to the laws of their most recent colonizers. The weapons of the weak could sometimes be drawn from the arsenal of the strong.

The report concluded with three recommendations regarding ownership and use rights at Nan Madol that were to be implemented by the high commissioner through the Congress of Micronesia: (1) that ownership to Nan Madol be vested with the *nahnmwarki* of Madolenihmw and that the Trust Territory government relinquish all rights it may have acquired over Nan Madol; (2) that the *nahnmwarki* restore use rights at Nan Madol to Salvador Alexander as originally granted to his father during German times; and (3) that visitors' rights to Nan Madol be maintained. Johnny Hadley, son of Nahnmwarki of Madolenihmw, Samuel Hadley, signed as committee chair. Edwel Santos, a representative in the district legislature from Kiti municipality or chiefdom, added his signature as recording secretary for the Special Committee. The committee report was then sent to High Commissioner W.R. Norwood on 8 October 1968, who forwarded it to his attorney general for review and then transmittal to the Congress of Micronesia's House of Representatives and the newly formed Historic Sites Commission.[17]

The Trust Territory attorney general's office first sought comments from several administrative divisions. Jonathan Koshiba, a researcher for the Land Administration Branch, commented on the Special Committee's report.[18] He wondered why the Japanese government's acquisition of Nan Madol by coercion and force was considered illegal, while Isohkelekel's conquest was not. Someone wrote in the margins of Koshiba's 11 August 1970 memo: 'Japanese were non-Micronesians'. Kozo Yamada, a Pohnpeian and the Chief of the Division of Lands and Surveys for the Trust Territory, also reviewed the Special Committee's report.[19] In a memo dated 4 October 1971 to the Trust Territory attorney general, he disagreed with the assertion that the ownership of Nan Madol resided with the *nahnmwarki* of Madolenihmw, and saw no advantage to any conciliatory approach that sought to make the high commissioner and the *nahnmwarki* joint custodians of the site. Such a proclamation, Yamada argued, would effectively remove Nan Madol's designation as public land, and with a host of subsequent complications. Yamada recommended a resolution of the dispute over title to Nan Madol, and requested the attorney general's assistance in identifying 'an acceptable approach that will permit this area to be set aside and managed'.

In his criticism of a joint trusteeship for Nan Madol, Yamada was referencing an earlier review done by the head of the Land Resources Branch, Norman P. Knott, in June of 1970.[20] Knott had undertaken an extensive review of the title to Nan Madol as requested by the Trust Territory attorney general's office and in response to the Special Committee's report. Knott recommended that the *nahnmwarki* of Madolenihmw and the high commissioner sign a proclamation declaring Nan Madol to be a Micronesian heritage site under governmental administration to ensure its care and maintenance. The actual administration of Nan Madol was to be entrusted to the district administrator of Ponape, who would be assisted by a seven-member committee chaired by the *nahnmwarki* of Madolenihmw, and with its other members drawn from the district government, the Historic Sites Commission and the *nahnmwarki*s of the island's four other municipalities or their representatives. Pressed by Nahmmwarki of Madolenihmw, Samuel Hadley, as a way to acquire leverage, Ponape District Administrator Boyd Mackenzie had supported the recommendations from the Land Resources Division.[21] The attorney general's office was asked to draft the authorizing proclamation but instead issued a counter opinion.

In a letter of 2 September 1971 to Norman Knott, now the acting chief of the Trust Territory's Lands and Surveys Office, Attorney General Richard Miyamoto and Assistant Attorney General James A. Stanton argued that their office could not draft a proclamation for the high commissioner's signature creating a public trust over Nan Madol with the *nahnmwarki* of Madolenihmw as co-trustee.[22] The opinion reviewed the history of land tenure under the German, Japanese and American administrations, and concluded that Nan Madol was public land, and thus the property of the Trust Territory government. The high commissioner had no authority to grant by trust or otherwise the area to the *nahnmwarki* of Madolenihmw.

In reinforcing the position that Nan Madol was public land, the opinion acknowledged provisions in the German land deeds of 1912–14 that stated all land for which there was no title belonged to the tribe or state within whose boundaries it lay. The authors, however, noted that the Japanese administration had overturned this particular policy by decreeing that non-private land belonged not to the tribe or state within whose boundaries it lay but to the administration. The quitclaim signed by Salvador Alexander was thus not a transfer of ownership, but a relinquishing of all leasehold interests to Nan Madol that, in effect, recognized Nan Madol as Japanese government land. The letter also cited the theory of state succession in support of its determination that Nan Madol was public land. Since Nan Madol was public land under the Japanese, its ownership automatically passed to the succeeding American administration.

The attorney general's office was especially critical of the Special Committee's report. It regarded the report as suspect and not supported by the available evidence. The chairman of the committee was the son of the *nahnmwarki* of Madolenihmw; this, Miyamoto and Stanton wrote, was a clear conflict of interest. On Pohnpei, however, any *nahnmwarki*'s chief representative was usually his eldest son. The eldest son of a *nahnmwarki* would often rise to become *nahnken*, the highest title in the afore-mentioned secondary or junior line of chiefs, who acted in the administrative interests of their seniors and who were known collectively as the *serihso* or 'sacred children'. Johnny Hadley, the chairman of the Special Committee, would eventually receive the title of *nahnken*, but not in his father's lifetime.

The review by the attorney general's office also noted that the committee report could not be considered to reflect the unanimous opinion of the committee members, as it was signed by only the chairman and the recording secretary. In addition, the attorney general's opinion cited a provision within the Trust Territory Code that required actions for the recovery of land to be commenced within twenty years of the determination being contested, which, in this case, was the 15 December 1950 decision by Civil Administrator Bass. The period of limitations had expired and the *nahnmwarki* of Madolenihmw had lost his right of claim for recovery. The opinion went on to note that the *nahnmwarki* 'had ample opportunity to resolve the present dispute in the courts. Having declined this opportunity, it is not the province of the Government to grant him the land through executive action.'[23]

The report closed with the citation of an earlier opinion of 31 August 1970, which decreed that the high commissioner had no inherent authority to alienate public land. This power belonged to the legislative branch, which in this case was the Congress of Micronesia, as earlier mandated on 27 September 1967 by United States Department of Interior Order No. 2918 that returned all public lands to Micronesians through their elected representative body. The opinion concluded that it was only the Congress of Micronesia that could grant Nan Madol to the *nahnmwarki* or otherwise establish some form of trust. Given the political sensitivities of the situation and the likelihood of an uncomfortable precedent, the still fledgling congress declined such action.

Despite the opinion of the Trust Territory attorney general's office, the issue of Nan Madol's status went unresolved, though the challenges did not cease. In an 18 September 1973 letter written in English to High Commissioner Edward Johnston, the Nahnmwarki of Madolenihmw, Samuel Hadley, protested a planned aerial survey of the Nan Madol area.[24] Hadley wrote that no aerial survey should take place until the 'fundamental problems concerning ownership and future use' of Nan Madol were resolved. Hadley challenged what he understood to be the Trust Territory's claim to ownership, a claim contrary to the law of Pohnpei as it existed traditionally and as codified in the German administration's land-tenure documents. Hadley argued that Nan Madol had been entrusted over the centuries to those who held the title of *nahnmwarki*. Each had exercised control over Nan Madol 'on behalf of, and as a traditional leader of his people'.[25] This 'protective and sacred control' had gone uninterrupted since the time of the founding Saudeleurs.[26]

The *nahnmwarki* went on to assert that the title of Nan Madol had never been given or sold to any person, and could not be, as its ownership resided in the people of Madolenihmw. The letter continued:

> Because of its history, and because of its importance to all Ponapeans, any
> decisions concerning Nan Madol can and must be made by the people
> of Madolenihmw. It is therefore imperative that the Government obtain
> the approval of the people of Madolenihmw concerning the purposes of
> the aerial survey and the master plan proposals for Nan Madol. You must
> understand that Nan Madol remains a very important and very sacred place
> to the people of Ponape. Far from being a dead relic, Nan Madol is the living
> embodiment as well as the source of Ponapean traditional culture. For this
> reason, even well intentioned activities may be extremely inappropriate.[27]

The *nahnmwarki* closed with the statement that until the Trust Territory government disavowed its claim to Nan Madol, he could not approve any government activities affecting the area. Johnston responded on 5 October 1973.[28] He apologized for the distress and confusion surrounding the aerial survey, but asserted it had nothing to do with title or ownership, and was simply part of a larger information-gathering project designed to facilitate the development of infrastructure and facilities, and to accelerate the cadastre and homesteading programmes on the island.[29]

Reflections

The above narrative invites a long and critical reflection. There is the 1950 proclamation from the Trust Territory government declaring that Nan Madol belonged to all of the people of the Trust Territory, a statement later amended in the Trust Territory Law Code that gave the Trust Territory government authority for all historic properties to be administered through a Historic Sites Commission. There is, too, the deployment of loose, shifting, slippery terms such as 'ownership', 'control' and 'joint trusteeship'; overtly colonial interpretations of what constituted public land and of the precedents of preceding colonial regimes; and the general discrediting of Pohnpeian responses upon procedural grounds and a lack of any real knowledge on the part of Trust Territory administrators about land tenure, social relationships and the roles of chiefs on Pohnpei. There was also a denial of the colonialism imposed upon the island through an increasingly bureaucratic system of control that required Pohnpeians to represent themselves through committees, reports, at hearings and in meetings.

At the same time, it should be acknowledged that oppositions are neither polar nor absolute. Pohnpeian notions of chieftainship and land tenure have always been somewhat fluid, contingent, sectionally variable, subject to negotiation, and affected by the nearly three-quarters of a century of formal colonial rule that preceded the 1950 proclamation by the Trust Territory Civil Administrator. The history of the Madolenihmw chiefdom also comes into play here. Despite its ritual primacy derived from its direct link to the conqueror of Nan Madol, Isohkelekel, and the establishment of a new chiefly polity for the island, Madolenihmw has proven a contentious land. There is a phrase, '*wehi keredi, kereda*', which translates as 'a land of constant political turmoil' (Hanlon 1988:276). Different clans and regions within Madolenihmw have contested the primacy of the Dipwinpahnmei – the ruling clan, the *nahnmwarki*'s clan – in the time since Isohkelekel. And within the Dipwinpahnmei there were at times tense, internecine struggles for power. The intrusion of whalers, traders, missionaries, naval ships and colonial regimes complicated even further a local polity that had been contentious and unsettled since its inception.

The ritual primacy of Madolenihmw and its ruling chief did not translate easily into those areas of life affected by the modernist project: government, economy, education and development. Pohnpeians most important differences and distinctions tended to be amongst themselves. The efforts of the descendants of Alexander confronted not only the impediments raised by two successive colonial governments, but the ambivalence and uncertainty of later *nahnmwarki*s less inclined than Nahnmwarki Paul to grant personal access and usage rights to Nan Madol.

The Congress of Micronesia, created in 1965, added an alien and limited albeit ultimately useful forum through which Pohnpeians addressed their concerns about the disposition of Nan Madol. Beginning in 1979, Pohnpeians had to contend with not just the United States of America but the Federated States of Micronesia, which eventually established its own law code. The FSM law code includes provisions for the maintenance and preservation of historic properties through an institutional entity called the Micronesian Institute for History and Culture. These new arrangements came with their own jurisdictional complications and administrative layering. Still, the phrase that rings loudest among these local articulations comes from the 1968 report of the Special Committee: Nan Madol is 'where the Ponapean customs originated from'. Masao Hadley, a high-ranking chief of Madolenihmw and the son of Nahnmwarki Moses Hadley, expressed a similar sentiment in his history of the site (1980a:1, 1980b:1). '*Nan Madol wasa sarawi oh waun ehu oh pil lingan*' – 'Nan Madol is a place of sanctity and respect, and it is beautiful.'

In examining the influence of cultural heritage on future political alternatives, it is important to keep in mind the very different colonialisms in Oceania, and their varying effects on islands' pasts and presents. *The Americanization of Micronesia* is the title of a book written by Roger Gale, published in 1979, that sounds dated in this era of globalization. A survey of American colonial rule over the islands, Gale's study details a time when, under the liberal rhetoric of development, the people called Micronesians were being asked to become other than they were. The islands were being remade into places that had the look, feel, sound, speed, smell and taste of America about them. Historic preservation extended this refashioning to the past, and the ways in which that past would be remembered, and its surviving properties and artefacts preserved. Local historical knowledge was thus drained of its specificity and mystery, and rendered in simpler, more general terms that allowed colonial administrators to better manage and control it. Frederick Errington and Deborah Gewertz (2001) call this process 'generification'. Understanding historic preservation in Micronesia as part of a larger process called development requires us to look under Gale's blanket of Americanization to see the resistance and alterity that can lie under the guise of bureaucratic compliance. Resistance and alterity are two very prominent themes that emerge from the histories Pohnpeians tell about themselves and their island. These histories resist the codification that would render the deeper Pohnpeian past static and lifeless, a reductionism that Thomas Ernst (1999) refers to as 'entification'.

Geoff White (1991) reminds us of how people express their identity through the histories they make about what is important to them. To quote Nahnmwarki Samuel Hadley again, Nan Madol 'remains a very important and very sacred place to the people of Ponape'. Despite the differential relationships that varying groups of Pohnpeians have toward the site, a consciousness of Nan Madol and its past is still very much a part of what it means to be Pohnpeian. Pohnpeian identity was at stake in the violent, localized responses to Spanish and German incursions at the end of the nineteenth and beginning of the twentieth century. Pohnpeian identity has also been at issue in more recent engagements over power, control, autonomy and development with the Federated States of Micronesia government, and these have included Nan Madol. Talk of secession from the FSM that began as early as 1981, persists. A deeper appreciation of Nan Madol's place in Pohnpeian understandings of themselves and the larger world makes possible a recognition of the future alternatives the site encourages by so consistently linking past to present.

Shifting the view from Peirot

I close with a story from Nan Madol. On the islet of Peikapw within the Nan Madol complex, there was once a pool of water known as Peirot (Hadley 1980a:80). In its waters, the rulers of Nan Madol were said to have been able to see what was transpiring on Pohnpei and beyond. Such intelligence was critical to the maintenance of their power. Things have changed. Peirot has long since dried up, but the patterns of the Pohnpeian past persist. Nan Madol may once again prove a place through which Pohnpeians envision a political future that is at once linked to and significantly different from their present. It will not be without more space wars, however. They continue in these contemporary times and with increasing intensity.[30]

In a reassertion of chiefly power, the current *nahnmwarki* of Madolenihmw, Kerpet Hadley, has claimed ownership of Nan Madol and the sole right to collect entrance fees to the site from all foreign visitors. The *nahnmwarki's* insistence on his rights has led to several unpleasant confrontations with visitors who were either unaware of the fees or unwilling to pay them. Residents of Temwen Island, whose property must be crossed to access Nan Madol by land, have also asserted their right to charge transit or access fees. The descendants of Nahlaimw Alexander and his son Salvador Alexander, whose property abuts the islet of Pehi en Keital on the western, land border

*Figure 3   An aerial photograph of Nan Madol that offers a partial view of the
site. Temwen Island is to the immediate left of the ruins. (Courtesy of J.
Stephen Athens, International Archaeological Research Institute, Inc.,
Honolulu, Hawai`i.)*

of Nan Madol, have challenged the *nahnmwarki*'s claim to sole ownership;
they have moved beyond their ancestors' claims to gathering rights and now
argue for partial ownership of Pehi en Ketal, as well as the right to charge
entrance fees through the islet. These contestations within Madolenihmw led
the *nahnmwarki* in April of 2010 to proclaim Nan Madol closed to all visitors
until further notice.

Ownership and entrance fees are not the only issues around which
foreign and local interests compete. There are more ominous challenges to
Nan Madol's past, present and future in the form of development plans. In
July 2009, the Governor of the State of Pohnpei, John Ehsa, who is himself

from the north of Madolenihmw, signed a Memorandum of Understanding (MOU) with Unicorn Star International Holdings Limited, a subsidiary of the Taiwan-based, venture-capital investment firm, Hotung Investment Holdings, Ltd (Jaynes 2009). The MOU stipulated that the governor would submit legislation to the Pohnpei State Legislature that authorizes the construction of a major resort, hotel and casino complex at Lukop, in the Sapwalap area of central Madolenihmw. Cultural tours and other tourist related activities focused on Nan Madol figure prominently in the proposed development project. The idea was not a new one; Rancho Verde, a British and Australian investment group, proposed a resort complex for Lukop in 1994. A Korean group later made a similar proposal through a local businessman. Neither plan survived public and legislative scrutiny. The Hotung proposal looked headed for a similar fate. The Pohnpei State Legislature took no action for almost a year. With the MOU set to expire in December, exasperated executives of the Hotung Group flew to Pohnpei to lobby for legislative action on the MOU in June of 2010. Their visit had its effects.

In late May of 2011, the Pohnpei State Legislature, despite the strong opposition of the local Catholic Church, passed the Micronesian Tourist Development Act, which allows for the establishment of a resort hotel and casino in Lukop. The bill gave authority to the Public Lands Trust Board of Trustees to execute a 55-year lease agreement for land in Lukop. The hotel was to have not less than 300 rooms, was to be built in three phases, and required a minimum investment of $150 million. Unicorn Star International Holdings Limited's initial proposal had called for a 1,000-room hotel and an initial investment of $50 million. The bill specified competitive procedures and requirements for the submission of development proposals, amended the Pohnpei State Law Code to permit gaming, established a Pohnpei Casino Gaming Commission, detailed the authority and jurisdiction of the commission, set regulations for the conduct of gaming activities, and added a gaming tax to the Pohnpei code. Upon passage of the bill, the Pohnpei State Governor's office issued a formal call for proposals. Unicorn International indicated its intention to submit a proposal, but with no expectations, its spokespeople added, of favour or advantage because of its previous efforts. A multitude of local questions and objections involving land use, access, ownership and the identities of local benefactors, however, stalled the process. The death of one of the principal Hong Kong investors caused further delays that appear for the time being to have effectively ended the likelihood of any casino and resort complex being built in Madolenihmw (Raynor 2013).

A casino and resort complex at Lukop is not the only development initiative involving Nan Madol. Previously, representatives from the government, the private sector and non-governmental organizations had gathered on

Pohnpei in mid-May of 2010 to consider a nationwide economic development plan centred around the World Park concept (FSM Information Service 2010). If approved, Pohnpei and the other three states of the FSM would become a wholly protected area, adhering to development and conservation standards designed to safeguard the country's unique cultures and rich marine biodiversity. The plan calls for Pohnpei and the other three states to transition to a tourism-based economy that features cultural sites and related activities; not surprisingly, Nan Madol is at the core of the Pohnpei plan, and would be dramatically affected by the major infrastructure and facilities development required in advance of its implementation. The World Park concept is a form of ecotourism on a national scale; its proponents argue that it will generate jobs, income, and help develop the FSM national economy.

Opposition to the plan on Pohnpei comes from the conservation community that views the World Park concept as straight-up tourism backed by foreign researchers out of touch with local values. Others worry that the plan would envelop not just land but people, creating in effect a cultural zoo frozen in time and designed for tourists to gawk at. The effects of such a plan on land-tenure systems on the 607 islands and atolls that make up the FSM is a major concern. How families, clans, individual landowners, state land boards and local businessmen would respond to the restrictions placed upon land use is a serious question. Complementing the World Park concept and the national government's emphasis on tourist-industry development, Pohnpei State paid for the renovation of its main airport terminal and the extension of the airport runaway to accommodate larger jets presumably coming from East Asia. State-sponsored advertisements on local television in early 2010 called for the tripling of the island's hotel rooms.

What drives all of these development plans, both local and national, is the continuing dependency of the FSM national government and its constituent states on American financial assistance provided through the Compact of Free Association. The current version of the compact, revised in 2003 and set to expire in 2023, has placed strong oversight and authorizing controls on that assistance. In addition, provisions within the revised compact call for a gradual reduction in direct funding over the life of the revised compact, to be replaced by contributions to a national trust fund, the interest from which is supposed to cover the costs of government functions and services following the expiration of the compact. In the estimation of most observers, the interest income generated by the trust fund will come nowhere near providing the FSM national government with the financial resources needed to sustain, let alone develop, itself economically. Hence, there has resulted an intense, almost desperate focus on tourism development on Pohnpei and the FSM.

Amidst these intensified efforts at tourist development, consideration has been given to proposals from more global agencies that seek to preserve and protect Nan Madol. The FSM Office of National Archives and Cultural and Historic Preservation has filed an application with the United Nations Economic, Social and Cultural Organization (UNESCO) to designate Nan Madol as a World Heritage site (Mauricio 2010). The application has the support of the *nahnmwarki* of Madolenihmw, who has created his own advisory committee to deal with issues that include ownership, administration, visitors' rights and access fees. Whatever the benefits, the designation of Nan Madol as a World Heritage site would add yet another layer of bureaucratic regulations to a piece of sacred geography already awash in a sea of conflicting claims and jurisdictions.

Nonetheless, Nan Madol endures. Its future and that of the island with which it is so intimately bound remain to be determined. All of this is not to say that things will necessarily end well or for the better. There is in the deeper Pohnpeian past the story of Liahnensokole, the turtle mother of Pohnpei, who offered her body as sacrifice to the Saudeleurs or stranger kings who built Nan Madol (Hanlon 1988:14–15). Hers was a submissive act that sought accommodation between the island and those who came from afar to dominate it. Amidst the increasingly anxious concerns for the development of tourism and a more self-sustaining national economy, there is the possibility that Nan Madol, like Liahnensokole, could become a subject of sacrifice to local ambitions, national needs and foreign investment. Conversely, and ironically, the failure to transform Nan Madol into a tourist site could well contribute to the dissolution of the FSM and require a different political reconfiguration for the island of Pohnpei. I suspect, however, that the power struggles over Nan Madol will not resolve themselves so easily or neatly as this. My four years of involvement with the Pacific Alternatives project has convinced me of the capacity of cultural heritage to encourage a visioning of the future beyond the nation-state. This is in a sense why there continue to be struggles over Nan Madol. I have also learned that, in the case of Nan Madol, struggles for power are more complicated, messy and fraught than imagined or theorized. Ongoing contestation over cultural heritage on Pohnpei underscores just how important are the stakes involved, and how intimately linked are that island's past and present.

Notes

1 'Historic preservation' is the vernacular in the USA and FSM for what in UK English would be termed 'heritage preservation'.

2 Nan Madol received designation as a National Historic Landmark on 16 September 1985; see *National Union* 6(22):4.

3   While I am highly critical of the historic preservation programme in Pohnpei and the Federated States of Micronesia, I hold a great deal of respect and admiration for those on the ground who struggle valiantly to make it serve local preservation needs.

4   Negotiations between representatives of the United States and what became the Federated States of Micronesia governments lasted from 1969 to 1982. The various procedures required for approval of the draft Compact of Free Association and the termination of the Trusteeship Agreement took another four years. The formal end of the Trusteeship and the official implementation of the Compact of Free Association occurred on 3 November 1986.

5   This section expands substantially on a narrative account first presented in Hanlon 2011:132–4.

6   A copy of this two-page proclamation can be found in the United States Trust Territory Archives (TTA), reel no. 2101, frame no. 0149. A copy of this microfilmed archive is housed in the University of Hawai`i at Mānoa's Hamilton Library.

7   Pohnpei and surrounding islands constituted one of the then six administrative districts of the territorial government; the Marshalls, the Northern Marianas, Palau, Truk (now Chuuk), and Yap were the other five. Each of the six districts was further divided into municipalities that were usually based on local divisions and boundaries. On Pohnpei, these divisions mirrored the island's five chiefdoms with separate municipalities established for the six outer islands included in the district.

8   John Richard Steincipher, Esq., ed., *Law Code of the Trust Territory of the Pacific Islands*, revised and re-codified, vol. II, Title 31-83. Seattle: Book Publishing Company, 1970, p. 22.

9   Administrative Directive 68-8, *Establishment of Special Nan Madol Committee*, 11 March 1968, TTA reel no. 2101, frame no. 0149.

10   Deputy High Commissioner to District Administrator, Ponape, 15 March 1968, TTA, reel no. 2101, frame no. 0149.

11   Special Nan Madol Committee, 'Report and Recommendation on the Legal Status and the Future Disposition of Nan Madol', 2 August 1968, TTA, reel no. 0445, frame no. 0115.

12   A somewhat different account of the land-use agreement for Nan Madol is contained in the papers of anthropologist John L. Fischer, 'Notes on Ponape', typewritten manuscript, 3 boxes, MS Case 5, PO 2, Bernice P. Bishop Museum, Honolulu, Hawai`i. See especially Fischer's translated and transcribed interview with Nahlik Lapalap of Melolenim (*sic*), 31 August 1950, folder D6 S1, and his translation of a letter by Lorenz Henry, the Chief Magistrate of Madolenihmw, dated 17 September 1950, miscellaneous file.

13   Subcommittee of (the) Special Nan Madol Committee, 'Report on Status of Nan Madol, Madolenihmw Municipality, Ponape District, Trust Territory of the Pacific Islands', 8 April 1968, TTA, reel no. 5033, frame no. 0141. The subcommittee's

report also includes testimonies given at public hearings held on Temwen Island in Madolenihmw municipality.

14   Special Nan Madol Committee, 'Report', 2 August 1968, TTA, reel 0445, frame no. 0115, p. 3.
15   Ibid.
16   Ibid.:4.
17   High Commissioner to Attorney General, 26 December 1968, TTA, reel no. 0545, frame no. 0156.
18   Research Officer, Land Administration Branch, to Record (File 178.67.9), 11 August 1970, TTA, reel no. 2101, frame no. 0149.
19   Chief, Division of Land and Surveys, to Attorney General, 4 October 1971, TTA, reel no. 2101, frame no. 0149.
20   Norman P. Knott, 'Nan Madol: Status of Title', June 1970, TTA, reel no. 2101, frame no. 0149.
21   Mackenzie to Johnston, 14 April 1971, TTA, reel no. 2101, frame no. 0149.
22   Miyamoto and Stanton to Knott, 2 September 1971, TTA, reel no. 0445, frame no. 0115.
23   Ibid.: 4.
24   Hadley to Johnston, 10 September 1973, TTA, reel no. 2101, frame no. 0149.
25   Ibid.:1.
26   Ibid. Legal issues have been further complicated by the municipal charter of Madolenihmw, which recognizes the *nahnmwarki* of Madolenihmw as the owner of Nan Madol; see *National Union* 6(12):7.
27   Hadley to Johnston, 10 September 1973, TTA, reel no. 2101, frame no. 0149, p. 1.
28   Johnston to Hadley, 5 October 1973, TTA, reel no. 2101, frame no. 0149.
29   Nahnmwarki Samuel Hadley later agreed to allow federally funded clearing and archaeological investigations of parts of Nan Madol.
30   This account of current and local controversies involving Nan Madol is drawn from observations and conversations that occurred during my visit to Pohnpei in April 2010. I wish to acknowledge Dr. Manuel Rauchholtz, the Consulting Cultural Anthropologist with the FSM's Office of National Archives, and Culture and Historic Preservation, for the information and insight he imparted to me. I also thank Bill Raynor of the Nature Conservancy office on Pohnpei for his updates on Nan Madol via email in October of 2013.

References

Benton, L. 2002. *Law and Colonial Cultures: Legal Regimes in World History, 1400–1900*. Cambridge: Cambridge University Press.

Bhabha, H.K. 1987. Of mimicry and man: the ambivalence of colonial discourse. In *October: The First Decade*, A. Michelsen, R. Krauss, D. Crimp, and J. Copjec (eds), 318–22. Cambridge, Mass: MIT Press.

———— 1994. *The Location of Culture.* London: Routledge.

Castañeda, Q.E. 1996. *In the Museum of Mayan Culture: Touring Chichén Itzá.* Minneapolis: University of Minnesota Press.

Clifford, J. 2001. Indigenous articulations. *The Contemporary Pacific* 13(2):468–90.

Ernst, T.M. 1999. Land, stories, and resources: discourse and entification in Onabasulu modernity. *American Anthropologist* 101(1):88–97.

Errington, F. and D.B. Gewertz 2001. On the generification of culture: from blow fish to Melanesian. *Journal of the Royal Anthropological Institute* (NS) 7:509–25.

Federated States of Micronesia 1980–1996. *National Union: An Official Publication for the People and the States of the Federated States of Micronesia.* Honolulu: Pacific and Hawaiian Collection, University of Hawai`i at Mānoa, Hamilton Library.

Federated States of Micronesia Information Service 2010. Pohnpei explores economic development office. *Pacific Islands Report* (3 June) http://pidp. eastwestcenter.org/pireport/text.shtml

Fischer, J.L. n.d. Notes on Ponape. Typewritten manuscript, 3 boxes, MS Case 5, PO 2. Bernice P. Bishop Museum, Honolulu, Hawai`i.

Foucault, M. 1977. Nietzsche, genealogy, history. In *Language, Counter-Memory, Practice: Selected Interviews and Essays,* D.F. Bouchard (ed.), 139–63. Ithaca, NY: Cornell University Press.

Gale, R. 1979. *The Americanization of Micronesia: A Study in the Consolidation of U.S. Rule in the Pacific.* Washington, DC: University Press of America.

Guha, R. 1983. *Elementary Aspects of Peasant Insurgency in Colonial India.* Delhi: Oxford University Press.

Hadley, M. 1980a. A History of Nan Madol. Unpublished, English-language version. Trans. and ed. P.M. Ehrlich. Copy in author's possession.

———— 1980b. Koasoai en Nan Madol. Unpublished, Pohnpeian-language version. Trans. and ed. P.M. Ehrlich. Copy in author's possession.

Hanlon, D. 1988. *Upon a Stone Altar: A History of the Island of Pohnpei to 1890* (Pacific Islands Monograph Series 5). Honolulu: University of Hawai'i Press.

———— 1998. *Remaking Micronesia: Discourses over Development in a Pacific Territory, 1944–1982.* Honolulu: University of Hawai'i Press.

———— 2011. Nan Madol on Pohnpei: the future of its past. In *Made in Oceania: Social Movements, Cultural Heritage, and the State in Oceania,* E. Hviding and K.M. Rio (eds), 121–40. Wantage, Oxon.: Sean Kingston Publishing.

Jaynes, B. 2009. Pohnpei courting 1,000-room casino resort. *Pacific Islands Report* (30 July) http://pidp.eastwestcenter.org/pireport/text.shtml.

Kirshenblatt-Gimblett, B. 1995. Theorizing heritage. *Ethnomusicology* 39(3):367–80.

Mauricio, R. 2010. Personal communication. 12 April. Kolonia, Pohnpei.

Meskell, L. 2012. *The Nature of Heritage: The New South Africa.* Malden, MA: Wiley-Blackwell.

Raynor, B. 2013. Personal Communication. 27 October. Madolenihmw, Pohnpei.

Scott, J.C. 1998. *Seeing Like a State*. New Haven: Yale University Press.

Steincipher, J.R. (ed.) 1970. *Law Code of the Trust Territory of the Pacific Islands* (revised and re-codified, 2 vols). Seattle: Book Publishing Company.

Trust Territory of the Pacific Islands. 1952–1986 Microfilmed Records of the Trust Territory Government. Honolulu, University of Hawai'i at Mānoa, Hamilton Library.

White, G.M. 1991. *Identity Through History: Living Stories in a Solomon Islands Society.* Cambridge: Cambridge University Press.

David Hanlon is Professor of History at the University of Hawai'i at Mānoa.

CHAPTER 3

Feasts, festivals and phantoms

The predicament of cultural policy
in a Solomon Islands society

✳

GEOFFREY WHITE

The term 'cultural policy' is deceptively straightforward. It connotes a kind of disciplining of the unruly concept of culture, making the abstract concrete, the intangible tangible, so that 'it' can be recognized, discussed and acted on. The word 'policy' also locates culture in the realm of state agencies and organizations that need policy to *do things* with culture. It is that bridge, between culture and action, as well as between the (trans)national and the local, that concerns me in this chapter. Similar to Ralph Regenvanu's discussion in his distinguished lecture on Vanuatu's attempt to 'mainstream culture into national development on a policy level' (in this volume), my focus in this chapter is the border zone between the national and the local in which state-sponsored interest in culture meets local practices. However, my particular interest is in the points of disconnection where national policies meet the local with little effect, passing like phantoms that never quite materialize in daily life.

In a previous publication (2011), Lawrence Foana'ota and I discussed the absence of a national cultural policy in the Solomon Islands, asking why something that had been discussed for decades had yet to be produced. That changed in 2012 with the publication of the first national cultural policy for Solomon Islands, a document titled 'Solomon Islands Nasinol Policy, Framework blong KALSA: Mainstreaming KALSA in Nation-building and Development', notably using Solomons Pijin terms for 'national policy' and 'culture' to inflect the document with a distinctive element of national identity (Ministry of Culture and Tourism 2012). The publication of this document (compiled by the Solomon Islands Division of Culture in the Ministry of Culture and Tourism, and copyrighted by the Secretariat of the Pacific

Community (SPC)) was stimulated by the country's hosting of the South Pacific Festival of the Arts in 2011 and supported by the SPC and the European Union. The predicament for cultural policy in Solomon Islands and Melanesia, however, is the intensely local nature of traditional cultural practices that are only tenuously (if not contentiously) related to the national institutions where policy statements are produced in concert with regional and global organizations. In this chapter, I explore this Melanesian conundrum by focusing on one locale, the island province of Santa Isabel, to reflect on the kinds of social activity signified by talk of 'culture' or '*kastom*', and the degree to which such activities do and do not articulate with national visions of cultural policy.

In a context where central government offices are as often a conduit for extractive policies that align more with foreign corporate interests than local communities and their subsistence-oriented lifestyles, directives from central offices may be as much a formula for conflict as for cooperative efforts aimed at cultural strengthening. When the new cultural policy speaks of 'harnessing' culture as a 'sector' for development (Ministry of Culture and Tourism 2012:1), and elaborates on the various dimensions of the cultural 'industry' that may benefit the Solomons, the language is that of development planning where success is most often measured in terms of monetized growth rather than the intangibles of knowledge production and social relations. On the one hand, the new Solomon Islands policy makes an important and long-awaited intervention aimed at strengthening indigenous practices in areas such as language, traditional medicine, justice, education and cultural copyright. Yet its implementation runs the risk of subordinating local actors to a newly legalized authority of the state empowered to regulate cultural practice using templates for 'best practices' articulated by regional organizations.

Cultural transformation in twentieth-century Melanesia generally proceeded in the guise of modernization and Christianization, with the aim of replacing or reforming elements of traditional culture. In the postcolonial era, as noted by Ralph Regenvanu for Vanuatu, these polarities are turned around, with the valorization of indigenous practices a means of decolonization. Following national independence, global talk of 'heritage' became a tool (or weapon?) put to use in movements for local empowerment. In asking about the purpose and politics of cultural policy, I continue a conversation begun in 1994 at the Honiara conference on Developing Melanesian Cultural Policy (Lindstrom and White 1994) and extended with Lawrence Foana'ota in our chapter on Solomon Islands national cultural policy (2011). Here I follow the thread to more localized activities, at the level of the province and village and ask, what is cultural policy for these more *local* contexts? Or what might it be? If policy depends on the apparatus of the state, what kind of cultural policy is possible in a society where the state is notoriously 'weak' (if not absent) in its organizational capacity, where centralized government is historically remote and disconnected from the rural villages where most people live, and where culture itself is often an object of guarded contention (Lindstrom 1994)? Given the diverse character of Melanesia, how can cultural traditions or *kastom* become an object of regional or national policy without subverting the very politics and epistemologies they profess to support?

To get at these questions I first trace a short genealogy of discourses of tradition in Santa Isabel, and then consider more recent developments, focusing on a cultural festival produced by the provincial government of Santa Isabel in July 2005 and an effort launched in 2010 to create a 'cultural heritage programme' for the island (Baines 2010). The 2005 Isabel Cultural Festival was one of the largest cultural events sponsored by the provincial government up to that time. Typical of a genre of regional custom events that had been expanding in scale throughout the Solomons since independence (see Edvard Hviding's chapter in this volume), the 2005 festival gave material and performative substance to the idea of island-wide Isabel identity – an imagined community aligned with the geographic boundaries of the island encompassing six distinct language groups, some of which are more closely connected to neighbouring islands than to other Isabel populations. I take up the 2005 festival not because it is in some way unique, but because it illustrates the ambiguous and at times absent role of the state in underwriting activities marked as 'cultural'. In principle, the festival involved the cooperation of church, state and traditional leaders in ways that reflect the distinctive alignment of church and state in Santa Isabel, where ideas about traditional leadership have evolved in close concert with church history on the island (see below). It also illustrates the often ambiguous and informal means through which the agency of the state is exercised in conjunction with other local actors, including the Isabel Council of Chiefs – itself an emergent and contested presence on the local political scene (White 1992, 2004, 2012).

At the 1994 Honiara conference on Melanesian cultural policy, numerous presenters described efforts to create local and provincial cultural offices, most notably in the Western Solomons (Cole and Roga 1994) and Guadalcanal (Roe *et al.* 1994). Indeed, the appendices to that book include 'Solomon Islands Western Province Policy on Culture' and 'Guadalcanal Cultural Preservation and Development – Draft Policy Statement'. There was considerable optimism at the Honiara conference that these efforts and their tentative successes might provide a model for creating such offices in other provinces. Thus, Catherine Cole and Kenneth Roga's optimistic note in their chapter on Western Province, 'Guadalcanal Province has a cultural centre (a program but not a facility); Isabel, Choiseul, and Temotu provinces are all currently considering or initiating the establishment of similar offices' (1994:113). Instead, to a large extent, the opposite has happened. None of the offices mentioned by Cole and Roga were created and the programmes in Western Province and Guadalcanal have largely dissolved. There are many reasons for this, including the period of violence, economic decline and government collapse in the years 1998–2003 – a period referred to locally as the 'Tension'. Given a country already known for a 'weak state' and disposition to distrust centralized authority, it is not surprising that earlier visions of centre-driven cultural development have not been achieved. But economic and political problems are not the only explanation. Looking more closely at the local level (in Santa Isabel) exposes some of the more fundamental social and cultural disjunctions that often render state-sponsored initiatives hollow or unsustainable.

It is important to point out that this chapter's focus on policy, and hence more formalized cultural practices, yields a more pessimistic account of Isabel cultural practices than would emerge from consideration of the wider range of activities that are generally alive and well at the local level. The dissonance between robust local cultural lives and anaemic state-sponsored initiatives is very much a marker of the 'predicament' of cultural policy I want to address. Whereas recent history suggests that there may be good reason to be pessimistic about the capacity of national or provincial offices to pick up the banner of 'culture', the topic continues to generate local interest and support. In Santa Isabel, as in other provinces, state-centred policies at the Provincial level are often disconnected from local and nongovernmental initiatives. In the Isabel case these disjunctions are precisely one of the reasons why political actors have, for decades, sought ways to better integrate the institutions of church, state and *kastom*, finding discourses of 'culture', especially as embodied by traditional leaders and 'chiefs', to be useful vehicles for empowering local agency.

In Solomon Islands, the years between independence (1978) and the end of the Tension in 2003 were a period of active exploration and production of traditional cultural activities in rural locales (Foana'ota and White 2011). In addition to canoe-building projects (Hviding 2014:113–15; Nielsen 2005; Pule 1983) and cultural centres or 'custom houses', provincial governments began to sponsor custom festivals, often in connection with their anniversary celebrations (often referred to in bureaucratic parlance as a province's 'Second Appointed Day'). Most provinces have organized 'custom dance festivals', 'cultural shows' or even 'custom queen (and/or king) pageants' that use a cultural idiom to define regional political formations (much as Hobsbawn and Ranger 1983 described for European states). As an example of the Western-inspired 'custom queen' shows, the *Solomon Star* reported that Malaita Province's Second Appointed Day festivities included a 'custom queen and king show', in which contenders competed for prizes 'dressed in their cultural costumes depicting the original identity of their ethnic groups.'(*Solomon Star* 1995). This trend gained national expression in the Melanesian Festival of the Arts held in Honiara in 1998 – an initiative of the Melanesian Spearhead Group.

Why is it, then, that the imagined communities held up in these provincial cultural activities, especially activities that appear to project customary forms of culture and the arts, have not been able to sustain cultural programmes or offices, whether in education, tourism or everyday life? One possible answer is that very often the stimulus and/or economic support for cultural programmes and projects come from outside interests such as foreign agencies, donors, NGOs and so forth – a point acutely evident in cultural projects at the national level (Foana'ota and White 2011). On the one hand, we might say that this is largely a matter of a weak state or a weak economy that simply cannot afford the luxury of large-scale cultural productions. While the economic-political situation is certainly a factor, the tendency to resort to economic explanations obscures other, less visible issues, such as questions about the social and political significance of 'culture' and its relevance in people's everyday lives. Especially for cultural formations that are self-consciously held up as emblems of culture and identity, we should ask, 'Whose culture is it?' and 'What are the motivations for and meanings of producing cultural events and activities?'

The economic problems in creating cultural policies and programmes belie other, more complex, cultural disconnects. First is the difficulty of articulating policies crafted in national or provincial centres that make sense for 86 or so language groups. Second is the incommensurability of the bureaucratic language of policy and the largely oral knowledge practices of Melanesian communities. The first point is related to the extensive debate about the social and cultural basis for national (or regional) identities in the Solomons archipelago (Jourdan 1995). Indeed, throughout Melanesia, much has been written about the challenges of forming meaningful national narratives in populations attuned to recognizing and accentuating cultural distinctions (Foster 1995; Kabutaulaka 2001; Kelly and Kaplan 2001).

It is important to note that the context for the decline of cultural offices in Guadalcanal and Western Province was the sharp economic and political destabilization of Solomon Islands from the late 1990s to the arrival of an international peacekeeping force in 2003 (the Australian-led Regional Assistance Mission to Solomon Islands or RAMSI). As Edvard Hviding notes in his discussion of the rise of the Christian Fellowship Church in New Georgia (2011), the period of collapsing state services also reaffirmed the importance and strength indigenous social organization in rural locales. The forced self-sufficiency of those years reminded many communities of the value of local-level indigenous practices of all kinds. Certainly in Santa Isabel, the disintegration of the state during the Tension was a factor in the renewed interest in the status of traditional leaders as a bulwark in the social life of local communities. Specifically, Paramount Chief and retired bishop Dudley Tuti led efforts to formalize the role of traditional leaders in local governance by empowering an island-wide Council of Chiefs. These political developments, outlined briefly below (and see White 2004), were focused largely on the hard economic and political issues of land and natural resources, but also encouraged greater interest in cultural education – the softer side of *kastom*.

A brief history of Isabel *kastom* and its contemporary conjunctures

During the twentieth century the overriding theme in Isabel religious history was the dominance of a single church, the Anglican Church of Melanesia (earlier the Melanesian Mission), in the century-long process of Christianization. I have written about this elsewhere (White 1991), but reference it here in order to note that the unusual alignment of one church (the Church of Melanesia) and one government unit (Santa Isabel Province) throughout most of the twentieth century produced an early history of coordination (or negotiation) between church, state and local political leaders (White 2012). Even though the island-wide role of the Church of Melanesia has been eroded by new evangelical churches and a breakaway Anglican church, the coordination of (Anglican) church and (provincial) government was formalized around 2004 with an agreement between the Church of Melanesia, the Province of Santa Isabel and the Isabel Council of Chiefs to create a leadership 'Tripod' to cooperate in matters of social and economic importance to the island. This cooperation, emergent and fraught with ambiguity, helped to underwrite the production of cultural activities such as the 2005 cultural festival. By the same token, the Tripod and the Council of Chiefs gain a greater degree of legitimacy through these very same activities. The reality of 'chiefs' in Santa Isabel depends as much on their performative presence in meetings, gatherings and festivals as any type of institutionalized authority gained through the legal or bureaucratic apparatus of the state.

Santa Isabel does not currently have a cultural office or programme sponsored by the provincial government, although periodically the authorities have indicated an intention to create one. In 1992 for example, when the province sponsored a large 'cultural show', the provincial minister responsible for education and cultural affairs was quoted as saying that 'the Province has set up an Office called Cultural Affairs to look after and coordinate cultural activities'(*Solomon Nius* 1992). I am not sure of the longevity of that office, but two years later when I visited there was no evidence that it existed. Since that time, a provincial 'Five Year Development Plan' produced in September 2003 set out as the first action step under 'Community Affairs' to 'Prepare and implement a cultural affairs programme through the Education Division and in association with the Isabel Council of Chiefs.' (UNDP 2003). The province has yet to take that step. What has developed, however, is a 'Cultural Heritage Programme', initiated in 2010 with assistance from a long-time expatriate advisor, Graham Baines, support from the Church of Melanesia, endorsement from the Council of Chiefs and even funding from the University of Bergen 'Pacific Alternatives' project. As has been the case with many cultural projects and programmes in Solomon Islands, the alliance of outside support and interest with local non-government actors proved to be catalytic in developing a cultural programme in the absence of cultural policies.

The history of forgotten policies pertaining to the protection or preservation of culture in Santa Isabel predates independence. In 1976, mirroring developments at the national level in the lead-up to independence, the precursor of provincial government, the Santa Ysabel Council, wrote in its three-year operational plan that 'the Council is making an attempt to sponsor the carving of custom artefacts. It has also plans to build a Custom House on Ysabel, where old artefacts or custom objects can be kept.' (Santa Ysabel Council 1976:12). To my knowledge, no custom house was ever built. As a sign of the durability of these ideas, however, nearly thirty years later the Isabel provincial government proposed a new chiefs house and cultural centre, to be built in the middle of the provincial capital.

The history of efforts to codify cultural policy in Isabel includes legislative actions at the very moment of Solomon Islands independence, in 1978, when the Isabel Council passed the Prevention of the Sale of Traditional Artefacts Bye-Laws prohibiting the sale of 'traditional artefacts', defined as any object made for traditional purposes, excluding 'articles specifically made for export or sale as curios' (*Solomon Islands Gazette* 1978). More recently, in 1995, the province passed an ordinance to register sacred sites around the island (a move that followed archaeological work on Isabel in 1990 and 1991 for the National Sites Survey). Like many legislative acts, however, there was no plan for making the public aware of the act or implementing its objectives. In talking to the premier in 2005, he worried that there was no enforcement, even in areas where logging was being conducted.

The enigma of these phantom cultural policies is analogous to the difficulties that traditional leaders have had gaining recognition from the state (and, specifically, from the provincial government). There is a long history of efforts to define a role for chiefs in local governance in Santa Isabel (White 1992:2012). Yet, even though the Isabel Council of Chiefs was established by provincial resolution in 1984, their status regularly slips into oblivion, out of the view of mainstream government. Thus, a report about a large convocation of chiefs and other Isabel leaders in 2000 noted that almost none of the chiefs were even aware of the 1984 resolution establishing an Isabel Council of Chiefs '99.8% of the chiefs do not know or are not aware of the existence of the document and its use' (White 2004:11).

Following the period of the Tension after the coups of 2000, the United Nations Development Programme (UNDP) decided to work more directly with provincial authorities and, as a kind of test case, created the Isabel Province Development Project (IPDP) in 2003 with the aim of improving the capacity of provincial government in all its functions. An important part of that project involved expanding the role of traditional leaders in governance – a goal that led to my own involvement, recruited as a consultant to work with the IPDP project for several months in 2004 and 2005.[1] The IPDP project initiated several years of efforts to codify and support Isabel chiefs in local governance, focused especially on the Isabel Council of Chiefs, headed by the paramount chief, a status that originated in the colonial period with encouragement from the Melanesian Mission (White 1991). From 1975 to 2006 the paramount chief was retired bishop, Dudley Tuti. Two years after his death in 2006, the Isabel Council of Chiefs appointed a new paramount chief in the person of Reverend James Philip Mason, a nephew of the late Dudley Tuti and also a former bishop in the Church of Melanesia. At the time of appointment, however, James Mason was serving as a vicar and assistant bishop in the Church of England in the United Kingdom – a sign of the importance of the connection between the church and chiefs in Santa Isabel, but also an indication of the fragile nature of the institution of paramount chief, given the selection of someone not resident on the island (White 2012).

The UNDP's project plans called for a review of institutional structures that would 'Examine and make recommendations on practical and legally valid means of engaging the Isabel Council of Chiefs and the Church of Melanesia in a "tripod" arrangement for governance in the Province that is effectively linked to village communities, and make the results available for public debate.' In line with this, the UNDP staff working with the Council of Chiefs in 2004 assisted the parties of the Tripod to draft a Memorandum of Understanding (MOU) that would spell out the terms of coordination with representatives of each of the bodies appointed to participate in the deliberations of the others.

Creating a Council of Chiefs that can articulate with state agencies required formalizing a structure analogous to the bureaucratic structure of local government during the colonial era (after which districts became provinces and sub-districts became wards). For the Council of Chiefs, eight 'Houses of Chiefs' replaced local wards (which had essentially ceased functioning), each with its own representative to the Isabel Council of Chiefs.

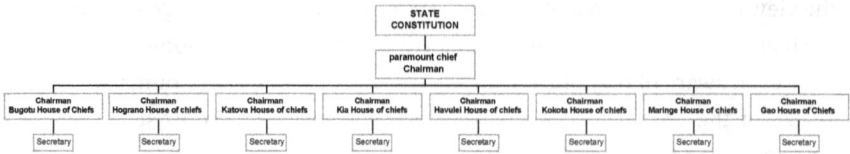

Figure 1   Isabel Council of Chiefs Organizational Chart (Henry Marau).

The effort to empower traditional leaders by codifying the status of chiefs in local governance runs the risk of transforming the very idea of the 'chief' into just another part of government. Indeed, these risks were not lost on those involved. When the late paramount chief discussed a memorandum of understanding that had been drafted in 2004 to coordinate cooperation between the province, the Church of Melanesia and the Council of Chiefs, he asked if, according to 'culture and tradition', it was necessary to have such a document. 'We are all church people; we are all people of the province,' he said. *'No gud iumi legalize evri samting an no moa traditional lida nao.'* ('We shouldn't legalize everything and then realize there are no longer any traditional leaders.')

In this instance, Dudley Tuti's words resonate with worries that have been noted repeatedly in discussions of chiefly authority. On several occasions, discussions of traditional leadership have noted the possibility that legislating custom may diminish its importance by rendering indigenous practices as subsidiary to Western law. For example, in its discussion of 'Foundations of Chieftain Authority' a 1999 leaders meeting observed that, 'Custom is law, therefore to give chiefly authority by a legislation would not strengthen but weaken the system. Recognition of customary law is good enough.' (Rojumana 1999). Similarly, in advice to the Council of Chiefs the following year, the provincial legal advisor noted that, 'Where a legislation is made the power of chiefs and the power of custom is withdrawn and given to those whose responsibilities are to make laws and imported court system.' (Isabel Council of Chiefs 2000; cited in White 2004:12–13).

In light of this apparent contradiction or double-bind, consider the proposal to build a major chiefs house and cultural centre in the middle of the provincial capital, Buala. Beginning in 2004, Isabel leaders in the Province and the Council of Chiefs began discussing plans to construct a headquarters building and cultural centre that would provide meeting space and office space for chiefs. By some accounts, the idea originated with efforts to find funding for a new provincial parliament building. However, prospective donors such as Japanese Foreign Aid were interested to support *cultural* projects, as well as economic development and 'humanitarian' assistance such as health supplies. Hence the plan shifted to a 'cultural centre'. In the words of the provincial finance officer, this proposal was 'more marketable' (that is, more consistent with the priorities of donors). Whatever its origins, the provincial government agreed to take responsibility for architectural design and construction, and then work with the chiefs and the church to decide on the content and activities supported there.

The point I want to make about this project is that even though it is conceived as an icon of chiefly power, the process of conceiving and funding it is primarily directed by the provincial government (which paid SI$83,000 [US$11,560] for conception and architectural design). The Province chose the location for the new structure and even called in earthmoving equipment (loaned by a logging company working at the time in the western end of the island) to level the area where the foundation would be built. This project, even though it never reached fruition, was a somewhat unusual example of close cooperation between two legs of the Tripod (Province and Council of Chiefs). It also illustrates well the singular role of the state in mediating the flow of resources between the island and the (inter)national community.

The most significant cultural development in recent years has been a 'Cultural Heritage Programme' organized by the former chief advisor to the UNDP Isabel Development Project, Graham Baines, with sponsorship of the Isabel Tripod (paramount chief, Church of Melanesia bishop and provincial premier) (Baines 2010). This programme was launched in March 2010 with a three-day workshop focused on the documentation of cultural valuables. That activity was led by Evelyn Tetehu of Kia, who began her own work on the importance of heirloom artefacts with a fellowship at the British Museum in 2006 as part of the 'Melanesia Project' that brought indigenous 'owners' to the museum to engage in interpretation and documentation of objects in their collection (Bolton *et al.* 2013; Burt and Bolton 2014). Although the Isabel Cultural Heritage Programme owes its origin to outside encouragement (and funding), it found local support from the Church of Melanesia, thanks to Bishop Richard Naramana, who provided office space and a staff position to support an 'archive' located in the church headquarters in Santa Isabel. Indeed, the bishop's initiative is one element of broader support provided to the Isabel Council of Chiefs, the latest instance of close cooperation between the church and traditional leaders in Santa Isabel.

The Isabel Cultural Festival

I want to explore these multiple dimensions of Isabel cultural politics by considering the organization and production of a cultural festival conducted in 2005. In this case, also, it is possible to interpret the event as both an expression of the robust state of Isabel culture and arts, and as evidence of the increasing role of the state (here the provincial government) as the dominant

Figure 2   Canoes at the 2005 Isabel Cultural Festival. Photo by author.

author of large-scale cultural events. In July 2005 the province sponsored an island-wide cultural festival that marked its twenty-first anniversary. Beyond the anniversary, the organizers conceived of the festival as an island-wide cultural celebration with co-sponsorship from the Church of Melanesia and the Council of Chiefs. That year the festival was the largest feast-gathering held on the island, more than a year in the planning with considerable provincial resources dedicated to support it.

So what kind of event was the Isabel Cultural Festival? To begin with, there was no tourism component at all. This was strictly a home-grown affair, with various groups and dignitaries attending from around the island and from the national capital, Honiara. Interpreting what the event was, for those involved, entails looking both inward to the feasting traditions and exchange practices of Santa Isabel, as well as outward to find precedents elsewhere in the Solomons. A first point to note is that when plans for the festival were originally set in motion by members of the provincial parliament, they called the festival a 'Solowata Festival' (saltwater/sea festival) that would focus especially on the production of traditional-style canoes, to be paraded and raced in the Maringe Lagoon offshore from the provincial government headquarters. However, it was not long before the communities of Isabel with inland ancestries and few ties to maritime technology stated that such a theme had little meaning for them. They argued successfully for changing the name to a 'cultural festival' so as to be more inclusive. The original influence for this came through the

Figure 3   The RAMSI stall at the Isabel Cultural Festival. Photo by author.

western end of Isabel with its ties to Western Province, where a large 'Festival of the Sea' has been held in Gizo off and on in December since the 1990s (see Hviding, this volume). An even earlier precedent for these events was the Maritime Festival held at Point Cruz in Honiara in the 1960s, and involving both indigenous canoes and European boat technologies (Lawrence Foana'ota, pers. comm.).

A second set of outside influences on the shape and organization of Isabel's Cultural Festival is that of the modern 'trade show', with food stalls and booths promoting various programmes and products active in Solomon Islands. This connection was brought home to me in 2005, when I observed a large National Trade and Cultural Show in the town square of Honiara just prior to travelling to Isabel where the cultural festival was about to be produced. It was apparent that the idea of mixing together entertainment with an array of food stalls and booths representing various businesses and organizations provided a template for the celebrations.

The trade-show format temporally converts a central, public space with a stage for entertainment and temporary booths for food stalls, and for commercial enterprises, non-profit and non-governmental organizations to promote their products and programmes. In Honiara the location of the trade show I visited was the Town Ground (since built over with a shopping mall) and in Isabel the space for the festival was the central, open ground in front of the government buildings in the provincial capital, Buala. In this way a central civic space is converted to festival space over the course of two or three days, with a schedule of entertainment activities, focused on a main stage and loud speakers for music, and programmes that accompany a convivial scene of crowds wandering among the booths sampling food, making conversation, attending to the entertainment and so forth.

Although in many ways an event typical of the times, influenced by the style and modalities of large events elsewhere in the Solomons, the Isabel Cultural Festival can also be read as an expression of longstanding exchange practices. In the Maringe area of Santa Isabel, there is a customary mode of feast-exchange called *diklo* in which the chief(s) of one area invite chiefs from another area, along with their kin and followers, to a feast, with days of feasting, speechmaking and entertainment. With the arrival of the (Anglican) church and the demographic consolidation of scattered groups into larger Christian villages, this mode of feasting shifted somewhat to the celebration of village 'church days', and is now taking on new forms, fuelled by the cash resources of church and state (White 1991). The ceremonies to install a paramount chief in 1975 and again in 2010 (both held in Sepi village, south-eastern Isabel), could be seen as especially large versions of this format, funded in large measure through the resources of the Church of Melanesia, which was celebrating its independence in 1975.

If *diklo* feasts are an expression of the power and identity of the hosts, it becomes relevant to ask, whose 'feast' was the provincial cultural festival? One answer is that, with the province as sponsor, the provincial premier and other government leaders embody the role of 'hosts'. A less obvious answer is that Buala village and its neighbours in the Maringe Lagoon also become hosts, with local leaders playing key roles in organizing and in welcoming guests. In terms of the ritual production of the festival, speeches by the Premier James Habu and the member of parliament from the Western District were a focal point for the opening ceremonies. For his part, Premier Habu took the unprecedented step of reading a kind of annual report (in English) on the state of the province, its economy and development activities.

At the same time, however, the event took place in a specific location – the provincial centre of Buala – where resident villagers also came to regard the festival as their event, providing much of the food through contractual catering arrangements with the Province organizers. Here it is important to comment on the complex spatial demographics of Buala, which is *both* a government station with Provincial offices, hospital, post office, RAMSI police station etc. *and* a village of landowning groups located in hamlets that spread out to the west of the government station. (To further complicate the residential topography, the headquarters of the Church of Melanesia Isabel Diocese is located less than a mile to the east, with its complex of offices and church housing.) Importantly, however, most of the food distributed at the festival event was prepared by villagers and either sold in food stalls or purchased by the Province for distribution at a culminating feast. Further evidence that the festival was not equally regarded as everyone's event was a conflict that emerged with another, competing celebration that had been planned by another community just down the coast. The village of Poro in the Gao district had for some time been planning a large 'Thanksgiving' feast to honour the Paramount Chief Dudley Tuti. Although Tuti himself asked to have the two events combined, the Poro chiefs went ahead with their event as a separate celebration. Just two weeks following the Isabel Cultural Festival they convened their Thanksgiving event for the paramount chief and invited dignitaries.

This glimpse of the emergence of a kind of competitive feasting gives rise to another question, 'Whose culture is the subject of cultural activities produced with state sponsorship, in this case the Province of Santa Isabel?' How does the province become an agent of cultural production? In a structural sense, the festival provides a framework for each locale to enact its membership in the larger identity of the island (being 'Isabel') – not unlike the way guests at a *diklo* feast express their connections with the hosts and, in the process, enact a larger regional identity. From the earliest moments, planning and implementation of the cultural festival were organized through the eight local districts or 'wards' of the province. Of course, wards and districts are themselves artificial groupings created by colonial maps that usually do not coincide with boundaries of language and culture. To further complicate the picture, the local level of government administration had essentially evaporated even before the Tension. The fact that the *de facto* dissolution of local-level government in the 1990s was hardly noticed is testimony to the continuing relevance of more informal structures of power associated with local leaders referred to as 'chiefs'. Where do state institutions end and indigenous modalities of power begin? The closer one is to localized practices, the more these lines of authority intersect and blur.

One of the first ideas for the event, when it was still discussed as a 'Solowata Festival', was that each ward would build a traditional style canoe and paddle it to the festival, where they would open the festivities with canoe racing. Each ward was given a grant of SI$3,000 (approximately US$420) for their festival project. Five of them completed construction of canoes that were vigorously paddled into the lagoon by decorated warriors on festival day. In addition to the canoe paddling, all of the activities of the festival were organized around participation from the list of participating wards (or a subset thereof). These included a 'custom queen' competition, musical performances and sports events. In each case, the master of ceremonies for the festival, using a microphone, would call up groups by ward, signifying local groupings that, collectively, form the island-wide or provincial identity of 'Isabel'.

One other feature of the cultural festival that replicates a longstanding practice of Isabel feasting was the presentation of a dramatic skit as one part of the event entertainment. The festival hosted a performance by a Honiara-based drama troop that enacted a play titled *Winds of Change* about the armed conflict associated with the period of the Tension. The play, authored by Tarcisius Kabutaulaka (indigenous to the island of Guadalcanal, currently a professor at the University of Hawai'i), represented a kind of morality tale in which guerrilla fighters shown attacking innocent people are finally won over by forces of peace and national solidarity. What struck me, seeing this drama in the Isabel context, was the way in which the performance enacted much the same vision of identity transformation, narrated as a deeply moral story of violence and peaceful resolution, as that of the Christian conversion plays that have been a staple of Isabel ceremonial life for decades (Errington and Gewertz 1994; White 1991). In 2005, it is this more contemporary national narrative of shared history that provides the tableau for festival goers to imagine their shared past and present. The theme of peace that has been a major organizing motif of Christian histories, told and retold in Solomons communities through the twentieth century, found new meaning in the years after the RAMSI intervention, as many citizens turned their attention to the work of reconciliation and peace-making following years of violent disruption centred around the national capital. In this case, just two years after the arrival of the multinational force, the theme of the peace and reconciliation expressed in the play also found support in several of the festival stalls in which Honiara-based non-profit and civic groups distributed information materials (see Figure 3).

Church, state and *kastom*: cultural policy as *bricolage*
In presenting these examples of cultural activity in Santa Isabel, I am interested to raise the question, 'Does it matter that the province has no cultural policy?' Judging from the level of activity and creativity in local cultural life, the answer would seem to be 'no'. Yet the question is worth asking, in so far as the provincial government has at various times announced its intention of creating a cultural office and/or supporting cultural programmes. Consistent with historical patterns, the cultural heritage programme discussed above is housed in the headquarters of the Church of Melanesia Diocese with sponsorship of the Isabel Council of Chiefs. Is the absence of state-sponsored 'policy' just a matter of weak governmental capacity and economics? Or does it signify something more fundamental about differences in epistemology and political practice? If nothing else, the examples of cultural activities

and projects discussed here suggest that, at the local level, actors inside and outside of government work through and across governmental, non-governmental and traditional institutions to accomplish their goals – a kind of *bricolage* of roles and relations in which persons who occupy bureaucratic positions use the imprimatur of institutional sponsorship to organize activities that suit local purposes. The Isabel Cultural Festival depended on funding from the provincial government, but for its organization and implementation, drew upon local social practices, at least some of which we would regard as 'traditional'.

This type of blurring of institutional boundaries is characteristic of local level political activity throughout the Solomons. In Isabel, however, it finds unique expression in the effort to integrate segmented spheres of power with the idea of the Tripod. Whether or not the term 'Tripod' is accepted, the issues that it addresses, of connecting the domains of church, state and *kastom*, are deeply ingrained in Isabel history, as they are in many Melanesian societies. It is important to note that this history is one marked by explicit recognition of the importance of indigenous 'culture' (or '*kastom*' or '*kalsa*') whether embodied in the figure of the chief or the value placed on land and ancestry. The driving force behind long-standing efforts to recognize and formalize traditional authority in local governance is the need to resolve land disputes, which always arise around projects that seek to develop or commercialize land holdings (cf. Weiner and Glaskin 2007). The constitutional right of landowners to regulate access to ancestral lands is the bedrock connecting 'tradition' with 'development', evident in debates about everything from hydroelectric schemes to massive forestry and mining projects.

Even though the institutions of the Isabel Council of Chiefs and its head, the paramount chief, continue to establish their own legitimacy, the very presence of a body of traditional leaders has proven significant for the latest effort to create a cultural programme for Santa Isabel – the Isabel Cultural Heritage Programme. The initiative for this project originates outside Santa Isabel (inspired by the British Museum's project on heirloom objects[2] and partially funded by the Pacific Alternatives project with which this volume is associated), but has obtained a degree of sustainability on the basis of endorsement from the Isabel Council of Chiefs and logistical support from the Church of Melanesia. In short, this configuration brings together a novel combination of institutional structures that sustain this most recent project. Perhaps because Bishop Naramana is himself an ethnographer and historian who has published on Santa Isabel (Naramana 1987), he has demonstrated a willingness to utilize larger institutions (in his case, the Church of Melanesia) to advance local projects, even in the absence of state involvement.

The mix of outside funding and support, combined with local efforts to empower traditional leaders, is not unique to the cultural heritage programme. Other examples can easily be found, even if they exist largely 'off the radar' because they are conducted in rural locales and leave little trace in the print media of national culture. Consider briefly the example of one locale, in the Maringe area of Santa Isabel, that found outside funding to support their own culture projects, fully organized by the people of nine villages interrelated by marriage and history. With a small grant from Australian People for Health, Education and Development Abroad (APHEDA), the people in a cluster of nine villages conducted a 'custom education seminar' in January 2003.[3] In good Melanesian style, the 'seminar' was organized as a gathering of several hundred people that effectively turned an education project into an inclusive participatory activity that mobilized the same social and cultural resources that go into major ceremonial occasions and feast-making. Whereas the outside grant proved an important catalyst, the motivation and implementation of the custom education seminar was entirely 'home grown'.

One of the risks to note in any discussion of cultural policy is the tendency, especially in funding agencies interested to support indigenous cultures, to equate 'culture' with pre-European custom. The view of intact traditional societies not yet well connected to the global modern economy tends to see 'culture' as pre-European practice, separate from anything 'modern'. This binary is one of the liabilities of the idea of cultural policy, which is often associated with '*kastom*izing' culture, construing indigenous culture as just those practices that are separate from the modern, from arenas of engagement and adaptation to new ways (as in Christianity, for example). While this kind of opposition of tradition and modernity can serve to highlight practices threatened by intrusive forces from outside, it can also artificially essentialize indigenous culture to mean only that which is pre-European and in danger of extinction. By implication, then, the overriding concern with cultural policy becomes preservation or protection (as when the important work of protecting sacred sites or cultural artefacts becomes iconic for 'cultural policy' as a whole). Thus the new national cultural policy document begins with the premise that indigenous traditions have been disappearing and need to be protected. The focus on preservation and 'revitalization' is clearly stated in the first lines of the document's statement of purpose:

> Unfortunately, many aspects of this **national treasure** have been lost
> over the years for numerous reasons. These include marginalisation and a
> dwindling pool of elders who are **repositories**, or libraries, of traditional
> knowledge.
>   Reversing the loss of culture is an immense task, requiring the

guidance of a national policy framework, coordinated action and
involvement by all stakeholders.

(Ministry of Culture and Tourism 2012:1, emphasis in original)

The authors of the new policy clearly recognize that focusing only on
preservation is self-limiting, and make a point of expanding the goals of
cultural policy to include the promotion of culture, especially the creative arts,
in contemporary society. The move beyond preservation is framed primarily
in terms of (socio)economic incentives, bringing '*kalsa*' in line with national
development planning: 'Revitalisation should not be the sole or ultimate goal
of the policy: equal emphasis should be placed on making the culture sector
visible and fostering its socioeconomic potential.' (Ministry of Culture and
Tourism 2012:1).

An excellent example of the rise of a new form of cultural activity (inspired
by older traditions) is the phenomenon of Santa Isabel youth pan-pipe groups.
During the time of the Tension small groups of mostly young musicians
began to form a new style of pan-pipe ensemble. The music spread quickly
throughout Santa Isabel in the 2000s and has since become a staple of large
ceremonial occasions. I first encountered the new style of pan-pipe music in
2002, when I returned to the island after a ten-year absence. I was astounded
by the creativity and innovation of these groups, assembling musicians in
their teens and twenties, playing songs ranging from custom songs to pop
songs and even the national anthem. Little did I know that two years later one
of those groups would be a knock-out hit at the South Pacific Festival of the
Arts in Palau in 2004; and two years after that another group would tour my
home islands of Hawai'i, performing to enthusiastic crowds at the East-West
Center in Honolulu and selling out an inventory of CD recordings. Despite
their marked success, which later included additional tours to Australia
and Singapore, most of the musicians (and dancers) are now back living in
their home areas, mostly reintegrated in the subsistence economy, with little
involvement outside the island. There has been no promotion of their music
for sale, no efforts to develop educational programmes around their craft,
and certainly no national programmes seeking to create new venues and
opportunities for these musicians.

The lives of Isabel's young pan pipers embody the contradictions in today's
efforts at making cultural policy. The pan-pipe 'new wave' emerged from
Solomon Islands villages around the same time that central government was
collapsing in the early 2000s. Drawing on the support of regional organizations
and international invitations, this new performance genre has now travelled
widely, crossing local/national/transnational boundaries along the way. Yet
these successes occurred with little support from state offices, with the

Figure 4   Pan-pipe group at the Isabel Cultural Festival. Photo by author.

important exceptions of the coordination of Solomon Islands participation in the South Pacific Festivals of the Arts in 2004, and the assistance of the national museum director for the group that travelled to Hawai'i in 2006. Despite moves toward formalizing cultural policy in national offices of tourism development, it is the creative and youthful energy of the 'grassroots' (as in this case, where young Isabelians have seized on local musical techniques and recrafted them for the sheer pleasure of performance) that is the driving force behind indigenous cultural production. Although Isabel pan-pipe groups have shown they are ready and able to navigate the circuits of national and international travel, they emerge from and are sustained by their role in local feasts and celebrations, where their performances are part of the *habitus* of social relations in their home villages and regions. It is not surprising, perhaps, that the discourse of national cultural policies, with one eye set on preserving pre-European practices and the other on national 'development', finds so few connections with practices that are at once innovative and firmly embedded in local contexts.

In this chapter, drawing on my experience with one Solomon Islands locale (primarily the Maringe district of Santa Isabel), I have argued that the language of cultural policy as formulated in the national arena often fails to gain traction at the local level for reasons that might be expected, given the predicament of national cultural policy in a region where cultural practices are rooted in highly local(izing) oral cultures. On a more optimistic note, however, Solomon Islanders working in the border zones of local and national cultural production have themselves articulated many of these same issues. For example, a recent document prepared in response to a regional 'cultural mapping' exercise in Solomon Islands, noted 'the prevailing problem of continuous failure by the mainstream tourism sector to develop robust all-year-round cultural promotion programmes' and called for 'community-based' approaches that foster 'wider participation' and 'instil a sense of ownership by local people' (Lidimani 2011:68).[4] The language of this recommendation points to the same sort of gap between policy and practice discussed in this chapter. Its inclusion in a policy document suggests that Melanesian cultural policy might well find points of intersection between the (trans)national and local that make translation and dialogue possible. Whether or not such connections develop in the future, local events and practices in Santa Isabel will continue to generate the kinds of robust cultural activity that have been characteristic of island life for as long as written accounts have described it.

Acknowledgements

The research for this chapter is based on fieldwork in Santa Isabel in 2004 and 2005 and again with brief visits in 2009 and 2010. I want to thank Edvard Hviding and the Bergen Pacific Studies Research Group for support obtained from the collaborative 'Pacific Alternatives' project. In Santa Isabel I am grateful to friends and mentors who have sustained my work there over time. I am especially indebted to the late Paramount Chief and Bishop Sir Dudley Tuti for his support and generosity. He, along with Premier James Habu, Bishop Richard Naramana (Church of Melanesia), and UNDP project coordinator William Pryor made it possible for me to participate in their conversations about formation of the Isabel Tripod. I particularly want to thank Graham Baines for information and insights on many issues taken up in this chapter, as well as Edvard Hviding and three anonymous reviewers for their close reading of an earlier draft.

Notes

1   Graham Baines, working as the principal coordinator of the UNDP Isabel Province Development Project, invited me to participate in the project as an anthropological advisor consulting on efforts to institutionalize traditional leadership in local governance (see White 2004:11). Although the experience left me with a more clear sense of the limits of academic work in effecting change, I am grateful for the chance for collaboration with Isabel friends and colleagues at an important time in the island's political history.

2   For more on the accomplishments of the British Museum's Melanesia project, conducted from 2005 to 2010, see Bolton *et al.* 2013; Burt and Bolton 2014; and

documentation on the project's website: http://www.britishmuseum.org/research/projects/melanesia_project.aspx.

3   APHEDA was created in 1984 as the overseas-aid agency of the Australian Council of Trade Unions. The next year, in 2004, APHEDA ' started a new 3-year project to build the capacity of a wide range of Community Based Training Centres, which focus on short courses and community training'. Members of the Isabel community working in Church of Melanesia offices in Honiara alertly noticed the possibility and drafted a proposal to address the programme goals.

4   As written, this recommendation reads as follows:

> ... community-based tourism provides the best approach to the revival of cultural inspiration at the community level. Wider participation in community-based tourism initiatives instils a sense of ownership by local people, and would lead to tourism oriented cultural programmes within villages. This mechanism would address the prevailing problem of continuous failure by the mainstream tourism sector to develop robust all-year-round cultural promotion programmes. (Lidimani 2011:68)

References

Baines, G. 2010. Santa Isabel Cultural Heritage Programme Report on Maringe District Workshop 'Skills for Investigating our Culture' (9–11 March 2010) (with a note on awareness activities in Kia and Baolo). An initiative of the Isabel Tripod. Unpublished report, files of the author.

Bolton, L., N. Thomas, E. Bonshek, J. Adams and B. Burt (eds) 2013. *Melanesia: Art and Encounter*. London: The British Museum Press.

Burt, B. and L. Bolton (eds) 2014 *The Things We Value: Culture and History in Solomon Islands*. Canon Pyon: Sean Kingston Publishing.

Cole, C.C. and K. Roga 1994. The relationship between cultural policy and programming in Western Province, Solomon Islands. In *Culture-Kastom-Tradition: Developing Cultural Policy in Melanesia*, L. Lindstrom and G.M. White (eds), 105–13. Suva: Institute of Pacific Studies, University of the South Pacific.

Errington, F. and D. Gewertz 1994. From darkness to light in the George Brown jubilee: The invention of nontradition and the inscription of a national history in New Britain. *American Ethnologist* 21(1):104–22.

Foana'ota, L. and G. White 2011. Solomon Islands cultural policy? A brief history of practice. In *Made in Oceania: Social Movements, Cultural Heritage and the State in the Pacific*, E. Hviding and K.M. Rio (eds), 273–99. Wantage: Sean Kingston Publishing.

Foster, R. (ed.) 1995. *Nation Making: Emergent Identities in Postcolonial Melanesia*. Ann Arbor: University of Michigan Press.

Hobsbawm, E. and T. Ranger (eds) 1983. *The Invention of Tradition*. Cambridge: Cambridge University Press.

Hviding, E. 2011. Re-placing the state in the western Solomon Islands: The political rise of the Christian Fellowship Church. In *Made in Oceania: Social Movements, Cultural Heritage and the State in the Pacific*, E. Hviding and K.M. Rio (eds), 51–89. Wantage: Sean Kingston Publishing.

——— 2014. War Canoes of the Western Solomons. In *The Things We Value: Culture and History in Solomon Islands*, B. Burt and L. Bolton (eds), 103–15. Canon Pyon: Sean Kingston Publishing.

Isabel Council of Chiefs. 2000. Meeting Report Two, Section 2.7.2. Files of the Author.

Jourdan, C. 1995. Stepping stones to national conciousness: The case of the Solomon Islands. In *Nation Making: Emergent Identities in Postcolonial Melanesia*. Robert Foster (ed.), 127–50. Ann Arbor, MI: University of Michigan Press.

Kabutaulaka, T. 2001. Beyond Ethnicity: Understanding the Crisis in the Solomon Islands. Working Paper. Canberra: State, Society and Governance in Melanesia Project, Australian National University. http://rspas.anu.edu.au/melanesia/tarcisiusworkingpaper.htm

Kelly, J.D. and M. Kaplan 2001. *Represented Communities: Fiji and World Decolonization*. Chicago: University of Chicago Press.

Lidimani, D.B. 2011. Cultural Mapping Report: Solomon Islands. Secretariat of the Pacific Community on behalf of the Culture Division, Solomon Islands Ministry of Culture and Tourism.

Lindstrom, L. 1994. Traditional cultural policy in Melanesia (kastom polisi long kastom). In *Culture-Custom-Tradition: Developing Cultural Policy in Melanesia*, L. Lindstrom and G.M. White (eds), 67–81. Suva: Institute of Pacific Studies, University of the South Pacific.

Lindstrom, L. and G.M. White (eds) 1994. *Culture-Custom-Tradition: Developing Cultural Policy in Melanesia*. Suva: Institute of Pacific Studies, University of the South Pacific.

Ministry of Culture and Tourism, Government of Solomon Islands 2012. Solomon Islands Nasinol Policy Framework Blong Kalsa: Mainstreaming Kalsa in Nation-building and Development. Secretariat of the Pacific Community, Fiji and the Division of Culture, Ministry of Culture and Tourism, Government of Solomon Islands (eds). Suva, Fiji and Honiara, Solomon Islands: Secretariat of the Pacific Community (SPC).

Naramana, R.B. 1987. Elements of culture in Hograno/Maringe, Santa Ysabel. *'O'O: Journal of Solomon Islands Studies* 1(3):41–57.

Nielsen, C.B. 2005. *A War Canoe Heading for Christianity*. Hoejbjerg, Denmark: Intervention Press.

Pule, R.T. 1983. *Binabina: The Making of a Gela War Canoe.* Suva: Institute of Pacific
     Studies, University of the South Pacific.
Roe, D., R. Regenvanu, F. Wadra and N. Araho (eds) 1994. Working with cultural
     landscapes in Melanesia: Problems and approaches in formulating cultural
     policies. In *Culture-Kastom-Tradition: Developing Cultural Policy in
     Melanesia*, L. Lindstrom and G.M. White (eds), 115–29. Suva: Institute of
     Pacific Studies, University of the South Pacific.
Rojumana, C. 1999. Recommendation 3.1.1. Rojumana Report, Appendix C. Files of
     the author.
Santa Ysabel Council 1976. Santa Ysabel Council Plan of Operation 1976–1979.
     Mimeograph. Files of the author.
Solomon Islands Gazette 1978. Supplement (Friday 13 October). S.I. (19):337.
Solomon NIUS 1992. Province supports preservation of culture and custom (31
     July):17.
Solomon Star 1995. Custom Queen and King Show Attracted 14 Contestants (16
     August):7.
UNDP 2003. Santa Isabel Development Plan 2003–2007. Volume I: Basis for action.
     United Nations Development Programme.
Weiner, J.F. and K. Glaskin (eds) 2007. *Customary Land tenure and Registration in
     Australia and Papua New Guinea: Anthropological Perspectives.* Canberra:
     ANU E Press.
White, G.M. 1991. *Identity Through History: Living Stories in a Solomon Islands
     Society.* Cambridge: Cambridge University Press.
——— 1992. The discourse of chiefs: Notes on a Melanesian society. *The
     Contemporary Pacific* 4(1):73–108.
——— 2004. Traditional Leadership Report. Consultancy report for Isabel Province
     Development Project. United Nations Development Programme and Santa
     Isabel Province.
———2012. Chiefs, church, and state in Santa Isabel, Solomon Islands. In *The Politics
     of Christianity in Oceania*, M. Tomlinson and D. McDougall (eds), 171–97.
     New York: Berghahn Books.

Geoffrey White is Professor of Anthropology at the University of Hawai'i at
Mānoa.

II

THE CULTURAL POLITICS OF LAND AND SEA

CHAPTER 4

Absentee landowners, gifted lands and 'economies of affection'

✳

Vilsoni Hereniko

Filming the land

In July 2000 I decided to go to Rotuma to conduct final pre-production work on my feature film *The Land Has Eyes* (see Howard 2006). The title of this film derives from an ancient and potent Rotuman proverb: *Pear ta ma on maf, Pear ta ma on al, Ma ineajema ne sei ta nojo.* This translates as 'The land has eyes, the land has teeth, and knows the truth.' Let me explain. In what follows, I craft a reflection that draws on multiple aspects of my work in Rotuma, as filmmaker, playwright, as scholar and interpreter of culture (Hereniko 1995), and as a Rotuman. I offer this in a form that, in the spirit of this volume, explores alternatives in the modalities of research and representation.

Rotumans living on Rotuma believe that the land is like a human being: the land can see, the land can 'bite' you, and the land is all-knowing. Human beings may hide the truth, but the land can reveal the truth when called upon to deliver justice. Although there is a Western-style court on the island that hears land disputes and attempts to deliver justice, sometimes it is unable to uncover the truth. When Rotumans believe that the court is ineffective, they often resort to Rotuman ways of uncovering the truth, which in large part means appealing to the spirit world to take appropriate action.

I tried to capture this belief in the efficacy of the spirit world in the climactic scene of *The Land Has Eyes.* This scene also underscores the crucial role of the language interpreter in a court case. The film itself is available at www. thelandhaseyes.org, but for the purposes of this chapter and understanding the scene below, it is sufficient to know that Viki is a young Rotuman girl whose goal is to redeem her father's honour and win a scholarship to further her education in Fiji. Her inspiration is the warrior woman, the first inhabitant to arrive on the island of Rotuma and now regarded as a powerful supernatural figure. Before the scene begins, Viki and her sister had been fighting over some money outside the courtroom. Viki, now dirty, is being called in to the interview.

CHARACTERS:

Mr Clarke – District Officer (D.O)
Poto – corrupt interpreter for the D.O.
Viki – protagonist and daughter of Hapati (defendant)
Three Chiefs – respected elders

SCENE 119. INT. COURTROOM – AFTERNOON

Mr Clarke scowls at Viki when he sees her unkempt long hair, her dirty clothes, and the fire in her eyes. He notices the stick in Viki's hand. The three chiefs in the room are also shocked by Viki's appearance. Poto shakes his head at Viki, then indicates to her to sit on a chair facing the chiefs. It's the same chair Viki's father was convicted in.

POTO   *Viki Teretume, le han on Hapati.* (to the District Officer) Viki Teretume, daughter of Hapati Falelei.

Viki surveys the room of three chiefs, Mr Clarke and Poto as she sits down on the chair. Carefully, she lays the stick across her lap. Poto starts writing.

CLARKE   Was that you fighting out there?

Viki remains still, not answering.

CLARKE   (to Viki) What's the stick for?

POTO   We should send her out sir! She's insulting us by the way she's shown up.

CLARKE   But her name's on the list, Poto.

POTO   Look at the way she's dressed sir.

Clarke nods in agreement.

CLARKE   (to Viki) Viki, is that your name?

Viki nods in agreement.

CLARKE (cont'd)   Speak up! Explain how you managed to score 95 out of 100 in English.

POTO   (to Viki) *Ae la faeg ka se togak uat. Ae eam se goua, ne ae po tapen mah sivaghul ma liam ta.*

CLARKE   Poto, translate for the chiefs only. She's supposed to be able to speak good English.

POTO   I know she can speak English sir. I just don't want her to misunderstand anything you might say to her.

Poto is about to translate for Viki but Viki beats him to it. Viki's words are now coming out more clearly than before.

VIKI   I like to read. My auntie in Fiji sent me a storybook of Greek mythology. I have a Bible too in English. I also read books in the library. And I work hard.

Poto doesn't translate for the chiefs because he's annoyed with Mr Clarke and is distracted.

CLARKE   (to Poto) Well, aren't you going to translate what she said to the chiefs?

POTO   Sorry sir, I didn't get what she said.

CLARKE   Pay attention, I won't repeat myself.

CLARKE   (to Viki) I understand that your father died about two weeks ago.

POTO   *Gou afai ne ou ofa kota al se.*

VIKI   Yes … sir

POTO   *O ko gagaj.*

CLARKE   I heard that you ran away when your father died, then later
caused a pig stampede through your village. Is this true?

VIKI   Yes.

CLARKE   Why?

VIKI   My father told me 'The land has eyes and the land has teeth' and
always knows the truth.

POTO   *Otou ofa ta ea, Pear ta ... pear ta lag maha ka ... ka ma on ala
ma ineajema te ne aire.* My father told me: 'The land is a strong wind and a
death' and always knows the truth.

The chiefs mutter under their breaths. They look at each other, surprised at
Poto's inaccurate translation of an ancient proverb.

CLARKE   That's wonderful. What a visual metaphor!

POTO   What did you say sir?

CLARKE   No need to translate that. Viki, why did your father tell you the
land has eyes and teeth?

Viki hesitates, looks around.

POTO   *Ka po e tese ta ou ofa ea se aea 'Pear ta lag maha ka ma on ala?'*
Why did your father tell you that 'the land is a ... a strong wind and the land
is ... death?'

The chiefs look at each other, perplexed.

CHIEF 1   *Pear ta lag maha ka ma on ala!* The land is a strong wind and
the land is death?

Chief 2 and 3 have a grin on their faces, knowing that Poto did not translate
correctly.

SCENE 120. EXT . COURTHOUSE – DAY

Cut away to Maurea, Hanisi, and Pili taking cover from the strong wind blowing outside the courtroom.

SCENE 121. INT. COURTROOM – BACK TO SCENE

CHIEF 2   *Poto, ka sei ta famorit ne rakak se aea ag on is famor Rotuma?* [Poto. Who is your teacher?]

CHIEF 3   *Gou ahae ia rakom e pa puak ta. Pear ta lag maha ka ma on ala?* [He learnt from the pigs in the sty. The land is a strong wind and the land is death?]

Poto looks flustered and angry.

Chiefs 2 and 3 burst into laughter.

CLARKE   Will someone explain what's so funny?

POTO   Sir, the chiefs are ignorant fools, because they can't speak or understand English!

Chief 2, the youngest of the chiefs, understands some English. He looks offended.

CLARKE   Nonsense Poto. What did you say that's so funny?

CHIEF 2   *'Pear ta lag maha ka ma on ala?'* ['The land is a strong wind and a death?']

More chuckles from the chiefs.

CHIEF 3   *(to Viki) Hante, ka tes ta Poto kota ease?* [What did Poto say just now?]

VIKI   *Ia ea aus gagaj hal ta gat ke famor uathaf po e aus kat inea ra la faeag fifis.* [He said you chiefs are ... blockheads because you don't understand English.]

The laughter stops abruptly. Chief 2 pulls back his chair and lurches toward Poto.

Poto is now at the front of the room, sparring like a boxer.

POTO   *Leum ae. Aelem se tei la gou kaoa ou mafa.* [Come closer. I'll punch out your eyes.]

Chief 2 looks like he's going to rush at Poto. Viki remains in chair.

CLARKE   What's going on now! Get back to your seats! (to Poto and the chief who is standing up). The two of you. I demand order in this courtroom! Sit down!

The chief obeys Clarke.

Sounds of banging at the back door of the room, as if someone's trying to get in.

CLARKE (cont'd)   Who's that at the door? Poto, see who it is.

Poto pulls open the door. A strong wind sends Poto reeling against the back of the room. Papers on Mr Clarke's desk fly everywhere. Poto keeps trying to stand up but keeps falling back. Viki is the only one in the room who doesn't fear the wind. The chiefs remain in their seats and hang on to the side of their chairs to prevent being blown away.

INTERCUT BETWEEN WHAT MR. CLARKE SEES AND WHAT THE CHIEFS SEE.

MR CLARKE'S P.O.V.: Poto falls on the floor, seemingly in a seizure. There are papers flying all around him as the wind blows and blows. Finally the wind subsides. Poto remains on the floor, unconscious. During all this, Viki remains seated on her chair.

THE CHIEFS' P.O.V.: Viki stands up in front of her chair and takes out the red feathers in the palm of her hand. Releasing the feathers into the whirling wind, Viki holds out the ceremonial staff toward Poto. Poto tries to pull away the staff. As he makes contact with the staff, he starts to shake, as though electrified by the object's *mana.*

Viki pulls back the staff and twirls it round and round, faster and faster until the action looks like a windmill. This twirling motion terrifies Poto, who is now in a seizure on the floor. Every time he tries to stand up, a red feather, like an arrow, knocks him back, until finally the warrior woman's image appears accompanied by a loud thunderclap. All of Poto's energy is spent, and he falls back, groaning and moaning. Finally, Poto is unconscious, the wind dies down, and the chiefs are no longer frightened.

BOTH P.O.V's converge.

CLARKE (cont'd)   Poto! What the hell…!

Chiefs 1 and 2 rush over to Poto, then lift him up and carry him out the door to rush him to the hospital nearby. Chief 3 closes the door and sits back in his chair. Clarke shakes his head in disbelief.

CLARKE (cont'd)   We've lost our interpreter!

VIKI   Sir, I can translate for you.

Clarke looks surprised.

CLARKE   Then tell the chief this meeting is adjourned.

VIKI   *Gagaj pure ea os tauna te is vahia.* [Sir, this meeting is adjourned.]

With a slight bow of the head to the District Officer to acknowledge his departure, the chief leaves. He bows his head slightly before Viki as if she's someone important.

CHIEF 3   *Gou inea ou ofa ta, fa ag nonojo. E ta teranit ka omus asa la peneis.* [I knew your father. He was an honest man. One day your family's name will be a sweet fragrance.]

Little did I know that when I decided to make a fictional film about the land having eyes and teeth that I would experience the efficacy of this ancient Rotuman truth in real life. I had been living in Honolulu for nine years by this time, having taken up a teaching position at the University of Hawai'i in 1991. Prior to this, I had lived away from Rotuma (in Fiji mainly, with a short stint in England) for thirty years. Although I had paid return visits to Rotuma during this time, these visits were few and far between, and lasted no more than one or two weeks at any one time. I still had memories of Rotuma in the 1960s and 1970s, when land disputes were common. During this time, the proverb *Pear Ta Ma On Maf*, when uttered in anger, would be met with fear and trepidation. I wanted to capture the mood of this period, not realizing as I do now that Rotuman land still holds deep within its womb the *mana* of the ancestors, and that its power, at least in 2000, had diminished but little.

About a year before my 2000 trip to Rotuma, my relatives at Hapmak (a sub-district of Itutiʻu, the largest district on Rotuma) cleared the bush at the edge of Mea village (one of several villages that make up Hapmak) and built several thatched houses in order to create our movie set: a large community hall elevated on a rock foundation, a thatched house where the family cooked and slept, and a traditional boys' hut on long poles. A tropical flower garden, planted by my sister, completed the movie set.

In July 2000, I caught an Air Pacific flight from Honolulu to Nadi then to Suva. In Suva, I bought a generator, tables and chairs, several beds, two refrigerators, lots of toilet paper, various props for the film such as a huge electric fan, food to feed the cast and crew for about a week, and all kinds of odds and ends associated with filmmaking. I then caught a cargo boat bound for Rotuma that took three days and two nights to get there.

In May of the same year, a Fijian by the name of George Speight carried out a military coup in Fiji, justified and necessary, he claimed, in order to protect Fijians from having their native lands wrested away from them by the Indians whose ancestors had migrated to Fiji to work in the sugar plantations in the late 1800s and had made Fiji their home. It is not just Rotuma that has land problems, then. Indeed, land is the cause of so much conflict all over the Pacific region, and although my focus here is Rotuma, the same issues still apply to many other islands in the Pacific Ocean (Crocombe 1987).

I started rehearsing with the actors on the set soon after I arrived in Rotuma. I was confident that my dream of making a feature film to document Rotuman culture and language would become reality. But then I heard rumours that a certain Vinesh from Fiji, whose parents used to live on the site of the set, had returned to the island and was making noises about wanting compensation for the use of his land. I paid little heed to the rumours because I knew that Rotuman land is owned communally, and that other clan members living on the island had given their permission for the use of their land for my film project. This man Vinesh was but an absentee landowner, one of many who had claims to the land. It seemed to me then that clan members who lived on the island and cared for the land should have more authority over its use. But I was mistaken.

During one of the workdays on the set, Vinesh appeared and joined the villagers working there. At the end of the day, we held a meeting that I chaired. I thanked everyone, including Vinesh, and explained that at the end of filming, all the houses on the set would go to the clan members who owned the property, to do with as they wished. Vinesh was pleased to hear this and spoke up, saying he was glad to hear that Rotuma would have its own feature film and he wished the project every success. He even gave us his blessings and support.

About the same time, I learned from my sister that when she was planting the flower garden for the film, some women in the village would walk by and mock her efforts. They derided her for her naivety in thinking that her brother's film project would ever happen; they told her she was living in fantasy land. This was during the weeks after Fiji had its third military coup of 2000, and the thinking then was that all plans for a film on Rotuma would be abandoned. But instead of giving up, I was determined more than ever to press on, and to view the coup as just another challenge to overcome, much like the isolation of Rotuma and the lack of regular electricity supply on the island.

Then reality set in. I went to the set one morning only to discover a wooden sign written in English and nailed to a coconut tree that said: 'No movie will be made on my land. If you don't like it, see me. Vinesh.' Concerned that if I didn't go to see Vinesh the whole enterprise would fall apart, I took my older brother (he was also the chief of the village at this time) and the church minister (for moral support), to try and get Vinesh to change his mind. Vinesh revealed that he wanted to be paid for the use of his land, even though the villagers had already cleared the bush before he arrived and the houses on the movie set could be his at the end of filming. This was not enough he said, and when pressed to tell us the amount he wanted was FJ$100,000. This was way beyond my means of course. Even if we had the money to pay, this would open a can of worms, as then all the landowners would want to be paid, and from then onwards, everyone on the island would expect to be paid handsomely for their assistance.

Surprised that the Rotuman way of doing things had been ignored, I found myself at a loss as to how best to proceed. I realized that we had no precedent to emulate and that if I didn't play my cards right, we could end up with a confrontation on the movie set. Working against me were the rumours circulating that my American wife and I had Hollywood connections, which then meant that we had a lot of money to spend. The truth was that we were independent filmmakers who had maxed out our credit cards, taken a second mortgage on our home, cashed all our savings and life insurance, begged and borrowed from friends and supportive individuals, and were still worried that we could go bankrupt as we had decided to start filming even though we knew we had not raised all the money necessary to go into production.

Vinesh's refusal to back down resulted in an improvised court case being held on the movie site. The Fijian district officer, the interpreter who was also the chairman of the Rotuma Council at that time, and I sat on a mat on one side, while facing us was Vinesh and other embarrassed landowners who had helped to clear the bush for the project. My oldest brother (and chief of the village) sat to my right while other interested relatives sat to the side some distance away, but within earshot. There were no verbal directions as to where people should sit, but somehow we ended up taking positions that we intuitively felt were most appropriate for us, given the circumstances.

A year before all this happened, I had visited Rotuma and gone to the Council of Chiefs' meeting and had asked them for their permission and their blessings for the project. After a number of questions, one of which required me to explain the story behind the film, the highest chief on the island spoke in favour of the movie project (on behalf of all the chiefs present) and gave it the council's blessings. Vinesh's intervention then, unbeknownst to him, was therefore a challenge to the council's (and by implication the district officer's) support of the film project.

During the court case, the chairman of the Rotuma Council (a Rotuman) acted as interpreter for the district officer (a Fijian), who didn't speak or understand the Rotuman language. As the hearing progressed, it became obvious that the chairman and the defendant Vinesh had no respect for each other. The chairman, who was a prominent banker in Fiji before his retirement to Rotuma, decided to veer away from the formal proceedings and address the defendant directly. 'Do you know what's the problem with you?' he demanded. 'What!' Vinesh challenged, his eyes flashing. 'You've got some Indian blood in you. That's why all you want is *paisa* [money], *paisa* all the time!' This was the last straw for Vinesh, whose anger had been building up during the proceedings of a court case that seemed heavily stacked against him, as no one present sympathized with his position on the land issue.

'You can talk!' Vinesh mocked, his body taught, his fists clenched, for he had been insulted by the court interpreter who was now making it clear that he was not an impartial observer of the court's proceedings. Vinesh pointed at the chairman: 'How can the pot call the kettle black! Everyone here knows your story. You robbed Fiji's National Bank then came here and built that huge house that looks like the Sheraton Hotel. Think we don't know where all that money came from?!' No-one on the island had ever accused the tall and well-built Chairman of the Rotuma Council of theft, at least directly to his face, and now this young upstart (he was in his late 30s) was making accusations in public that everyone else on the island had only heard about in whispers or read about in the Fiji newspapers.

'How dare you speak to me like that?' the chairman thundered as he glared at Vinesh. 'That is not true!'

'Of course it's true! Our ancestors say that the land has eyes and teeth, and the land knows the truth. The land knows what you did in Fiji before you came here!' Looking as though he was capable of murder, the chairman rose to his feet. 'Who do you think you are! You are the greedy one, and the land knows it. The land will get you!' 'Me?' Vinesh mocked again. 'The land will get YOU!' The chairman lurched toward Vinesh and was just about to slug him in the face when my skinny brother pulled him by the arm and cautioned him. 'This is not the way to do things. That's enough.' my brother advised.

Of course Vinesh was already on his feet to defend his honour, his fists clenched. The chairman regained his composure and sat down again, while Vinesh stalked away angrily toward the main road. Later that the day, the police arrived at Vinesh's house and escorted him to the government station, where they locked him up in jail while we shot our film.

Four years later, and after we had completed post-production of the film, I heard rumours that Vinesh had become sick not long after we left Rotuma, though the doctors in Fiji and New Zealand where he eventually sought help could not find anything wrong with him. When my wife and I returned to Rotuma in 2004 to show the film around the island, we were told that Vinesh had passed away.

The chairman of the Rotuma Council was still alive then, and helped facilitate our free screenings on the island. He died about a year later.

Land as cultural heritage

Land is the most important cultural heritage for the Rotuman people (cf. Ravuvu 1983). Firstly, the island is only nine miles by two. However, it is a volcanic island, and the soil is so fertile it could grow almost anything. Unlike some other parts of the Pacific, where much of the land has been alienated to foreigners, Rotumans have managed to retain control of their lands, which are owned communally by clans that can trace their genealogy to a common *fuag ri* or original homestead. Information on land ownership was orally passed down from one generation to another. Before Fiji's independence in 1970, the emphasis was more on stewardship than ownership of land. People were generous in sharing the land's resources, to ensure that everyone's needs were taken care of, and it was not uncommon for those who needed to use certain land resources they didn't own to ask for permission from the stewards of the land.

This was what happened when I wanted to film on land adjacent to the village where I grew up. My family asked permission from *iris ne mata hanua*, the caretakers of the land, living on Rotuma. Vinesh's family was but one of many owners, but since his family had moved to Fiji, permission was not sought from him or his family, but from the caretakers living on Rotuma. Normally this approach would have been sufficient. It didn't work in this instance because Vinesh saw the film project as an opportunity for him to make money. More importantly, this incident illustrates a growing problem with 'absentee landowners', many of whom have moved overseas and have been away for decades, yet refuse to relinquish control to those who are the *mata ne hanua*, the caretakers of the land.

'Gifted' lands

Before the Rotuma Lands Act of 1958 was written, the sharing of land resources was the norm, and was a means by which people's relationships were not only maintained but reinforced and consolidated. If one day I asked to cut copra on your land and you gave me permission, I would feel obligated to help you at a later date should you ask me for assistance, perhaps with a funeral or wedding. If one day I became the head of a clan that owned a lot of land, then I might even show my gratitude by 'gifting' you with a plot of land on which to build your house. I might even give you permission to plant on surrounding lands. These transactions were oral in nature, informal, and could be revoked at a later date should there be a falling out between the original owner and the one gifted with a plot of land. It was therefore in the interest of the one receiving the gift to not only be a good steward of the land but to maintain good relations with the original owner.

The new 'landowners', who were not genealogically connected, built their homes on these 'gifted' lands but often failed to pass on to their descendants information on how they came to be living where they were. Such information is not necessarily in their favour, and it is only human to want to suppress the facts or hope that the passage of time will cloud the memories of the original owners or their descendants.

The practice of gifting land worked well when Rotuman values of sharing, reciprocity, and communalism reigned supreme. But times have changed. Over the years, Western values of materialism, capitalism and individualism have slowly eroded Rotuma's social, cultural and economic landscape, and wreaked havoc with Rotuma's traditional land-tenure system. This shift, reinforced by the materialistic values of the market economy, has encouraged Rotumans to think about land as a valuable asset that could be owned by an individual. Rotumans have been led to believe that you need to have proof of ownership in writing. This is of course the way the modern world works, and Rotumans are now no longer content to depend on the oral word. They want their names recorded in the land register, a common result in the history of state regulation of land in Fiji (Humphrey 2009).

The Rotuma Lands Act is illustrative of this trend towards individual ownership. Rules of ownership that were oral became translated into the written medium. Attempts were made to devise rules of ownership and inheritance that assigned all land to specific named individuals. Many landowners discovered to their chagrin that their names had been left out of the records, either deliberately or by mistake. These errors of commission or omission were often undiscovered until an incident arose that forced you to go to the government station, where the written records are kept, to check their accuracy. Most Rotumans assumed that the records were accurate, and didn't think it was good form to be carrying out inquiries or making investigations that could be seen as indicating a lack of trust in our leaders.

In the present economic climate, where land ownership seems to have become more important than sharing, some Rotumans who claim to be *kainaga* 'clan members' are now challenging each other in court over their rights to ancestral lands, only to find that the court is ill equipped to resolve their cases. Part of the reason for this is that the present Lands Act is not tailored to Rotuma's unique situation.

When Rotuma was ceded to Great Britain in 1881, Britain made Rotuma a part of Fiji (already a British colony then) to be administered from Fiji instead of Britain (see Howard 2007). Fiji's laws became Rotuma's laws, and when the government of Fiji devised a land-tenure system for Fiji (France 1969), it was assumed that the same rules would apply to Rotuma, even though Rotuma has a different social structure and its inhabitants speak Rotuman, not Fijian. So, for example, unlike Fiji, where land was passed down along paternal lines, land on Rotuma was inherited along both paternal and maternal lines.

Attempts by the Fiji government to record land ownership on Rotuma according to paternal lines only were resisted by Rotumans living on the island as well as overseas. This was understandable, as it would result in many people losing their claims to land. The Rotuma Land Act has therefore never been fully endorsed by the Rotuman people, who saw it as an imposition that would be detrimental to Rotuma and its people. However, this didn't stop this imperfect document from being used to adjudicate land cases on the island, simply because it was the only written legislation available.

The original Rotuma Lands Act makes no provision for the practice of gifting land as compensation or to consolidate relationships. Its main concern is that landowners must prove genealogical connections to the original landowner. Now that the original Rotuma Lands Act is being overhauled to take into account Rotuma's bilineal system of land inheritance, there needs to be a special provision for individuals living on land that Rotumans customarily call *pear na hanisi* (land given out of affection). If this is not done, many Rotumans will be evicted from their place of residence.

Fearful that they could lose their homes and the land under their feet, families scramble to find ways of getting their names into the land register, and, in the process, wreak havoc and tear apart strong communities that were once harmonious and tightly knit. A recent court case involving my immediate family and our neighbours on the island of Rotuma aptly illustrates the complexities of resolving land disputes that have come about as a result of land that was 'gifted' years ago.

Call for help

In *The Land Has Eyes*, the protagonist's father is falsely accused of stealing coconuts that from someone else's land. He is hauled before the court and fined. Humiliated and stricken with tuberculosis, he eventually dies. Viki, his youngest child and daughter, is determined to clear her father's name, so that when she finds herself face to face with the district officer, she advocates on behalf of her father. She acts like the lawyer her father wanted her to be, and manages to convince the district officer of her father's innocence.

Below is the relevant scene in the screenplay.

SCENE 122. TWO SHOT – CLARKE AND VIKI

CLARKE   Tell me what happened there. I think the chiefs understand but I don't.

VIKI   Poto is an evil man. He mistranslates in court so his relatives and his friends will win their cases. Most people on the island are aware of this, but they don't want to make waves.

CLARKE   Why?

VIKI   Because we are all related, and we like harmony here.

CLARKE   And the chiefs? Are they afraid of him too?

VIKI   Some of them. Some are his close relatives.

CLARKE   Now I'm beginning to understand.

VIKI   He killed my father.

CLARKE   Poto?

VIKI   My father was an honest man but Poto made him out to be a liar and a thief. My father lost his case. But he told me the truth always prevails. Sometimes we have to wait a long time, he said.

CLARKE   I had heard about him from one of the chiefs. Tell me, is there one thing you want me to do?

Viki nods her head as she looks Mr Clarke in the eye. Mr Clarke reaches out and takes her hand.

CLARKE   Tell me.

VIKI   I want you to clear my father's name. Promise me you'll reconsider the case, now that you know the truth.

CLARKE   I promise you. I'll recommend to the chiefs that you take this year's scholarship. With their backing, the scholarship will be yours.

Viki looks up at Clarke, shocked, but elated. She grabs Mr Clarke's hands and shakes them vigorously. Then she realizes what she's doing and stops. She turns and hurries toward the door. Mr Clarke calls after her.

CLARKE   You forgot your stick.

Viki smiles as she sees Clarke holding up her stick, their eyes meet. She walks back to retrieve her father's ceremonial staff.

CLARKE   Tell me, what do you want to be when you grow up?

VIKI   I want to be like my father. He always told the truth.

Viki feels a flood of emotion rushing back to overwhelm her. She hurries out of the room. Mr Clarke is deeply moved.

When I was writing the screenplay of *The Land Has Eyes*, I had no idea that two years later, I would find myself in a similar position to Viki. As some would say, this was a case of real life imitating art. It all began with a frantic phone call in 2006 from my sister in Rotuma. She told me that she had had an argument with one of the neighbours, whom I shall call Raksaa. That was not unusual, I thought. She added that the neighbour had shouted at her that she should not be living in Mea village, but on the reef where she truly belonged. When she pressed to know why, the neighbour told her that the land our home is on does not belong to her. She was speechless, as our family had lived in Mea for as long as she could remember. She decided to go to the government station to check the land register. To her dismay, she discovered that the neighbours' names have been entered (they weren't there before) into the column 'New Owners'. Our family's name was nowhere to be seen.

When my sister discovered that the lands that belonged to our grandfather Kaitu'u Karaini had been transferred to our neighbours, she was livid. She broke the news to our brother Tonu, the oldest of eleven children. Tonu was 73 years old at this time. For almost all of his life, apart from a few short trips to Fiji, Tonu lived on Rotuma. Tonu had a reputation for integrity, hard work and humility. He was also highly regarded as a gifted fisherman and farmer. A quiet and unassuming man, who valued peace and harmony above material prosperity, he lived a simple life unaffected by the money economy and Western influence.

My sister La, on the other hand, had left the island when she was nineteen and had grown up in Fiji. Prior to her return to Rotuma in 1999, at the age of 55, she was married to another Rotuman and was working in Fiji as a librarian. She gave birth to four children whom she raised with her husband. Because of physical abuse, my sister La divorced her husband and returned to the island to take care of our brother Tonu, whose health was deteriorating. My sister's behaviour was shocking to many Rotumans, who are not used to women taking such a strong and independent stance on her own life, particularly when married.

When Tonu learned that the land upon which our home had been built did not belong to our grandfather Kaitu'u Karaini according to the records at Ahau, he was devastated. He felt helpless because he could not read or write, or speak English. What could he do when the district officer, a Chinese-Fijian man, could only speak English and Fijian but not Rotuman? Incidentally, in the film *The Land Has Eyes*, Viki's father could not speak English, mirroring my own father's lack of English.

Tonu's response to the news was to leave Mea village altogether and go to live with relatives in another village. When my sister called me from Rotuma, I advised her that it would be a mistake to abandon our home. After all, we had lived there for as long as we could remember. At the back of my mind, I was wondering where I would stay in Rotuma should I return for a visit. My brother and sister abandoned our home temporarily, but they returned eventually. The neighbours on either side continued to treat them with disdain. The stress was more than my frail brother could bear, and before long, he became bedridden and later hospitalized.

As for my sister, she would not let a slight of any kind pass her by without a response, and she did not hesitate to call the police whenever she felt that the neighbours had gone too far. The policeman in charge, however, is a close relative of one of the neighbours, and was not sympathetic to my sister's claims. It wasn't long before my sister realized it was useless for her to call the police, and that she had to deal with the neighbours herself, which often meant a tit-for-tat response that only led to further conflict. While engaged in this running battle with the neighbours, she continued to be a full-time nurse for our brother, who never returned from the hospital. I made a special trip from Honolulu to Rotuma to say my goodbyes just before he died. Just as well that he passed away, because the court case that soon followed would have broken his heart twice over.

Meeting the neighbours in court

After several failed attempts by the district chief of Itu't'iu to resolve the impasse between my family and the neighbours, the case was taken to court in 2006. From Honolulu I flew over to Fiji, where I carried out research at the Fiji Archives in Suva in order to prepare for the hearing. My family was the plaintiff and the neighbours on either side were the defendants. My only other living brother in Vatukoula flew over to lend moral support. The fourth person in our party was an elderly woman relative living at a nearby village.

As for the neighbours, they hired a truck to take all their supporters to the courtroom. Among the supporters was the wife of the chairman of the Rotuma Council. There were about twenty of them, and four of us. We sat on different sides of the room facing the front, where the jury was seated. The chairman of the Rotuma Council, also a close relative of the defendants, chaired the meeting. The District Officer (the equivalent of Mr Clarke in the film) was present too. He was a Chinese-Fijian man, who neither spoke Rotuman nor understood its culture in any depth. Also at the front was a representative of the chief of Itu'ti'u, the chief being away in Fiji.

Right from the beginning, I felt that the cards were stacked against me and my family. My only comfort was that I had prepared well and had with me photocopied evidences from the archives to prove that Raksaa's family had no connection to my grandfather, whose name appears as the original owner of the lands in dispute. I also had evidences to prove that Raksaa's family moved into their present residence in 1923, and that my grandfather had gifted the land upon which their present house is located to Raksaa's auntie.

The defendants, on the other hand, did not have any written evidence to support their argument, which basically was to assert that we were related and that they had been on their present location long before any of us was born. They had no coordinated plan of action and were improvising as they went along. They resorted to shouting and accusations when they felt challenged to prove their assertions.

On my family's side, I had told my older brother and sister that only I was allowed to speak, as I was the best educated among us and, besides, I was the one who had done the research at the archives and had the proper evidence to prove our case. This didn't sit too well with my older brother, who also wanted to speak, but I refused to let him (by holding his knee down when he wanted to stand up during the hearing), mainly because I knew he would resort to the same tactics as the other side.

I was also surprised that the district officer, who was in truth the only judge and jury of the case before him, did not have an interpreter. I knew he could not speak Rotuman, and I was suspicious that he was being left out of the proceedings on purpose. I also knew that he took his advice from the chairman of the Rotuma Council as well as the chief's representative, and I decided that I would present our version of events in Rotuman first and then translate it into English, so that he would understand what was going on. I also made clear in my opening remarks that my use of English was for the sole purpose that he would understand what was going on. I also held up several photocopies of documents I had discovered at the archives. The defendants, however, made no efforts to translate for the district officer. They seemed to think that in order to win they needed to flood the courtroom with supporters. It is possible they also thought that the verdict would be decided by a show of hands, hence the need to have so many people present.

It would take too long to describe all that happened in court, except to say that when the time came for the verdict, the district officer declared that my family had won. He added that the names in the column that had the heading 'New Owners' were to be removed, and that the name of my grandfather was to remain as the original owner of the lands in question. He then told us, as though we were naughty children, to get up, walk around, and shake hands with each other as a sign that we forgave one another. We did shake hands, with great reluctance and embarrassment.

My brother, sister, elderly aunt and I returned from the government station elated and vindicated. On the way out of the courtroom, the defendants invited us to their feast at Raksaa's home. Anticipating a win, they had prepared a cooked pig and delicious food to celebrate after the court case. On the other hand, we were so focused on the court case that we did not prepare a special meal. I decided to accept and show a willingness to reconcile, but the rest of my family refused to join me. I told the defendant's side that I was representing my family and I even made a request that we let bygones be bygones and to return to the days of old when we all shared our resources and lived harmoniously. A few days later I left for Fiji then Honolulu, thinking that harmony would return to Mea village.

One thing that I was certain about as a result of my research at the Fiji Archives was that the Raksa'a family came to Mea village because a house builder from Futuna was friendly with my grandfather. As compensation for work this Futunan man had done for my grandfather, he was given permission to build a limestone house in Mea village. This man later married a woman called Ana, who had a sister called Jieni. Ana had no children from the Futunan man, but Jieni had four children, one of whom is Raksaa.

Sometime later, Raksaa's mother and her children moved to live in Mea village. After the death of Ana and her husband, Raksaa's immediate family made it their mission to establish firm foundations in the village. When I was growing up, my family was poor, because we didn't have enough lands from which to cut copra, and my father often had to ask Raksaa who was the 'pure' or chief of the village.

My research at the Fiji Archives revealed to me that my grandfather, whose name appears in the land register as the original owner of the lands in dispute, was the chief of the village of Mea when he was alive, which means that his descendants, myself included, have a direct link to this chiefly lineage. When I was growing up, I always thought that the chiefly family was the Raksaa family, as they had the biggest limestone house (located next to ours) and they had the best lands. My discovery came as a shock to me.

'Economies of affection'

Should the Raksaa family be allowed to remain where they are? What would be a humane response to their situation? To this day, Raksaa refuses to accept the fact that his mother came to be in Mea because his auntie was married to a man who had been gifted with a piece of land by my grandfather. His story is that he is genealogically connected to my grandfather, even though the family tree that he provided in court does *not* link him and his family to my own family. My family tree also does not link his family with ours. If our two family trees do not intersect at any point, how could we be related?

It appears that Raksaa's efforts to link up his family tree with my grandfather's are motivated primarily by fear that without any genealogical connection, his family would be evicted. To resolve this anomaly in Rotuma's land-tenure system, we could learn from an approach taken by some tribes in Africa that use a guiding principle known as 'economies of affection' (Hyden 1980, 1983; Waters 1982).

Using the principle of 'economies of affection', persons living on gifted lands would have a claim to remain where they are today, as long as they could demonstrate that they had been good stewards of the land on which they now reside. If so, then ancestral practices that fall outside genealogical connections could apply in the present. This is what 'economies of affection' is about: putting people and their needs first and foremost.

Winning the battle but not the war

My sister La eventually packed her bags and abandoned our home and lands in Rotuma and moved back to Fiji. She found being sandwiched by neighbours on either side that hated her too stressful, and she feared for her health. She had fallen sick several times and, living on her own, couldn't put up with the neighbours anymore, as she was without support, her two living brothers and two sisters having moved to live in Fiji, Samoa and Hawai'i.

By abandoning our home on the island, my sister was in reality giving in to the wishes of her neighbours. It was naive to think that because the district officer declared in court that the lands under question truly belonged to my grandfather, and that the records had to be straightened out to reflect this fact, that our neighbours had lost the case, and my family had won.

After the court case, the district officer thought that he had resolved a difficult land dispute and that the case could now be put to rest. This conclusion came about as a result of lack of experience of Rotuman culture or its people. By constantly harassing my sister – for example, throwing rocks at her chickens, stealing her pineapples, throwing rubbish across the hedge and into her compound when she isn't looking – Raksaa's family eventually succeeded in forcing my sister out of our family home through indirect means. Further, now that we are away from the island, what is to stop them from fiddling with the land records at the government station again? This may or may not happen, but only time will tell.

With my sister returning to Fiji, the neighbours could continue to do as they pleased with the lands that were under dispute. We had resigned ourselves to this possibility, as there was nothing we could do about it. But the thought of totally abandoning our home on the island was too much to bear, so we as a family met several times to figure out who among us was best suited to return to live in the family home.

My other sister (older than me but younger than La) is single and uninterested in living on her own in the family home. My only other living brother (older than La and myself) wanted to go, but his Tongan wife wasn't interested in uprooting the family in Vatukoula and moving to Fiji. And I, of course, was not ready to retire to the island. We eventually found an answer. We sent to the island a nephew (his father is Rotuman, his mother Fijian) and his Fijian wife and three little children. My nephew didn't have a regularly paying job in Fiji, and his family was finding it difficult to make ends meet.

Rotuma sounded more appealing to them than living at the fringe of urban Suva, and they agreed to be caretakers of the family home on the island.

As agreed, I paid for the family's boat fare and basic needs, and sent them on their way to Rotuma. Every month I send them money to buy basic supplies (for example salt, sugar and soap) and to pay for incidental expenses in relation to funerals, weddings and church donations, among other obligations.

There is a bittersweet ending to this story. As it turns out, my nephew and his wife and children get along well with the neighbours, and the old ways of helping each other and working together have been restored. For the moment, everyone is happy with each other again. When I first wrote this chapter, my sister La lived with me in Suva, while my other sister preferred to live with our Fiji relatives (instead of her siblings), giving her more freedom of movement. She has tried living with my nephew and family in Rotuma, but found that difficult because her authority has been displaced. After several struggles for control over the affairs of the family home, she eventually decided to live with relatives in another village.

Life in Mea village has returned to normal again and peace has been restored. The courtroom drama that we all had to go through would not have happened if Tonu and his family had felt secure in Mea village. His insecurity, and ours as well, came about when it became obvious that our fates regarding land ownership would be based on whose names appeared on the land register kept at the government station.

There is enough land owned by my grandfather, fourteen plots in total, to cater for everyone's needs, including Raksaa's. There is no humane reason why his family could not remain where they are. Under the present Rotuma Lands Act, however, there is no provision for this ancient customary practice in modern Rotuma. I believe that 'economies of affection' are the answer to this. Although values of basic survival, social maintenance and development have been destroyed as a result of capitalism in Europe and Asia (Hyden 1983), Rotuma remains very much a subsistence economy. It is therefore in the island's best interests (harmony, social cohesion, land use etc.) to ensure that gifted lands, as much as possible, remain in the hands of the original recipients.

Conclusion

This chapter identifies two areas in Rotuman land tenure that remain unaddressed by efforts to overhaul the present land-tenure system. The first has come about in more recent years because of out-migration by many Rotumans to Fiji or overseas, resulting in plots of land, and abandoned homes, that are not put to productive use. A possible solution is for the Rotuma Council to impose a time-frame for the period owners can be away overseas before they lose their land rights. Ten years seems a reasonable length of time. A variation to this approach would be to allow those who have cultivated abandoned land for at least a decade to be able to file claims to own such lands based on 'fair use'.

A second area that was not addressed in the Rotuma Lands Act of 1958 is that of 'gifted' lands – parcels of land given away by the original owners to individuals as compensation or to reinforce relationships. Using the concept of 'economies of affection', such individuals may be allowed to remain, possibly owning these lands, on the basis of certain prerequisites. A village or district council would need to hear these individual cases and make decisions based on criteria that should be agreed upon by all the community. This would allow those who are not genealogically connected to the original landowners, but who have built homes on these lands based on goodwill and good faith, to be treated with affection.

The trend toward commercialism and individualism poses a threat to the Rotuman values of *haihanisiga* and *hanisi*. *Haihanisiga*, translated as 'looking after each other', is the solution to absentee landowners whose lands are needed by residents on the island who want access, largely for farming purposes, in order to feed their families. *Hanisi*, which means love or affection, is embodied in the expression *pear na hanisi*, lands given out of love or affection. *Hanisi* needs to be practised when dealing with 'gifted' lands that occurred before the Rotuma Lands Act was written.

As long as Rotuman values of *haihanisiga* and *hanisi* are used as guiding principles when dealing with 'absentee landowners' and 'gifted lands', Rotumans should be able to adapt successfully to the challenges posed today by the forces of the market economy and other globalizing influences.

References

Crocombe, R.G. (ed.) 1987. *Land tenure in the Atolls: Cook Islands, Kiribati, Marshall Islands, Tokelau, Tuvalu.* Suva, Fiji: Institute of Pacific Studies of the University of the South Pacific.

France, P. 1969. *The Charter of the Land: Custom and Colonization in Fiji.* Melbourne: Oxford University Press.

Hereniko, V. 1995. *Woven Gods: Female Clowns and Power in Rotuma* (Pacific Islands Monograph Series 12). Honolulu: University of Hawai'i Press.

Howard, A. with J. Rensel 2007. *Island Legacy: A History of the Rotuman People.* Victoria, BC: Trafford Publishing.

——— 2006. Presenting Rotuma to the World: The Making of The Land Has Eyes. *Visual Anthropology Review* 22(1):73–95.

Humphrey, L. 2009. Land, Memory and the State: 'Official' and Other Histories in Waya Island, Fiji. PhD Dissertation, Department of Anthropology, University of Hawai'i at Mānoa.

Hyden, G. 1980. *Beyond Ujamaa in Tanzania: Underdevelopment and an Uncaptured Peasantry*. Berkeley: University of California Press.

——— 1983. *No Shortcut to Progress: African Development in Perspective*. Berkeley: University of California Press.

Ravuvu, A. 1983. *Vaka i Taukei: the Fijian way of life*. Fiji: Institute of Pacific Studies of the University of the South Pacific.

Waters, T. 1982. A Cultural Analysis of the Economy of Affection and the Uncaptured Peasantry in Tanzania. *The Journal of Modern African Studies* 30(1):163–75.

Vilsoni Hereniko is Professor of Creative Media at the University of Hawai'i at Mānoa.

CHAPTER 5

The Western Solomons and the sea

Maritime cultural heritage in

sociality, province and state

✳

EDVARD HVIDING

State, nation and ambivalence in the Western Solomons

There is an urgent need for closer, ethnographically grounded examination
of the provincial, non-local/non-national scenes of Melanesian politics,
viewed as a level of governmentality in which relations between the local
and the national, and channels to the global, are continuously negotiated
and reconfigured. While these topics are discussed in some detail in the
Introduction (White and Hviding, this volume), in this chapter I shall
examine a particular example of this problem-prone intermediate axis of the
Melanesian nation-state equation; that of the province. The analytical position
is thus located neither fully in the rural nor fully in the national.

It is the Western Province of Solomon Islands that is my point of departure
and focus of interest. Within a timescale that covers post-independence
Solomon Islands but gives some prominence to the cultural history of this part
of the Solomons, it is my intention to bring to the forefront some particularly
distinctive connections between cultural heritage and political innovation. As
in the national example of Vanuatu provided by Regenvanu (this volume), my
discussion of the Western Province of Solomon Islands demonstrates how
culturally distinct lifeways, ascribed as well as self-ascribed, may become
foundations for new forms of government.

A cluster of high volcanic islands and extensive reefs, rich in both marine
and terrestrial resources, the Western Province is a part of Melanesia whose
people have some notoriety with regard to participation in projects of nation-
making. On 7 July 1978, the day of independence, when the flag of the new
nation of Solomon Islands was raised, sentiment and situation were far

from celebratory in the small town of Gizo, administrative headquarters and infrastructural hub of the (equally new) Western Province:

> an attempt to raise the [new] Solomon Islands national flag ... led to a
> confrontation between Western people and migrants from Malaita, the
> home island of the Prime Minister. Three plane-loads of police were flown
> in to reinforce the police station. The next day, members of the British royal
> family arrived, fresh from the independence celebrations in [the capital]
> Honiara. In welcoming them, the President of the Western Council was
> careful to limit the symbolism: 'Your visit here is being acknowledged by
> our people as strictly a case of the British royal family visiting the Western
> people ...'
>
> (Premdas *et.al.* 1983: 164)

This was the outcome of a long and protracted chain of activities and events subsumed as the 'Western Breakaway Movement' (Premdas *et.al.* 1983). Rumours abounded in the late-colonial Solomon Islands as to what agendas the unpredictable 'Westerners' might develop from their ambivalent attitudes as independence was near. Some had thought that a merger with the huge island of Bougainville to the north was an option, until that island in 1975 became the North Solomons Province of the new independent nation of Papua New Guinea. Others, not least within the Western Solomons, pointed to the fact that the land mass, population and marine and terrestrial resources of 'the West' would be more than sufficient as a base for a nation of its own. As independence came in July 1978, the people of the western Solomons were generally not appreciative of the new Solomon Islands government's proposal for a nation based on what has been perceptively referred to as 'decreed affinities' (Dureau 1998). The Union Jack still flew in Gizo.

As provincial legislation was enacted in the new nation, the four rather thinly stretched 'districts' of colonial administration (Eastern, Malaita, Central and Western) became seven more compact provinces. In that process the new Western Province did join the 'decreed' nation, but its politicians and other spokespersons have ever since remained the strongest voices on the national scene for a radical transformation of Solomon Islands into a federacy of states. In 1995 the province experienced a split in which Choiseul, its largest single island, formed a separate province, though still with strong connections to Gizo given the lack of infrastructure on Choiseul itself. Following the establishment of Choiseul Province, the label 'Western Province' covered only the New Georgia group of islands, plus the Shortlands far to the north-west. Meanwhile, at a national level, Pijin terms like *olketa long west* ('the people of the west') retained their holistic coverage and from now on applied

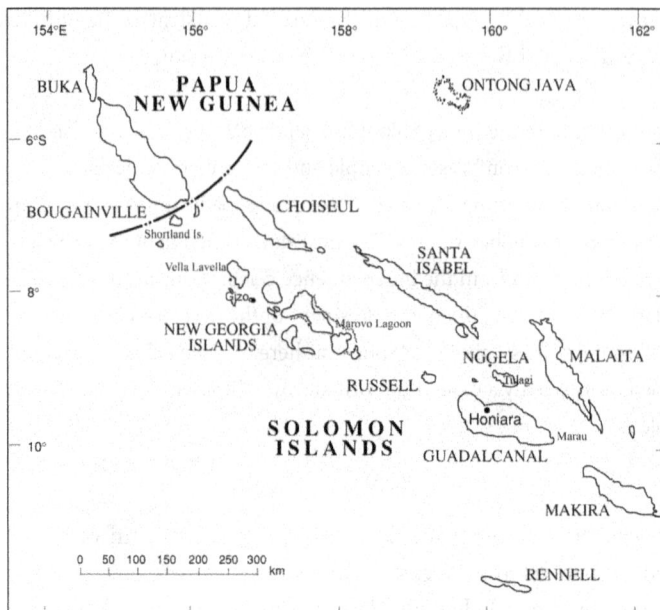

Figure 1   Solomon Islands, including provincial borders and place names in the
             Western Solomons mentioned in the text (University of Bergen).

to two provinces, not one. In a parallel vein, the English concept of the
'Western Solomons' became increasingly prominent in both governmental
and everyday discourses, in Honiara, Gizo and elsewhere, and by implication
referred to all islands in 'the west' including Choiseul (Figure 1).

Twenty-two years after independence, the Solomon Islands nation found
itself sliding rapidly into political chaos and governmental collapse in the wake
of armed clashes in Guadalcanal, failed government attempts to maintain
national integrity, and a *coup d'état* in Honiara on 5 June 2000 (Fraenkel 2004;
Moore 2004). The small seaside town of Gizo once more became the site of
a prominent departure from national ambitions. In the month following the
coup in Honiara, Independence Day saw the culmination of a political process
in Western Province referred to later as a 'coup that nobody noticed' (Scales
2007), involving the declaration of the Western Solomons by its leaders (for
the occasion being the combined executive assemblies of both Western and
Choiseul provinces) as a state-in-federation.[1]

Despite intermittent debates in twenty-first century Solomon Islands
about degrees of provincial autonomy, the unilateral declaration for all
practical purposes of a 'State of Western Solomons' has been unrecognized in
formal terms since it was made. The troubled nation has remained dependent
on the natural and human resources of the west, and the sheer dominance of
Western Solomons parliamentarians in national government has not exactly

promoted the autonomy aspirations of 'the west' in that field of political action. Those aspirations were and are grounded in decades of dissatisfaction with the management within Solomon Islands of national revenue, the greatest proportion of which has consistently been derived from the lands and seas of Western Province through the foreign-dominated logging and tuna-fishing industries. Western Province spokespersons have pointed to a consistent mismatch between the province's contribution to national export revenue and its share of financial returns from the national government. The rapid growth since the late 1990s of the logging industry in Choiseul Province and the continuing lack of infrastructure development in that large island have promoted similar observations from there.

The Townsville Peace Agreement aimed at resolving the Guadalcanal conflict was reached in Australia in November 2000 and explicitly took up provincial autonomy and scenarios of federal government in its visions of national reconstitution. The issues remained prominent in political discourse, if not action, during the years leading up to the arrival in July 2003 of foreign intervention into the Solomon Islands crisis in the form of the Regional Assistance Mission to the Solomon Islands (RAMSI, see, for example, Fraenkel *et.al.* 2014; Kabutaulaka 2006; Moore 2005).

Debates on a federal system of government continued in the post-2003 phase of national 'restoration' (Kabutaulaka 2006). Meanwhile, the State of Western Solomons, a political and territorial configuration formally limited to the far-flung islands of the post-1995 Western Province, quietly continued to fly its flag and at times even to communicate on state letterhead paper, while somewhat less quietly pursuing outspoken agendas of financial autonomy. Choiseul Province, also with its own flag, has been even quieter, but in that remote island there has been growing dissatisfaction with the lack of infrastructure and economic development. Taken together, the two provinces have, as 'the West', remained consistent in their critique of the prevailing political and financial systems of the post-colonial nation – while also, ironically, maintaining a massively prominent presence in national government.[2] Of the twelve cabinets since 1978, seven have had a prime minister from New Georgia or Choiseul, and the Ministry of Finance has, rather remarkably, had ministers from the West almost continuously since 1989. Meanwhile the people – the 'Westerners' – have retained their processes of ascription and self-ascription to distinctiveness, amounting to an implied sharing of ethnic identity (Barth 1969) and a difference from the rest of the nation that worried non-Westerners already during late colonial times as the national project emerged.

What, then, are the historical relationships and cultural affinities that have combined to generate claims of shared identity in the Western Solomons, beyond the strategic manoeuvres of politicians? Arguments concerning land, language, skin pigmentation, mission history and more have been brought forth (Premdas *et.al.* 1983:168–71) in ways that do not necessarily see the Western Solomons as different from any other locality where social groups organize themselves according to territorially marked and culturally defined boundaries. In the following, I argue that for the Western Solomons, particular and very significant territorial and cultural-historical dimensions are connected to the sea and the connectivity it affords.

Islands connected: maritime dimensions of cultural heritage and everyday life

Maritime orientations in everyday life and cultural history are far from unique to 'the West', and are characteristic of much of the Solomon Islands. There are well-known examples of locations – the artificial islands of 'salt-water people' in the Langalanga and Lau lagoons on the coast of Malaita, the small islands to the east of Makira (Santa Ana, Santa Catalina), and the even smaller islands in outer Temotu Province – where life is even more strongly sea-oriented than in the western Solomons. Moreover there is no lack elsewhere in the Solomons of regional long-term regularities of inter- and intra-island travel, marriage and exchange, such as the historically and genealogically defined Malaita-Guadalcanal entity described by John Naitoro (2000:3–4) with reference to the relevance of that pre-colonial indigenous configuration to mitigating the turn-of-the-century armed conflict on Guadalcanal.

What sets 'the West' apart in this regard, however, is the degree to which the entire New Georgia group of islands, with the Shortland Islands and Choiseul at the peripheries, has the sea, not the land, as the main channel for social and political connectivity. Across a distance of more than 200 kilometres, the New Georgia islands, as the core of 'the West', constitute a shared universe where linguistic diversity, local variations of shared cultural themes, inter-island marriages and frequent maritime travel generate an image of these high volcanic islands as a large, coherent social space in which the sea affords continuous interaction. In 'the West' everybody lives in coastal villages, by popular assumption owns a canoe or two, and more often than not has a spouse from another, related island speaking a different, related language. The hyper-connectivity among the islands of the western Solomons is thus different from the rest of the archipelago, where single, large continental islands (some also with inland populations) dominate the scene, complemented by a few cases of small, low, widely dispersed islands.

In his analysis of the emergence of the State of Western Solomons during 2000, Ian Scales suggested that a major factor in the distinct identity of 'the West' is:

indigenous understanding of pre-Protectorate history in terms of kin
and custom. At that time, the islands of the western Solomons formed a
maritime world of inter-island exchange, conflict and alliance, little involved
with the east. Local populations in the New Georgia Islands were by late
frontier times populated by a mixture of people from all the islands in the
West under the mantle of various local descent groups, each controlling
their own area.

Scales (2007:191)

Scales refers here to the constitutively inter-island nature of social life in
the New Georgia islands, a maritime world that has persisted into the present.
In the Western Solomons the sea is like land, most notably in the sense that
in the major languages there is one single term for the ancestral territorial
estate of land, reefs and lagoon held under customary tenure by most of those
localized descent groups, usually referred to as *butubutu* (Hviding 2003a). This
land-and-sea territory is *puava* in Marovo and *pepeso* in Roviana; the term is
similar to many other territorial concepts in Oceania, such as the Fijian *vanua*
and the Hawaiian *ahupuaʻa*, in that it encompasses the range of resource zones
from mountain tops to open sea beyond the reef (Hviding 2003b). And there
is more to it, as indicated in a statement from the submission made by the
politicians of the Western Council in 1975 to the late-colonial government's
'Special Committee on Provincial Government':

> The way our islands have been arranged by the creator has been such that
> the geographical locations have in numerous ways determined how far and
> with which islands groupings the majority of our people have identified
> themselves and have a growing emotional attachment. Geography tends also
> to have demarcated the territorial extent of such attachment.

(Premdas *et.al.* 1983: 169)

This implies a certain uniqueness in spatial terms, wherein the focus is on
'island groupings' rather than single islands. While the other major provinces
of the Solomon Islands nation – Isabel, Guadalcanal, Malaita, Makira – largely
consist of one large island, each a small continent in itself, the Western Province
is constituted by almost a dozen major and innumerable minor islands, fringed
by large lagoons and connected to each other across deep-water channels,
over open sea and along more sheltered seaways. The 'canoe', admittedly now
as often as not in the sense of a fibreglass boat with outboard motor, remains
the only real means of inter-island transport and communication here. In the
Western Solomons, the sea truly connects – it does not separate.

We are mindful of so many inspiring ideas left to us as scholars of the Pacific by the late Epeli Hau'ofa (1993, 2008; Waddell *et.al.* 1993). In his influential, widely quoted article 'Our Sea of Islands', Hau'ofa argued that Western scientists, the political elites of the Pacific and agents of aid-donor nations and organizations had all misunderstood the Pacific by envisioning human settlement and practice in this great oceans in terms of 'islands in a far sea' – isolated points harbouring separate human existences dependent on the exporters of development aid and trade goods and the importers of labour migrants. Arguing to the contrary that the Pacific must be seen in terms of the entire regional whole of Oceania as a 'Sea of Islands', Hau'ofa invoked the notion that 'home' may not be confined to a specific location, but is likely to include the entire Oceanic space within which Pacific peoples move. This part of Hau'ofa's argument echoes long-term migration patterns in the region's cultural history, specifically the settlement of the entire tropical and sub-tropical Pacific by the Lapita peoples over the last 4,000 years (Kirch 1997), and the longevity of such patterns in terms of the lives lived today among the islands.

So it is logical for me to return to the sea, that foundation of existence for so many of Oceania's people, in the Melanesian region of large islands not so remote from each other as the smaller land masses further out in what some would see as the 'real' sea of islands. While Hau'ofa's 'Sea of Islands' and the 'People of the Sea' examined by historian Paul D'Arcy (2006) are spatially positioned out in archaeology's 'remote Oceania' – beyond the eastern Solomon Islands – another sea of islands is constituted by the Western Solomons, particularly the New Georgia group. Contrary to the objections of some, whose analytical focus (or residential location) on the large islands of Melanesia have caused a resistance to maritime metaphors for Oceania's identities,[3] the notions of shared cultural heritage among people of the Western Solomons relate above all to the role of the sea as an environmental realm that enables high mobility and shapes the connections of persons, groups and histories. In a discussion of early encounters of New Georgians with European (or, in this case, American) ships, Nicholas Thomas (2010: 57) argues that the inhabitants of the small island of Simbo at the south-western corner of the New Georgia group did not, as contact with Europeans and their political economy intensified, constitute a circumscribed, easily demarcated 'island society'. Instead, through travel, warfare, exchange, marriage and shifting residence the people of Simbo lived lives that ranged across many islands and that were 'truly archipelagic'.

The notion among Solomon Islanders of 'the West' as an entity is not a new one, but is emblematic of an indigenous pan-Solomons view of the New Georgia group, Choiseul and the Shortland Islands as a particularly dense and dynamic interactional field with New Georgia as the core. In this pan-Solomons sense 'the West' co-exists with other island identities such as 'Malaita', 'Guale' (Guadalcanal), 'Isabel' and others, the main difference being that unlike the others 'the West' is not a single large land mass but a dispersed yet seemingly unitary cluster of large and small islands. The core of the Western Solomons is the spatially complex archipelago of the New Georgia group arranged like stepping-stones on a north-west to south-east axis of about 220 kilometres – Vella Lavella, Ranongga, New Georgia, Rendova, Tetepare, Vangunu, Gatokae, with the two small islands of Simbo and Ghizo being, respectively, a far western outlier (with high importance in early colonial encounters) and a central administrative hub of modern times. Tetepare is notable for being the largest uninhabited island in the entire Pacific, having been completely depopulated in the nineteenth century through warfare and epidemics. The south-west and south-east sides of the main island of New Georgia are fringed by the raised barrier reefs forming the Roviana and Marovo lagoons. Historically, the expanses of open sea between most of the lagoon clusters and larger islands have linked, rather than separated, the inhabitants of the different parts of the archipelago – an observation that echoes the proposal by navigator and scholar David Lewis (1972:15) that in the Pacific, the ocean spaces are 'highways rather than barriers'.

The maritime technology of New Georgia retains a firm grasp on the seasonal forces of erratic north-west monsoons and persistent south-east trade winds. Throughout the New Georgia group, maritime travel and inter-island trade, friendship and marriage remain significant features of everyday life. Now strongly influenced by loyalties to three different church denominations (to the level of denominational endogamy), these sociopolitical systems of sizeable scale formerly involved raiding, warfare and headhunting, including beyond the archipelago to other parts of the Solomons. Today, economic links between the various parts of the New Georgia group remain strong, as district centres and markets for copra and other cash crops are few in number and dispersed, and a high intensity of travel still characterizes everyday life in the New Georgia islands. Small and large islands, central or peripheral, densely or sparsely populated localities, all converge into the forms of social, cultural, political and economic connectedness referred to by Schwartz (1963) for the Admiralty Islands off New Guinea's north coast as 'systems of areal integration'. The steep and rugged volcanic topography of most islands inhibits ground transport; and air travel, although fairly well developed, is prohibitively expensive. Maritime travel thus remains the all-important means of transport throughout the New Georgia group, as evidenced on market days in Gizo, when large dugout canoes with outboard motors arrive from the islands of Ranongga, Vella Lavella, Kolobangara, New Georgia and elsewhere, congesting the harbour.

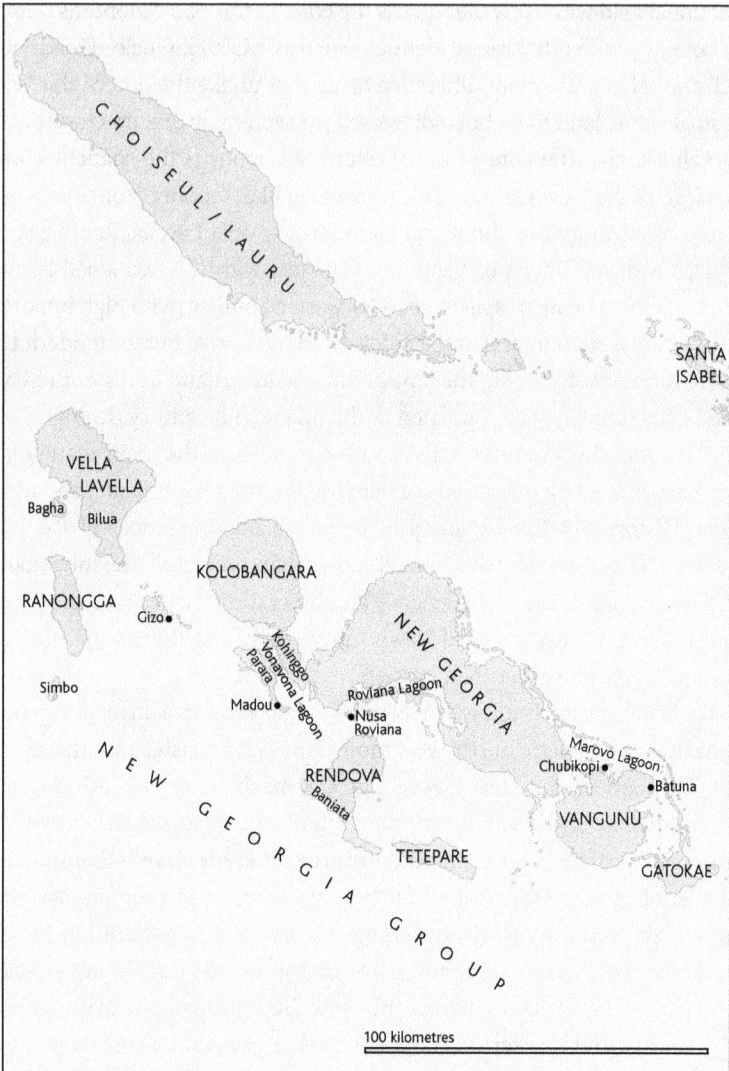

Figure 2   Map of the New Georgia group (University of Bergen).

Beyond its significant role in the Western Solomons as universal scene for travel through which social relations expand and connect, the sea is a key for the practice of everyday life itself, as demonstrated by the sheer numbers of canoes (relative to population) found in most villages, by the extraordinarily high reliance in the New Georgia islands on seafood (even in a nation said to have just about the world's highest consumption of seafood per capita), and by the presently heavy emphasis on tourism focused on the sea, waves and reefs. It is quite possible that in terms of population history, the sea is even more significant today than in the past, as all villages are now located on the coast.

Today, the forested hinterlands have timber, but not people. The cultural and cosmological significance of the sea is expressed by people in New Georgia in their dislike of maps that portray lagoons as flat monotone surfaces, unlike in air photographs and, most recently, Google Earth.

This is 'maritime Melanesia' proper (Hviding 1996). Everyday village-level interaction is, now as before, outwards-oriented and often multilingual in its cultural scope, a diversity that does not reflect separation over longer or shorter runs of history, but that is a result of continued, conscious efforts of linguistic differentiation whereby neighbouring peoples establish increased distinctiveness through the development of numerous different yet related languages, along the lines of the argument proposed for Melanesia in general by Laycock (1969, 1982). Twelve languages are spoken in the New Georgia group. While ten of them belong to the Northwest Solomonic group of Austronesian languages, the remaining two are non-Austronesian but not closely related, and are spoken at opposite ends of the archipelago: in Vella Lavella, and in southern Rendova. The spatial distribution of languages partly derives from distinct groups with sea- or inland-based histories.

There is no reason to assume that the distinct societies or 'ethnolinguistic groups' of the New Georgia area have ever been isolated, nor that they have been particularly stable over time. From a view of the history of overseas relations throughout the New Georgia islands, it may be argued that continuous inter-group and inter-island contact and long-term overall demographic stability (from a complex internal history of repeated migration, settlement and displacement) have provided a context for the conscious development of group difference, mainly through linguistic diversification. In this sense the close cultural similarities between neighbouring peoples speaking totally unrelated Austronesian and non-Austronesian languages are notable phenomena, as are the many tales of human migrations, linguistic change and animal dispersal encountered in New Georgia's oral traditions (Hviding 2003c:46–8). Those tales often range way beyond New Georgia to include putative historical and more concrete genealogical connections with the islands of Bougainville, Choiseul and Isabel, and on a deeper level there is the widespread notion that in a very, very distant past humans and birds were not present, but then arrived from the north-westerly direction of 'sunset'; also the direction in which the spirits of the dead of New Georgia make their final journey.

The large ethnolinguistic groups of the Marovo and Roviana lagoons on both sides of the large main island of New Georgia were and are the major movers of past and present inter-island politics, although the town of Gizo these days plays its own important role as infrastructural and administrative centre. From a history of raiding, trading and wide-ranging alliances of friendship and marriage, the Marovo and Roviana people of today retain kinship links throughout most islands of the New Georgia group, and beyond that to Isabel, Choiseul, the Russell Islands group, Savo and Guadalcanal. These long-term relations, in New Georgia often spoken of with reference to 'paths' (Hviding 1996:165–6)[4] – a powerful idiom with connotations of spatiotemporal sequence and regularized movement embodied also in established sea routes – still involve regular visiting through an institutionalized practice referred to as 'kinship travel'.

Inter-island relations and social scenarios are designated by New Georgians in terms that relate to anthropological categories of both kinship and friendship. As idioms of relationality, they are subsumed by overarching concepts whereby one may be contained by, and transformed to, another. The practice of transforming strangers into friends and subsequently into affines and ultimately kin (vice versa through ostracism and excommunication) runs deep in the history of the regional interaction systems. The term used in Marovo for 'stranger' is instructive in this regard for its implication of transition: it is *tinoni karovona*, 'person [who] crossed over', and presupposes that any person referred to in this way has somehow arrived from overseas and established a local connection.

Continuing involvement in well-established friendship among men in New Georgia could imply subsequent exchanges in marriage, leading to the establishment of kin relations. Such processes are echoed in today's importance of maintaining overseas friends for assistance in trade, and of regularizing inter-island marriages through alliances of long standing. Throughout New Georgia, the concept of *baere* or 'friend' has a multitude of uses with reference to 'same-sex' or 'cross-sex' relations, particularly the former. One specific usage relevant to pre-colonial regional systems referred to ritualized friendship, specifically to trading partners, of which most influential adult men would strive to have a variety in as many islands as possible. It is remembered today that *baere* relationships between men who were potential foes were strong and imbued with deep mutual respect. Such relations implied a predictable flow of prestigious exchange goods, and could imply shelter and provisions for travelling raiding parties – safe havens in enemy lands. In this sense, the regional exchange systems radiating from the pre-colonial New Georgia group had much in common with the famous *kula* systems of the Massim on the other side of the Coral Sea (Leach and Leach 1983; Malinowski 1922). To reapply the words used by Malinowski for the subtitle to his famous book on the *kula*: there was as at least as much 'enterprise and adventure' in New Georgia as in the Massim.

From their headhunting raids in other islands, Marovo warriors also brought home captives (see White 1991 for account of effects on Santa Isabel).

Some of these were destined for ritual death, but more often than not captives were brought home for pragmatic purposes such as labour in slavery, or marriage. It is said that the 'slaves' of former times were often treated well, and that they could even be assimilated into their master's family. *Pinausu*, the word used in Marovo for slave, also means 'animal pet' but connects semantically to the field of adoptive kinship. Whereas Nicholas Thomas (1991:48) concluded from the basis of archival material that among the headhunting groups of New Georgia captives from other islands were entirely removed, physically and symbolically, from their former homes, present-day New Georgians in fact continue to maintain a variety of inter-island links originating in genealogically positioned persons who were taken captive and subsequently incorporated into their captors' group(s).

The sea and the canoe are the main idioms of this history of intense maritime connectivity, now as before. Early European observers, from the first explorers to the colonial officers and missionaries who started arriving in the Western Solomons in the final years of the nineteenth century, were alternately fascinated by the superior maritime technology represented in New Georgia's war canoes, and horrified by the intensity of headhunting expeditions carried out in those canoes by the coastal dwellers. The people of the Roviana and Marovo lagoons, and of Simbo, Vella Lavella, Rendova and other islands of the group, went raiding and trading both within the group and further afield, across the ocean to Isabel, Choiseul, Russell Islands, Savo, Guadalcanal and other remote destinations, possibly even to Malaita. The raiding and trading systems of pre-colonial New Georgia were truly large scale – as attested, for example, by the existence in the Marovo language of a distinct numeral for ten thousand (*vuro*), used to count taro for the feasts organized by the great chiefs of the day. Because of their history as voyagers, the people of present-day New Georgia retain kinship links within and beyond the archipelago. Cognatic descent, prevailing in Marovo and Roviana, contributes to the maintenance of bilateral kin connections which are often traced to captives taken generations back. They are maintained today by frequent visiting and intermarriage, which also works to bolster land claims.

Icon of the sea: the Western Solomons war canoe

I did my first field research many years ago with a particular focus on the role of the sea as a scene for everyday practice, a source of history, and – through the tenure and political control of sea and reefs – a core focus of social relations in the Marovo Lagoon (Hviding 1996). Here in maritime Melanesia are large islands and spectacular lagoons, but also – very significantly – seascapes where signs of cultural continuity are under and above water, for those whose local knowledge enables them to see. In this chapter, aware that my perspective is shaped by my association with the maritime cultures of the Marovo Lagoon, I extend my argument about the sea as a focus for cultural identity and social relations to the Western Solomons more generally. I want to argue that the maritime-based history of these islands, the predominantly coastal living with a high emphasis on fishing and seafood consumption, and the continued reliance on sea travel for trade, marriage and other social and economic purposes, enable us to view the sea and its associated practices and histories as a distinct cultural heritage of Western Solomon Islanders, even those who may see themselves as inland dwellers first and maritime travellers second. Much of this, I argue, is signified in the famous large war canoe of New Georgia (see Hviding 2014, for a detailed overview). That war canoe, with its towering, ornamented prow and stern, is an icon of oceanic connectivity, connoting not only headhunting but also the transfer of living persons and the continuation across the sea of social linkages established through abductions, alliances and marriages, past and present.

The characteristic plank-built war canoe of the Western Solomons, with its plank-built single hull decorated with pearl-shell inlay and tall, richly ornamented prow and stern, is well known under its Roviana name *tomoko*, but goes by other names such as *magoru* in the Marovo area and *niabara* in Vella Lavella. This style of canoe, whose sleek and light build and high speed were commented on by most early European navigators who visited the Western Solomons, was built and used from Choiseul in the north-west to Marovo in the south-east and, by technological and cultural adaptation during past times of inter-island travel, raiding and trading, also in some locations in islands further afield, such as at Kia in north-west Isabel (White 1991:87) and in some smaller islands of the central Solomons. Don Alvaro de Mendaña y Neira, the first European visitor to the Solomons, noted how:

> Their canoes are very well made and very light; they are shaped like a
> crescent, the largest holding about thirty persons. They are so swift that,
> although our ships under sail started two leagues ahead of them, with a
> good wind and all the sails set, they caught us up within the hour. Their
> speed in rowing is marvellous...
>
> (Mendaña 1568, in Amherst and Thomson 1901:109)

Lieutenant H.B.T. Somerville of the Royal Navy spent several months during 1893–4 in and around the Marovo Lagoon in his capacity as leader of detachments from the HMS *Penguin*, a steam- and sail-driven sloop of 1,130 tons engaged in an ambitious nautical survey of the New Georgia group. While the *Penguin* steamed and sailed around New Georgia and adjacent islands for survey work, and regularly had to go all the way to Ugi near Makira in the

Figure 3   War canoe, New Georgia, 1890s (Amherst and Thomson 1901:566).

eastern Solomons to replenish coal, Somerville was frequently left with a few men, tents, a steam launch and a pile of coal to set up camp in the vicinity of coastal villages so as to survey the reef-studded lagoon in detail. Somerville was Victorian gentleman of scholarly persuasion; he was interested in 'natives and their customs' and carried a copy of the field manual *Notes and Queries of Anthropology*. He proved to be not just a dedicated nautical surveyor but also a diligent observer and note-taker with regard to the people he met under the remarkably peaceful circumstances of his mission. His ethnographic materials were published in a long descriptive article in the *Journal of the Royal Anthropological Institute*, and his enthusiasm for the canoes of the day was well expressed there, though apparently with some reservations concerning the level of civilization of their builders:

> The canoes of New Georgia are built, as in the rest of the Solomon Islands, on the Malay model, with high prow and stern post. Nothing can exceed the beauty of their lines, and carefulness of build – considering the means at disposal – or their swiftness when properly propelled. They are a most astonishing revelation of scientific art in a people little removed from complete savagery. These graceful boats are of all sizes, from that of the 'one-man' of 8 feet long, to the great war canoe, or *tómako* [*sic*], of 40 to 50 feet, which will hold perhaps thirty-five men.
>
> (Somerville 1897: 369)

The standard build of a Western Solomons war canoe included a heavy keel piece from which a spacious hull was built with four strakes, which were lashed together lengthways and to a complex support framework of internal ribs. Hardwood gunwales and towering prow and stern posts made from a much lighter wood were then added. Altogether twenty large and small planks are required for the proper construction of the war canoe, whose size, build and purpose have led archaeologist Matthew Felgate (2007:127) to view it as more than simply a canoe, instead as a 'keel-ship …, being of very complex sewn-plank construction on a vertically oriented central keel'. Today, this large water craft first and foremost symbolizes a distinctive maritime history and invokes the wide inter-island relations of the people of the Western Solomons.

Different versions of large, elaborately decorated plank canoes were also built in the past among many peoples elsewhere in the Solomons, and early European navigators from Mendaña onwards made observations of large, swift, beautiful canoes across the archipelago. As in New Georgia, the large ocean-going canoes of Isabel, Guadalcanal, Gela, Malaita and Makira were surrounded by much ceremonial and used for inter-island journeys of both raiding and trading. However, only the Western Solomons has experienced an enduring, even accelerating, agenda of revitalized war-canoe building (Hviding 2014; for an example from Gela, see Pule 1983). To New Georgians of today, the war canoe is seen as an essential emblem of their past, and the transmission of the skills of war-canoe building has become a powerful symbol of cultural revival and continuity. The distinctive Western Solomons *tomoko*-style canoe indeed expanded its presence on many scenes in the post-independence nation. For example, its characteristic sweeping profile (with prow and stern posts considerably taller than in any other canoe design from elsewhere in the Solomons) figures prominently on the national coat-of-arms, and as such is seen by many islanders of the West as a statement of their influential presence in the Solomon Islands nation-state.

Meanwhile, the characteristic *nguzunguzu* prow ornament of the war canoes, a small human-like image carved from wood and inlaid with pearl-shell, has become a representative object of the Solomon Islands as a whole in the eyes of the many tourists and other visitors who obtain one from handicraft shops or from the woodcarvers themselves. Holding a bird or a human head in its hands, a *nguzunguzu* was lashed just above the waterline to the bow of every departing New Georgian war canoe to ensure safe navigation and success in warfare. Originally carved from light wood and stained black, *nguzunguzu* are now produced in large numbers and many varieties for the tourist market, by village carvers who work in ebony and other exclusive woods and provide dazzling patterns of nautilus-shell inlay. A favourite souvenir, this former spiritual aid for Western Solomons warrior-navigators has become somewhat of a national symbol. *Nguzunguzu* are now encountered in all kinds of commercial and official logos and advertisements, and this small but significant part of the war canoe has emerged centre stage as akin to an international trademark of the Solomon Islands nation, its people and their history.

Canoes in action: development in a maritime state

Back, then, to the State of Western Solomons, which continues to exist on the national level as the Western Province, and remains in dialogue over state matters with adjacent Choiseul Province. Whereas the strong ambitions of statehood expressed on 7 July 2000 have hardly been fulfilled, successive elected provincial administrations have retained high financial ambitions, and a dedication to building up an economic system founded in solid subsistence resources, revenue from logging and industrial tuna fishing, and sea-based tourism in the form of diving, sports fishing, lagoon kayaking and lately even surfing. The maritime-dominated history of the Western Solomons thereby continues into the present, in that the sea is destined to be the main money earner when timber resources run out. There is a notable convergence between the maritime quality of 'the West' and the reef- and blue-water-related desires of the tourists who come there. In a notable sense, as its lands have, in the eyes of tourists, become defaced by logging, the Western Solomons relies more than ever on the sea for its participation in the global economy now that the logging industry by necessity declines.

So, in yet another historical era, the sea and its offerings make the Western Solomons distinct. To these encounters and convergences of globalization is added the ubiquitous war canoe (and certainly its stand-in, the *nguzunguzu*) with its associations with warfare and headhunting, the essential pre-Christian practices extinguished by the advance of colonialism and Christianity. In March 2005, then Prime Minister Sir Allan Kemakeza visited a number of tourist resorts in the Western Solomons and concluded that 'the province should be a role model for other provinces in the push for tourism development'. Kemakeza noted that with 'the attractions such as the reefs and blue sea for divers, beaches and landscape, flora and fauna and people's smile', the tourism industry should be able to 'earn billions of dollars for the country' (Wate 2005).

Meanwhile, the unrecognized State of Western Solomons has not been as financially successful as expected. But 'the West' has seen an interesting and entirely local social movement take centre stage, particularly by supplying rural areas with services that neither national nor Western Solomons governments were able to finance during the years of crisis. This is the Christian Fellowship Church (or CFC), founded in the 1950s by the charismatic layman Silas Eto (1905–83) as a breakaway movement from what was then the Methodist Mission. In an atmosphere of intense religious revival involving spiritual visions, revelations and trance, Eto soon became known as the Holy Mama, *mama* being a vernacular term of affectionate address for father (Harwood 1971; Hviding 2011; Tuza 1977). The Holy Mama built the CFC into a major force in the Western Solomons, bringing thousands of followers into what he defined as the 'new life': an existence based on the desired condition of 'fellowship', which is a respectful, mutually helpful and happy state of relationship among living persons within and outside of the church, founded in the Holy Mama's conceptual trinity of 'peace, love, unity' (in the doctrinal Roviana language, *binule, tinataru, kineke*). Building on the Holy Mama's original conception of a 'first creation' which opened the 'time of church and worship' (*totoso lotu* [Rov.]) / (*kolokolo lotu* [Hoa./Mar.])[5] and saw the church through its first three decades, a remaking of the CFC has taken place since the 1990s under the leadership of the Holy Mama's son and successor, the Reverend Ikan Rove. Having attained the mantle of the 'Spiritual Authority' of the CFC, Rove and his associates refer to the remaking as a 'second creation' that signals the advent of *totoso/kolokolo divelopmen* ('the time of development'). In this time, the organized accumulation of revenue from large-scale logging on the CFC's customary lands by Asian transnational companies, as well as the CFC's massively efficient system of communal labour, support large-scale tree plantation development throughout large parts of northern and western New Georgia (with an emphasis on teak), as well as the building of a financially autonomous system of business enterprise, infrastructure and social services.

The mantra of new life, as well as the arrival in 1902 of the Methodists and the Revd J.F. Goldie, came up for celebration in July 2004 (a year after the arrival of RAMSI), when the entire membership of the CFC, leaders of other churches and government dignitaries, including the governor-general and the prime minister, gathered at the large CFC village of Madou in the Vonavona Lagoon. The CFC leaders were the first to admit that this was exactly two years after the true centennial, which was duly observed by the (Methodist) United Church in 2002 – a far more low-key celebration in the midst of economic depression and government failure. As it turned out, what lavish consumption was present at the centennial celebration of the United Church in 2002 had actually been funded by the CFC as an expression of compassion and assistance to relatives in need from those more fortunate. We do not have to be reminded here about certain aspects of the gift (Mauss 1954), namely the potential position of power attained by the donor of a lavish gift that is happily accepted by the recipient.

It had been evident already in 2002 that the CFC wanted to mark its own strong relationship to the Revd Goldie, but that the leaders of the rapidly rising movement wished to do it separately from the church they had once separated from, and in their own distinct way, likely to emphasize local cultural heritage (or, New Georgian *kastom*). And so in 2004, as the CFC's week-long celebrations opened and a large framed photograph of Goldie was carried around at ecstatic church services by the Spiritual Authority's own children, no less than fifteen full-size war canoes, complete with traditionally dressed and ornamented crews, were presented and organized into several days of racing competitions on the lagoon (see Aswani and Haas 2005). The Spiritual Authority – who was to receive a knighthood in London in 2005 for 'services to religion and community' – had commissioned one complete war canoe from every CFC village around New Georgia with a labour capacity to make one. When I visited CFC villages in northern New Georgia in early June, work was fully concentrated on the making of large canoes (sometimes with the aid of electric tools) and the specialized large-scale production of masses of canoe decorations and ornaments for the entire fleet (each participating village would make large numbers of one particular ornament for ultimate distribution to all).

The modest activity of war-canoe replica building that had been going on for several decades throughout New Georgia and in some other parts of the Solomons, such as in the Nggela group (Pule 1983), had come full circle. Many early efforts had been influenced by outside initiatives to support the documentation and possible revival of cultural heritage, at least in terms of financial assistance from national or provincial government or from donors such as the Australian High Commission's Cultural Fund, and all were limited to the building of one canoe only by a single community. The entirely indigenous project of the CFC, however, had no outside sponsors and aimed to focus not so much on cultural documentation as on reviving aspects of the visual and political power of the war canoe through spectacular display of a great number, similar to the large raiding parties reported from late pre-colonial times. The well organized construction of the fifteen canoes was the means, but the mustering of a full fleet of fifteen from as many villages was the end, in the sense of being a demonstration of the sheer power of the CFC and its Spiritual Authority. That the aim was to enable spectacular visual display and seaworthiness for competitive high-speed paddling, and not to promote the revival of minute details of canoe construction, was seen in the fact that none of the fifteen canoes were of entirely traditional construction. There were a number of shortcuts that did not, however, lessen the stability of the canoes or the visual impact of the fleet when it came together for the first time. While the war canoe of olden times was considered to have a potential for 'dazzling' spectators through the contrast between blackened hull and dense patterns of shiny pear shell inlay, the canoes of the new CFC fleet were built in a simpler way, but with the aim to dazzle through their sheer number.[6]

Creative shortcuts aside, the CFC war-canoe fleet can be seen a major cultural-heritage project that has emerged from within the rural, not encouraged by any external agents (which is not to say that there are no connections between the CFC and government; this is discussed shortly). The scale of this independent effort was evident at the 2004 Goldie Centennial at Madou, and further elaboration was seen after the Spiritual Authority visited the British Museum canoe storerooms in 2005 en route to his knighthood investiture. The CFC canoe fleet is the Spiritual Authority's own demonstration of power and the manifestation of his own somewhat humorous self-definition as simply a variation on the great regionally powerful chiefs of the past. Today, still, the war canoe expresses political, economic and spiritual power, irrespective of headhunting.

The CFC's fifteen war canoes have remained prominent on the Western Solomons scene since they first appeared. On several occasions the canoes have welcomed national and international dignitaries arriving in Gizo, and they have provided the visible foundations of several provincial Festivals of the Sea. They followed into harbour yachts arriving from the Brisbane-Gizo race in 2006, and in 2007 they were filmed by a BBC crew for the opening scenes of the high-profile documentary series *South Pacific*. There has also been a spill-over beyond the Western Solomons: White (this volume) describes the manner in which Isabel islanders responded to the escalation of war-canoe building in 'the West' by organizing their own 'parade of canoes' at a provincial 'Cultural Festival' just one year after the Madou celebrations, in July 2005.

Although the fleet is far from a provincial government project, the CFC has been a partner with that government in several of the Festivals of the Sea. The CFC is a rural social movement that provides for many state-like functions in contexts where the state machinery of provincial and national government has little presence. Yet the movement's leaders have on occasion expressed public praise of the national government, and one of the CFC associate leaders, the Hon. Job D. Tausinga (a brother of the Spiritual Authority) served in the national parliament for the North New Georgia constituency continuously from 1984 to 2014 and has been a frequent cabinet minister. Several provincial premiers and provincial secretaries have been from the CFC, and in 2010 CFC's involvement in parliament reached a new stage when Silas K.V. Tausinga, a son of J.D. Tausinga, was elected for the first time, thereby providing the CFC with two seats in Parliament. The CFC thus stands for a solid, long-term connection between the lands, seas and peoples of New Georgia and the national government, in ways unlike any other church denomination in the Western Solomons.[7] It was in line with this strong capacity for both replacing and supporting the state that the war-canoe fleet was displayed in full racing magnificence for the first time at Madou, with the governor-general and the prime minister present.

In a spectacularly successful way, the *tomoko, magoru, niabara,* or in whichever of the languages of the New Georgia group it can be named, is a major bearer of the distinct cultural heritage of the Western Solomons. As we see from the example of the Christian Fellowship Church, the war canoe has also emerged as an icon of intense political-economic ambition, standing for the elevation of the CFC in the twenty-first century into a social movement with powerful influence throughout New Georgia, and beyond. The Western Solomons war canoe means different things, then, to different people and in different contexts. To some, perhaps mostly tourists, the canoe stands folkloristically for a chilling history of headhunting and other exotic practices. For practical money-oriented tourist operators, the war canoe is a magnet that draws in more tourist dollars. For the majority of the 70,000 or so people of today's Western Solomons, the war canoe stands for their maritime history of overseas travel, inter-island connections and multi-local sociality. But for the Christian Fellowship Church followers, the war canoe, in the form of a fleet always prepared for display, stands for the power of the Spiritual Authority and of the CFC as a spectacularly successful rural social movement. This particular invocation of war canoes embodies a uniquely dense relationship between cultural heritage and political innovation, in which the central cultural heritage of the Western Solomons' maritime history represents the highest level of political innovation in these islands (the CFC's 'time of development').

At the Festival of the Sea held in May 2006 at Gizo with the CFC fleet of war canoes on display and engaged in a series of races, Deputy Premier Holoti Panapio in his opening speech described the event as 'extra special to Western Province'. He highlighted it as 'relevant in contemporary Solomon Islands' in terms of it being 'a golden opportunity for the young generations as it is one of the channels in which they can learn about their cultural heritage'. The war canoe stands for this entire cultural complex of maritime history and inter-island relations, rather than just conveying the folklore of headhunting. The canoe more generally invokes the validity of relationships founded in generations of overseas raiding, abduction and headhunting, which are complemented today by the recognized existence of land owned by New Georgians in Choiseul and in the Kia and Bughotu districts of Isabel, from genealogical connections to the captives once taken.

The model of Oceanic sociality exemplified by the western Solomons would seem to be partly predicated on the notable prevalence in the New Georgia group of bilateral kinship, whereby everyone has more than one home locality and possesses by birth land and sea rights in more than one kin group (Hviding 2003b). The colonial administration was not sympathetic to this fluid foundation to sociality in the western Solomons, in which everyone has several home localities on different seashores, and introduced restrictions to curb what was regarded as a much too strong propensity by the islanders to leave their 'home village' for shorter or longer periods of time. The resident powers of British colonialism were far from prepared to appreciate a social world in which everyone could exist in a number of separate locations. But colonialism has had its day, and inter-island sociality grounded in the pre-colonial again flourishes in the post-colonial.

As noted initially in this chapter, the ethnography of contemporary Melanesia poses some particular challenges, but also gives specific potentials, for a close study of various types of actors in multiple systems of state and government. Indeed, the culturally diverse Melanesian countries are characterized also by diversity in governance, and in this region are found the most creative and complex interfaces between cultural heritage and political innovation in the entire Pacific – interfaces which remain largely unrecognized in governmental discourses about state-building because of the dismal views of Melanesian politics that are imposed from outside, with little understanding of the details of indigenous leadership or 'statecraft'. I have demonstrated in this chapter how such 'statecraft' may have its foundations not in imported models of 'governance', but instead in locally grounded models of sociality itself. The example of the politically volatile western Solomons as a 'sea' of rather large and resource-rich islands mostly in close proximity to one another, with an inter-island sociality generated and mediated by maritime travel, may be seen as indicative of aspects of a much wider model of Oceanic sociality. In this model, no one and nothing will be from one place only. All or most persons, ideas and objects are more or less derived from overseas, and there is a distinctiveness of overseas connections and inter-island relations in cultural and social history. As this social and political connectivity also informs the approaches taken to governance and identity formation on the levels of province and self-declared state, it seems that the Western Solomons, in the middle of Island Melanesia, is destined to become a sea-based state: perhaps the most Oceanic of all Pacific alternatives.

Notes

This chapter is based on long-term fieldwork since 1986 in Marovo, elsewhere in the Western Solomons, and in the urban power centres of Gizo and Honiara. During more than three years in the Solomons I have had the privilege of engaging with all levels of practice and power in this nation of people whose welcome to outsiders remains so generous. I am grateful for this generosity as well as for many special conversations over the years with Marovo-speaking rural and urban operators of cultural, political and/or economic power, in particular His Grace the Reverend Ikan Rove KBE, Spiritual Authority of the CFC (who passed away in 2014); Honourable MP Job Duddley Tausinga; Sam Patavaqara, Narcilly Pule and Wilson Liligeto (all sometime Provincial Secretaries of Western Province); educationalists Aseri Yalangono and Brian Bird; and many influential chiefs and rural leaders such as Vincent Vaguni, Erik Andersen, Allan Pulepae, and Kata R. Ragoso.

1   In this chapter I use the capitalized form 'Western Solomons' specifically for the late-twentieth century political formation and culturally distinctive geographical entity referred to by its own residents (and many other Solomon Islanders) as such; particularly in the context of the unilateral state declaration of 2000. There is deliberate vagueness in the term, since Choiseul may or may not be drawn in under its coverage. Conversely, the non-capitalized form 'western Solomons' is a simpler geographical reference, similar to what in everyday discourse in Solomon Islands is 'the West'.

2   The Western Prime Ministers are (in chronological order): Sir Francis Billy Hilly (1993–4; from Ranongga), Manasseh Sogavare (2000–1, 2006–7, 2014–; from Choiseul), Snyder Rini (briefly in 2006; from Marovo), Danny Philip (2010–11; from Rendova), Gordon Darcy Lilo (2011–14 ; from Kolobangara). Examinations of cabinet records show that the Ministry of Finance was, except during very brief periods following the cabinet reshuffles, from 1989 to 2011 continuously in the hands of a total of seven parliamentarians from the West, with Snyder Rini and the late Christopher Columbus Abe, both in their time Members of Parliament for Marovo, holding the cabinet post for Finance for a total of six and eight years, respectively.

3   Margaret Jolly (2001:423), reflecting critically on Hau'ofa's concept, reports on experiences at a meeting in Suva of representatives of Pacific museums and cultural centres. She notes how 'several of the representatives from Papua New Guinea, the Solomons, and Vanuatu opposed what they saw as an undue emphasis on the ocean and navigation on the part of the Polynesian and Micronesian delegates. The representative from Papua New Guinea pointed out that many Highlanders from the interior of his country had no sense of ancestral connections to the ocean, no knowledge of how to make canoes, and indeed had never seen the sea. There is a big difference between living in the interior of a large mountainous island and living in archipelagos of smaller islands or on coral atolls.' Another point has been made by Kuehling (2007:286) who argues that any sea-focused approach to Pacific life worlds 'reflects on the male bias in the West rather than on a Pacific reality, in which the sea is mostly observed while squatting on somebody's land'. In the light of these critical comments, I argue that it is all the more significant that a version of Hau'ofa's 'Sea of Islands' should be located right in the middle of

Melanesia, involving large, mountainous islands of considerable size where kinship and marriage are fundamentally of inter-island scope and scale.

4   Vernacular prototypical terms corresponding to 'path' or 'road' have been documented as central concepts of social organization throughout Oceania (see Parmentier 1987 for Palau; Bateson 1958:237 for the Sepik; Campbell 1983 for the Massim; Bonnemaison 1994 for Vanuatu; Roalkvam 2003 for Kiribati; Siikala 1996 for the Cook Islands; and Fox and Sather 1996 for Austronesia-wide examples). The point raised here is the more specific role of 'path' in the New Georgia islands as a pervasive organizational concept that implies regular maritime travel through which an inter-island, extra-local scope is generated for any local sociality.

5   Most vernacular terms in this chapter are in the Marovo language, one of the two major Austronesian languages of New Georgia (the other one being Roviana). For the CFC, which uses Roviana as the main doctrinal language but which has its cultural and linguistic roots in Hoava, a minor Austronesian language spoken in the northern Marovo district of Kalikolo, a few clarifications are made in the text by referring to terms in the three languages as Hoa./Mar./Rov., respectively.

6   Unlike previous village-level war-canoe projects around New Georgia, none of the new CFC canoes were made in the traditional planked style, as that was deemed too time consuming. As the aim was to build a fleet for display and inter-village competition, the chosen approach was that of taking a very large dugout hull and adding high prow and stern posts and one or two strakes, the latter fastened to the hull by means of traditional lashings through holes drilled along the edges. Decorations were painted on the black hulls rather than being made of pearl-shell inlay. The Spiritual Authority visited the British Museum in October 2005. At the museum's storerooms he and his entourage examined several largely intact Western Solomons canoes from the late-nineteenth and early-twentieth century, with particular attention given to the largest water craft in the museum's collection, an elaborately decorated 33-foot war canoe from the island of Vella Lavella, dating from c.1908 (BM Registration No. Oc1927, 1022.1). Although not from the areas in New Georgia where the CFC influence is the highest, the Vella Lavella canoe was considered to provide many lessons as to the historically correct patterns of decoration. A further linkage between this specific canoe and local interest in Solomon Islands was created in 2008–10 as the University of Bergen's Pacific Alternatives project collaborated with the British Museum, University College London and the Solomon Islands National Museum on a pioneering effort of three-dimensional scanning and modelling of the canoe for purposes of digital repatriation (Hess et. al. 2010).

7   The Spiritual Authority of the CFC died in June 2014 after a long illness, during which conflict over theology, wealth management and succession (which in June 2015 is still not clear) had led to the virtual banishment of Tausinga and his family

from the CFC. Outcomes of the conflict remain uncertain, but the rural power of
the CFC remains much the same.

References

Amherst of Hackney, Lord and B. Thomson 1901. *Discovery of the Solomon Islands by
   Alvaro de Mendaña in 1568* (2 Vols). London: Bedford Press by permission
   of the Hakluyt Society.

Aswani, S. and J. Haas 2005. *The Christian Fellowship Church One Hundredth Year
   Commemorative Celebration of the Arrival of Methodism to the Western
   Solomon Islands, June 2004*. DVD, Roviana, not subtitled. Santa Barbara,
   CA: University of California at Santa Barbara and Ethnovideo Productions.

Barth, F. 1969. Introduction. In *Ethnic Groups and Boundaries: The Social
   Organization of Culture Difference*, 9–38. Oslo: Universitetsforlaget.

Bateson, G. 1958. *Naven: A Survey of the Problems suggested by a Composite Picture
   of the Culture of a New Guinea Tribe drawn from Three Points of View*.
   Stanford: Stanford University Press.

Bonnemaison, J. 1994. *The Tree and the Canoe: History and Ethnogeography of Tanna*.
   Honolulu: University of Hawai'i Press.

Campbell, S. 1983. Kula in Vakuta: the mechanics of keda. In *The Kula: New
   Perspectives on Massim Exchange*, J.W Leach and E.R. Leach (eds), 201–28.
   Cambridge: Cambridge University Press.

D'Arcy, P. 2006. *The People of the Sea: Environment, Identity, and History in Oceania*.
   Honolulu: University of Hawai'i Press.

Dureau, C. 1998. Decreed affinities: nationhood and the Western Solomon Islands.
   Journal of Pacific History 33(2):197–220.

Felgate, M. 2007. Leap-frogging or limping? Recent Evidence from the Lapita littoral
   fringe, New Georgia, Solomon Islands. In *Oceanic Explorations: Lapita
   and Western Pacific Settlement*, S. Bedford, C. Sand, and S.P. Connaughton
   (eds), 123–40. Canberra: ANU E Press.

Fox, J.J. and C. Sather (eds) 1996. *Origins, Ancestry and Alliance: Explorations in
   Austronesian Ethnography*. Canberra: Research School of Pacific Studies,
   The Australian National University.

Fraenkel, J. 2004. *The Manipulation of Custom: From Uprising to Intervention in the
   Solomon Islands*. Canberra: Pandanus Books.

Fraenkel, J., J. Madraiwiwi and H. Okole 2014. The RAMSI Decade: A Review of the
   Regional Assistance Mission to Solomon Islands, 2003–2013. Submitted to
   the Prime Minister's Office, Solomon Islands Government.

Harwood, F.H. 1971. The Christian Fellowship Church: A Revitalization Movement in
   Melanesia. PhD thesis, Department of Anthropology, University of Chicago.

Hau'ofa, E. 1993. Our Sea of Islands. In *A New Oceania: Rediscovering Our Sea of Islands*, E. Waddell, V. Naidu and E. Hau'ofa (eds), 2–16. Suva: University of the South Pacific. [Reprinted 1994, *The Contemporary Pacific* 6:148–61.]

—— 2008. *We are the Ocean: Selected Works.* Honolulu: University of Hawai'i Press.

Hess, M., S. Robson, F. Millar, G. Were, E. Hviding and C. Berg 2009. *Niabara* – the Western Solomon Islands war canoe at the British Museum. In *Proceedings of the 2009 15th International Conference on Virtual Systems and Multimedia*, Vienna, 41–6. Los Alamitos, CA.: IEEE Computer Society.

Hviding, E. 1996. *Guardians of Marovo Lagoon: Practice, Place, and Politics in Maritime Melanesia* (Pacific Islands Monograph Series 14). Honolulu: University of Hawai'i Press.

—— 2003a. Disentangling the *butubutu* of New Georgia: cognatic kinship in thought and action. In *Oceanic Socialities and Cultural Forms: Ethnographies of Experience*, I. Hoëm and S. Roalkvam (eds), 71–113. Oxford: Berghahn Books.

—— 2003b. Both sides of the beach: knowledges of nature in Oceania. In *Nature Across Cultures: Non-Western Views of the Environment and Nature* (Science Across Cultures: The History of Non-Western Sciences 4), H. Selin (ed.), 243–75.. Dordrecht: Kluwer Academic Publishers.

—— 2003c. Between knowledges: Pacific Studies and academic disciplines. *The Contemporary Pacific* 15:43–73.

—— 2011. Re-placing the state in the Western Solomon Islands: the political rise of the Christian Fellowship Church. In *Made in Oceania: Social Movements, Cultural Heritage and the State in the Pacific*, E. Hviding and K.M. Rio (eds), 51–89. Wantage: Sean Kingston Publishing.

—— 2014. War canoes of the Western Solomons. In *The Things We Value: Culture and History in Solomon Islands*, B.Burt and L. Bolton (eds), 103–15. Canon Pyon: Sean Kingston Publishing.

Jolly, M. 2001. On the edge? Deserts, oceans, islands. *The Contemporary Pacific* 13:417–66.

Kabutaulaka, T.T. 2006. Parties, constitutional engineering and governance in Solomon Islands. In *Political Parties in the Pacific Islands*, R. Rich (ed.), 103–16. Canberra: Pandanus Books, Australian National University.

Kirch, P.V. 1997. *The Lapita Peoples: Ancestors of the Oceanic World.* Oxford: Blackwell.

Kuehling, S. 2007. Book review of *People of the Sea: Environment, Identity and History in Oceania*, by P. D'Arcy. *Anthropological Quarterly* 80(1):283–7.

Laycock, D.C. 1969. Multilingualism: linguistic boundaries and unsolved problems. In *New Guinea and Neighbouring Areas: A Sociolinguistic Laboratory*, S.A. Wurm (ed.), 81–99. The Hague: Mouton.

—— 1982. Melanesian linguistic diversity: a Melanesian choice? In *Melanesia: Beyond Diversity*, R.J. May and H. Nelson (eds), 33–8. Canberra: Research School of Pacific Studies, Australian National University.

Leach, J.W. and E.R. Leach (eds) 1983. *The Kula: New Perspectives on Massim Exchange*. Cambridge: Cambridge University Press.

Lewis, D. 1972. *We, the Navigators: The Ancient Art of Landfinding in the Pacific*. Canberra: Australian National University Press.

Malinowski, B. 1922. *Argonauts of the Western Pacific: An Account of Native Enterprise and Adventure in the Archipelagoes of Melanesian New Guinea*. London: Routledge and Kegan Paul.

Mauss, M. 1954 [1923–4] *The Gift: Forms and Functions of Exchange in Archaic Societies* (trans. I. Cunnison). London: Cohen & West.

Moore, C. 2004. *Happy Isles in Crisis: The Historical Causes for a Failing State in the Solomon Islands, 1998–2004*. Canberra, Australia: Asia Pacific Press.

—— 2005. The RAMSI intervention in the Solomon Islands crisis. *Journal of Pacific Studies* 28(1):56–77.

Naitoro, J.H. 2000. Solomon Islands conflict: demands for historical rectification and restorative justice. Asia Pacific School of Economics and Management, Update paper. Canberra: Australian National University.

Parmentier, R. 1987. *The Sacred Remains: Myth, History and Polity in Belau*. Chicago: University of Chicago Press.

Premdas, R., J. Steeves and P. Larmour 1983. The Western breakaway movement. In *Solomon Islands Politics*, P. Larmour with S. Tarua (eds), 164–95. Suva: Institute of Pacific Studies, University of the South Pacific.

Pule, R.T. 1983. *Binabina: The Making of a Gela War Canoe*. Suva: Institute of Pacific Studies, University of the South Pacific.

Roalkvam, S. 2003. Pathway and side: an essay on Onotoan notions of relatedness. In *Oceanic Socialities and Cultural Forms: Ethnographies of Experience*, I. Hoëm and S. Roalkvam (eds), 115–36. Oxford: Berghahn Books.

Scales, I. 2007. The coup nobody noticed: the Solomon Islands Western State movement in 2000. *Journal of Pacific History* 42(2):187–209.

Schwartz, T. 1963. Systems of areal integration: Some considerations based on the Admiralty Islands of Northern Melanesia. *Anthropological Forum* 1(1):56–97.

Siikala, J. 1996. The elder and the younger – foreign and autochthonous origin and hierarchy in the Cook Islands. In *Origins, Ancestry and Alliance: Explorations in Austronesian Ethnography*, J.J. Fox and C. Sather (eds), 41–54. Canberra: Research School of Pacific Studies, The Australian National University.

Thomas, N. 1991. *Entangled Objects: Exchange, Material Culture, and Colonialism in the Pacific*. Cambridge, Mass.: Harvard University Press.

——— 2010. *Islanders: The Pacific in the Age of Empire*. New Haven: Yale University Press.

Tuza, E. 1977. Silas Eto of New Georgia. In *Prophets of Melanesia*, G.W. Trompf (ed.), 108–45. Port Moresby: Institute of Papua New Guinea Studies.

Waddell, E., V. Naidu and E. Hau'ofa (eds) 1993. *A New Oceania: Rediscovering Our Sea of Islands*. Suva: School of Social and Economic Development, University of the South Pacific.

Wate, A. 2005. 'Western takes lead in tourism industry says PM.' *Solomon Star*, 2 March.

White, G.M. 1991. *Identity Through History: Living Stories in a Solomon Islands Society*. Cambridge: Cambridge University Press.

Edvard Hviding is Professor of Social Anthropology at the University of Bergen.

CHAPTER 6

Women and customary land tenure in Vanuatu

Changing understandings

✳

LISSANT BOLTON

In October 2008 the Vanuatu Cultural Centre held a workshop at which ni-Vanuatu women discussed customary relationships between women and land in ni-Vanuatu societies.[1] The Cultural Centre (known more usually as the Kaljoral Senta or VKS) is both a museum and a centre for cultural research and activism. It addresses the rich diversity of knowledge and practice across the archipelago's more than eighty islands and 110 language groups through a group of extension workers, known as fieldworkers. The fieldworkers are volunteers recruited to document and revive local forms of knowledge, and practice in their own islands and districts. The 2008 workshop was for thirty-eight women fieldworkers, and at it they considered aspects of women's relationship to land tenure, which they had researched in their own places through the previous twelve months. It was held because of pressures from both the Vanuatu government and from external bodies such as the Australian government to reform the nation's land-tenure legislation, and because of the recognized need to document the diversity of land-tenure systems in the archipelago.

At this meeting Rachel Iaken, a fieldworker from a traditionalist enclave in the middle-bush area of the island of Tanna, reported on her research into this issue in her district. She made the comment that if a woman marries into her mother's natal kin group, as an exchange for her mother, then she will be able to make a garden on her mother's land.[2] As in the past, so sometimes still today, marriages in Vanuatu are arranged and, arranged or not, they are usually virilocal. On Tanna arrangements follow the principle of sister exchange: such exchanges can occur within one generation, or, as in Iaken's example, can be made between one generation and the next. As the very term sister exchange suggests, such marriages are often described from the male point of view, as bringing women to join a descent group. Iaken's comment presents another perspective: a woman may marry to, and invest in, land with which she already has kinship connections. Specifically, such a marriage would enable her to invest in land with which her mother and her maternal grandparents have had strong connection.

The women fieldworker's workshop took place at the interface, so to speak, of different systems of thought in contemporary Vanuatu. There is increasing pressure on land in the archipelago: from expatriates wanting to buy land, and from government and businesses to 'develop' land. In both cases, a specific set of ideas about how land can be owned and transferred between people is taken for granted. As is true elsewhere in the Pacific, global economic and development thinking about land and land tenure, with its focus on individual ownership and on the legally binding documentation of ownership, is quite different from land-tenure arrangements in indigenous Vanuatu. Investment – the key concept in Iaken's example – is a foundational aspect of land-tenure practice in Vanuatu. It is not a basis for land rights that translates easily into global land-ownership models. Many of the assumptions that global economic and development thinking makes about land tenure are being absorbed into contemporary ni-Vanuatu thinking and are overwhelming such ni-Vanuatu principles. In particular, they often marginalize the subtle, but crucial ways in which women hold rights of tenure to land in Vanuatu. This chapter addresses this process.

✳

The Vanuatu Constitution clearly states that 'all land in the Republic of Vanuatu belongs to the indigenous custom owners and their descendants' (chapter 12:73) and 'the rules of custom shall form the basis of ownership and use of land in the Republic of Vanuatu' (chapter 12:74). The Constitution could not, and does not, specify what those 'rules of custom' might comprise, but both the constitution and land-related legislation enacted in the early years of the Republic are characterized by the 'clear view that the "custom owners" of land in Vanuatu are groups not individuals' (Lunnay *et al.* 2007:10).

A significant body of international economic thinking argues that development cannot occur where customary land tenure exists (Fingleton 2005:1). The Vanuatu government is under pressure from external organizations, such as banks and governmental aid organizations, to reform its land policy. For example, a 2006 Australian government White Paper advocated a Pacific land mobilization programme 'to explore ways to overcome the major land tenure constraints to growth in the region' (cited Daley 2009:4). In response to these pressures, attempts are being made to address customary land-tenure practices with a view to bringing about land reform. The Kaljoral Senta women fieldworkers workshop at which Iaken spoke was convened partly to provide data which might be used to ensure women's customary relationships to land be recognized under any new legislation.

The Vanuatu Kaljoral Senta, founded in 1956, became at Independence in 1980 an institution committed as much to the revival of indigenous knowledge and practice as to its documentation. At this time the VKS developed a network of volunteer ni-Vanuatu extension workers, known as the fieldworkers. The fieldworkers meet annually at the Kaljoral Senta both for training and discussion, and to present research reports on a nominated topic. Each year they agree a topic for the following year's workshop and prepare a report on that subject for their region, which they present to each other. There are both men's and women's fieldworker workshops, the men's group having been founded in 1981, the women's in 1994 (see Bolton 1999; 2003; 2007). I have had the privilege of chairing the women fieldworker's workshops each year since 1994,[3] and chaired the women and land workshop. Although the discussion at the workshop was always tied to specific local practices, here I discuss the subject in general terms – summarizing and analysing generalities that arose from the specificities of the discussion.[4] I begin with some background on the current land debates and on land-tenure practices.

Legislation and political economy

Vanuatu has been argued to have one of the worst records for fraud, misrepresentation and misunderstandings in land-alienation transactions in the colonized Pacific ([South Pacific] Forum Secretariat 2001:18). Certainly, as Howard Van Trease has argued, competition between France and Britain as joint colonial powers in the archipelago (forming the Anglo-French Condominium government of the New Hebrides 1906–8) led to the alienation of very large tracts of land, even where that land was never occupied or developed by the alienators (1987:xi). When Vanuatu became independent in 1980, all land was declared by the constitution to belong to customary owners. This constitutional change was substantiated in advance by land-reform legislation passed by the pre-independence Representative Assembly, which came into force at independence, by which all existing registered titles became null and void, and which addressed the means by which former title holders could negotiate with custom owners (Van Trease 1987:243).

A number of laws which addressed the tension between customary land tenure and pressure for individual ownership were also passed at Independence, initially with special reference to urban land. At the time, these laws seemed to address the challenges facing the new nation adequately.

Howard Van Trease concludes his survey of land issues at this period with admiration for what the new government had achieved, observing that by 'the end of 1983 ... Vanuatu had in existence a legal framework to deal with land transactions as provided for under the Constitution' (1987:264). Since the early 1980s a number of further laws have been passed, several of which focus on urban land issues. Rural land tenure was addressed in the 2001 Customary Land Tribunal Act, which was passed to establish a system of land-dispute resolution in accordance with the custom of those involved in the dispute. In 1995 a Supreme Court decision allowed the granting of long-term leases of up to 75 years. Some argue that under the terms of this ruling, customary owners can only recover their land at the end of the lease if the lessees are compensated for any improvements, for example for buildings constructed on the land, thus opening the door again to permanent land alienation (Cox *et al.* 2007:11); however, this interpretation is disputed (Regenvanu, pers comm. March 2009).[5]

Through the first decade of the twenty-first century Vanuatu has faced a booming real-estate market, especially on the island of Efate, where Vanuatu's capital, Port Vila, is located. As one report put it, 'land alienations ... have emerged ... on a scale that threatens the livelihoods of ni-Vanuatu, the authority of the government, and the country's social and political stability' (Lunnay *et al.* 2007:3), and 'land dealings (negotiations, leases, registrations, sub-divisions etc.) have got out of control' (Lunnay *et al.* 2007: 5). A very significant proportion of the island Efate has been sold by customary owners in long-term leases of up to 75 years. Purchasers of this land are primarily expatriates, who have often subdivided the land and resold it as house lots – often for holiday homes for Australians and New Zealanders. Ninety percent of the coastal land in Efate is now reported to have been alienated (Cox *et al.* 2007:9). Ironically enough, therefore, the alienation of land is not assisting the development of the Vanuatu economy in any substantive sense, except for short-term construction work, and the provision of domestic servants. Holiday homes on Efate often stand empty for long periods.

Approximately 80 per cent of the population is primarily supported by the subsistence economy (Daley 2009), which in turn depends on the land. Although some people on Efate support themselves through employment, even many residents of the peri-urban villages around Port Vila, such as Mele and Pango, sustain their families in part or in whole through subsistence, and this is even more the case in rural Efate. The loss of land, and the loss of access to the sea, has already had a significant impact.

Alongside the land boom there has been increasing pressure on Vanuatu to reform land laws. This comes from some of the nation's major aid donors, such as the Asian Development Bank and the World Bank, and from within the Vanuatu government, and is being enacted through the national Comprehensive Reform Program, or CRP. Specifically, there is pressure to create registered titles to land for custom owners: the registration of land titles facilitates land transactions. Within the wider region the South Pacific Forum's Pacific Plan supports the facilitation of land sales. As a 2001 Forum briefing paper outlines:

> Communal ownership of property – which allows shared decisions
> regarding use and transfer – is widespread throughout the Pacific. However,
> it creates difficulties through providing a barrier to the transfer of land to
> users outside the ownership group, or apparently reducing the security of
> any such transfer of tenure, as well as making access to credit on the basis of
> land ownership difficult. The constraints on its transfer to outsiders are the
> root of these difficulties in fitting traditional land tenure patterns into the
> modern economy.
>
> ([South Pacific] Forum Secretariat 2001:31)

There are also some ni-Vanuatu, within and without government, who have an interest in the individualization of land tenure. However, there are also opponents to this development. As Member of the Vanuatu Parliament, Ralph Regenvanu, a trenchant critic, argued in 2008, 'Determining customary land ownership has become an obsession of (the Vanuatu) government, reflecting its own obsession with promoting capitalist development.' (2008:67).[6]

Retrospectively, it becomes clear that the legal system established at Independence depended on the assumption that ni-Vanuatu would not willingly give up their land to outsiders. At that time the First Minister for Lands, Sethy Regenvanu, made the oft-quoted statement that 'land to ni-Vanuatu is what a mother is to a baby', continuing: 'Ni-Vanuatu do allow others the use of their land, but they always retain the right of ownership.' (cited Van Trease 1987:xi). The land alienation occurring now on Efate results partly from people valuing the cash they can obtain for their land more highly than the land itself, a concept inconceivable at independence.

In September 2006, the Ministry of Lands and the Vanuatu Kaljoral Senta organized a National Land Summit, with the goal of agreeing on resolutions that would form the basis of a new land policy for the next five to ten years. The first recommendation of the National Land Summit was: 'The Government to make laws that provide that all land in Vanuatu is owned by groups (tribes, clans, or families);' that 'not one person (individual) is an owner of any traditionally owned (kastom) land;' and that 'members of the (kastom) traditional owning group (male and female) must be involved in the decision-making about their land.' The distinction between individual ownership and corporate land tenure is critical to much of the contemporary debate about land.

The Australian government aid arm, AusAID, supported the Vanuatu government with research into land issues following recommendations from the National Land Summit: Anna Naupa was a key figure in supporting this research. The Kaljoral Senta has also undertaken land-tenure research. Joel Simo undertook the National Review of the Customary Land Tribunal Program in Vanuatu (2005), and also produced several lucid summaries of land issues for a ni-Vanuatu audience (2005, 2008).[7] Simo and Naupa co-authored a valuable study of matrilineal land tenure in Vanuatu (2008). The problem such initiatives face is negotiating the terms of the debate set by the reform agenda, that is, the intention or expectation that customary systems must conform to, or at least be comprehensible to, Western models of land ownership. Documentation becomes a process of making customary systems conform to Western thinking by analysing them in terms of key Western concepts such as ownership, rights and decision-making.[8] Key to this is the idea of individual land ownership. Leasing or sale of land is dependent on the identification of a landowner: an individual, or a small group, that 'owns' the land and has the 'right' to alienate it. As Simo remarks, the very use of the word 'landowner', as opposed to 'landholder', in Vanuatu's land laws has caused many land-dispute problems (Simo 2005:7n.4).

In 2007, Naupa and Simo requested that the Vanuatu Kaljoral Senta's women fieldworkers group focus their 2008 research programme on women and land. At that time there were about 38 women attached to the fieldworker programme.[9] One of the commonest assumptions in discussions about land in Vanuatu today is that women do not have rights in land, or rights to talk about land publicly. The subtext of the request that the fieldworkers discuss women and land was to discover what 'rights', if any, women might have in relation to land. Although generally aware of the ferment of discussion about land in Vanuatu at present, the fieldworkers' discussion was focused not on national-level issues, but on the specifics of their own district, and the issues there.

Attitudes to women

In Vanuatu, as in other parts of Melanesia, one of the most significant impacts of expatriate thinking relates to ideas about women: as I have argued elsewhere, introduced perceptions of the indigenous role and status of women are eroding customary practice in Vanuatu (Bolton 2003, 2007). From Captain Cook onwards, expatriate visitors have perceived women as disadvantaged in ni-Vanuatu societies. This perception partly arose because, in contradiction to then prevailing European ideals, many ni-Vanuatu women did significant amounts of labouring work. The colonial government enhanced existing gender divisions by excluding women from roles in the new contexts of church and government. Only men were given opportunities to take positions, and especially to take leadership, in these contexts. After independence women continued to be largely excluded from government and from other contexts of decision-making.[10] The exclusion of women from decision-making at a national level is nowadays assumed by both expatriates and ni-Vanuatu to reflect the exclusion of women from decision-making at a local level. But this classification of all women into a single, disadvantaged group is a misinterpretation of indigenous systems, in which a person's role and actions were determined by their kinship location and rank or status.

As Anna Naupa argues, the kinds of relationships women have with land have been blurred during the colonial era, 'leading to a common perception that women's land rights are secondary to men's and therefore lesser and/or negligible' (Naupa n.d.:1). My argument is that the very terms in which the issue is discussed are half the problem. Thinking about women as a single undifferentiated group, along with thinking about land in terms of rights and ownership, acts to separate women from their customary roles and responsibilities.

Attitudes to land

As elsewhere in Melanesia, in rural Vanuatu land is fundamental to life and to society: people were and are deeply tied to the land which supports them with all the resources needed. This is implicit in Sethy Regenvanu's formulation: the land is as a mother to her baby because it is the source of all nurture, the foundation of all life. People live, and garden and fish, in places where they hold agreed privileges of access, and only go beyond when invited. In contemporary Vanuatu, with the development of towns, roads, schools, hospitals and churches, the number of places where one can go beyond one's own land has greatly increased. In the pre-colonial past, such options were limited. Any land-holding group is likely to hold various plots of land that are not contiguous: in the past, and still today, people do not move freely across land to which they have no direct affiliation, but only along paths that are described in Bislama as *ol pablik rod*, i.e. as public roads. In the past, visitors coming from elsewhere would be greeted at 'the eye of the road', the point or gate where the road entered into a settlement (e.g. Deacon 1934:25). Unless invited, ni-Vanuatu did not, and still do not, freely visit other settlements where they have no close kin or trade connections, nor other gardens, nor possibly even forest areas to which they have no privileges. In the past the freest form of movement was over water.

The degree to which land is the foundation of everything in ni-Vanuatu conceptions is made clear in the importance of the relationship between a descent group and their land. In many parts of Vanuatu one could actually join a kin group by eating the food of their land. As Lane observes for the island of Pentecost, 'people are products of the land, through the substance transferred to them in food from the land' (1971:250). At the same time people had, and have, a strong sense of obligation to the land, to care for it. One's land is also the place of one's ancestors. Those ancestors, still visible in the landscape through their grave sites, are part of an invisible population co-resident in the land. John Taylor describes this concept for north Pentecost, where it is called *abanoi*. He says '*abanoi* is not a separate place but is present in the same space that people inhabit, and thus exists like an invisible mirror-world layered across or threaded through the lived world of human experience' (2008:86). Throughout Vanuatu each descent group is linked to the land by their familiarity with the lineaments of this invisible parallel dimension. Joan Larcom, describing the Mewun of south Malakula, talks about the importance of 'the focal idea of living together in the special sacred place of one's group' (1983:187). The descent group knows the key sites on their land for their group history, they know the specific environmental features, the sacred places and the non-human populations.[11] Part of the reluctance to venture into another group's land derives from a sense of being out of one's depth – of not knowing the dimensions of the parallel realm there, and thus of walking into unknown dangers. A distrust of other places lingers on today, often expressed in terms of anxiety about sorcery in other places.

Historically, affiliation to land was at the mercy of the constant adjustments caused by wars and raids. As Margaret Rodman details for east Ambae, men became leaders partly through 'the reputation they gained for committing ruthless acts of violence. Powerful warriors often seized land to which other, less influential Longanans had stronger rights.' (1984:65). The colonial era also impacted on land ownership, not only as the missions, the colonial government and the development of plantations enforced the relocation of populations away from their ancestral lands, often into settlements at the coast; but also as by the late 1930s Vanuatu's indigenous population dipped to only about 47,000 people (Douglas 1990:46).

The affiliation of a descent group to their land is of little importance if there is no next generation to take the connection forward. The provision of people for the land was the ongoing theme of the women's reports at the 2008 workshop. It was and is held to be of great importance that the affiliation between a particular descent group and their land should be sustained into succeeding generations.

Linking people to the land

In practice, women's customary access to land is not substantively different to men's. Although there are different specific formulas through which this principle operates, across the archipelago land is generally held by a descent group and allocated to group members by a senior male member of that group. Men, and sometimes women, access land by making presentations or offering other forms of respect to the man allocating the land.

In contemporary contexts, the responsibility to allocate land is sometimes conflated with ownership, so that senior males are described as landowners. Their responsibility to allocate land becomes ownership of land, and because men generally allocate land, women are said not to have rights to land. But the responsibility to allocate land did not, originally, equate with ownership in the sense of exclusive tenure and control. Joel Simo points out that in the languages of Vanuatu people speak of land using the first person plural, 'our land' not 'my land', drawing an example from his own island Anietyum: 'if someone wants you to accompany him to his land, he will say *apan akaja umaja*, which means "let's go to the place that looks after us (*umaja*)"' (Simo 2005:3). Contemporary characterization of senior males as landowners is a function of the impact of the lingua franca, Bislama. Bislama uses the English term *land ona* (landowner), and offers no alternative term which would provide a more accurate rendition of indigenous terminology. The use of '*land ona*' has affected people's understanding of their own local practice, and it makes it possible for unscrupulous senior men to lay claim to an ownership they may well know they do not have. A similar alteration to the understanding of the exchanges made at marriage has been effected by the use of the Bislama term *pem woman* (to buy a woman). The significance and purpose of marriage exchanges in linking two family or clan groups is now often overwritten by the concept of purchase.

The idea of ownership is also impacting on practice at a local level. This is particularly true of reef and beach resources. Most fieldworkers reported that in the past, both beaches and reefs were seen as 'community' resources, i.e. as accessible to co-resident kin groups, but that now, there is a stronger sense of exclusive ownership of them. It is my untested perception that this is part of a wider trend in which community and descent group ownership is fissioning into smaller and smaller units, as men think of themselves not as land-holders, but as landowners, and as monetarization diminishes community interdependence.

In most parts of Vanuatu, a woman moves to live on her husband's land at marriage. Almost universally, when a woman marries, she retains use rights to the land of her birth through her father and brothers. In some cases these continuing rights are made specific: her father gives her a piece of land called a 'basket', where she may make a garden for the whole of her life. This land rarely passes from the woman to her children, but at her death reverts to her natal group. In terms of access to land to make a garden, a woman is thus actually better provided for than men, for she is able to access land from her natal group, and also from the group to which she marries. At marriage she becomes a member of her husband's descent group, and that membership is made more real as she absorbs the substance of his group's land by eating the food grown from it, and as she bears children to it. It is thus my impression that she needs access to her natal land most in the early years of her marriage, until – by investing in the land, eating its produce and bearing children to it – she has become more fully a member of the group she has joined.

The importance of the connection between a descent group and land is most visible in areas where descent is reckoned matrilineally. Naupa and Simo set this out clearly in their account of land in North Pentecost. They quote an informant who said 'I will make sure that my sister's children come back to the land that is under my custody for the simple reason that they are the members of my tribe, and my children will always return to their mother's land because they belong to their mother's tribe.' (Naupa and Simo 2008:97). What became clear from the reports at the women and land workshop is that this principle of connection is not only a matter of linking men to their descent groups' land, the issue of personal affect for women is also important: marriages are often made that link a woman to land to which she already has kinship connections.

This is where Iaken's comment comes in to play. On Tanna the principles of marriage that involve two groups 'swapping' women can enable a woman to make a garden on land where her mother had made one before her. Similarly, in south Erromango the principle that a woman should marry into her grandmother's group enables her to move back to land with which she also has a personal connection.[12] Such marriages certainly strengthen the ties of a woman's children to that land, but for the woman herself they activate her personal attachment to the land of her female kin. A woman who marries to land to which she has a descent group affiliation will always have a stronger connection to it than a woman who does not. That is to say, in times of tension or difficulty a wife who has no personal descent connection is always more vulnerable. One of the issues discussed at the workshop was the problem of contemporary marriages between people from different islands. It is much harder for a woman who comes from another island entirely to be absorbed into a descent group. Again, this is especially the case in the early years of the marriage, before she has invested her labour in the land, has eaten its produce and borne children to it. When a woman moves to her husband's land, but is unable to invest in it by bearing children, her absorption into the group becomes more difficult, and her tenure much more shaky.

Over and over again the fieldworkers discussed marriage as the key strategy for ensuring the ongoing connection between a descent group and their land, and gave specific examples of such marriages occurring in their own generation, so as to provide people for the land. Marriages ideally bring two people who have strong connections to land into a productive relationship, producing children whose descent relation to that land is strengthened by the kinship connections of both their parents. It is hard nowadays to grasp the critical importance of creating the next generation. In the past child-bearing was a strength belonging to women that balanced the contributions men made in other contexts. Bearing children to the land was a powerfully important role for women. Customary childbirth is still the most taboo topic for women, a subject which the women fieldworkers have consistently refused to discuss in a workshop. I take it that this relates to the powerful importance of bearing children.

The provision of people for the land operates on the same principles as in other contexts of investment. It is not enough, for example, to be a parent, one must demonstrate that parenthood in acts of care and provision for the child. It is not enough to have access to land; one must demonstrate that relationship by activating it. The work of women and men together in making the land productive through gardening and other land-management techniques is crucial. Today, if people who live in town want to sustain their land access privileges, then they must return regularly to their home island to participate in kin-group events, and must support those who are working the land in their absence by contributions of various kinds. Town dwellers who do not do this will lose their ability to access their land.[13] The relationship must be activated. This is true in death as in life, it is important that a person who dies in town is buried in the island, on their land, in order to ensure their children's ongoing connection to it. Sometimes when a marriage is contracted in town between people from different islands, the wife is unwilling to move to her husband's natal land, and they remain in town. In this case, unless the husband works especially hard to maintain the connection with his land, both they and their children become gradually more and more isolated from it. Connection to the land needs to be maintained by both partners to the marriage in order to ensure that the children of the marriage have rights to it.

It is not only the case that a given relationship must be demonstrated in acts of care, but also that acts of care can create a relationship. One's affiliation to land is thus both a matter of investing in the land by taking care of it in gardening and other land-management techniques, and a matter of being cared for by the land – by living on it, by eating the food it provides, by using the resources it provides. Hence the significance of the Aneityumese expression quoted above – 'let's go to the place that looks after us' (Simo

2005:3).[14] This sense of mutual investment and care, land and people looking after each other, is less between an individual and land, than between a group and land. It is not only a matter of caring for the land but of caring for, and being cared for by, the people of the land. Concepts like ownership do not adequately encompass the depth of this connection. Investment is and was a key principle in land tenure: investment in relationships through acts of provision or care, investment of labour into the land itself, investment by the land into its inhabitants.

This sense of investment is the second aspect of Iaken's comment: if a woman marries back into her mother's kin group, as an exchange for her, then she will be able to make a garden on her mother's land. Iaken did not say that the woman would be able to live on her mother's land. Rather, she specified a relationship of investment: the bride, returning to her mother's land, invests in it by making a garden.

Adoption and *bladlaen*

If marriage was a key aspect of land-holding discussed by the fieldworkers, then the other major issue in the workshop was adoption. Adoption is a key principle of kinship. Children are adopted when a person invests parenting into a child. Margaret Jolly, describing the Sa of south Pentecost in the early 1970s, comments that although people there recognized biological parentage, nevertheless 'insofar as there is a notion of "real" mother or father, this seen to be the person who nurtured the child' (1994:95–6). Food and nurture creates kinship equal to genealogical connection, and investment of parenting in a child creates a relationship which is reckoned to be 'real' in a way that is difficult for expatriates, schooled in ideas of biological connection, to fully grasp.[15]

On the first day of discussions in the workshop, Nauli Batik, from south Epi, discussed adoption strategies in her own family, which were implemented to provide a next generation to work the large piece of land they hold. This led to the first of several debates about adoption through the workshop. These debates were premised on a sense of social change: strategies that worked in the past do not necessarily work today. Jean Tarisesei (from Ambae) commented that in the past adoption was an effective strategy because the issue was lack of people, not lack of land. Lisiel Rantes, from Southwest Bay, Malakula, responded by saying that it is now important to adopt a child from close family, a child whose link to the land is also reinforced by their biological descent. She specifically identified the adoption of a child with descent from another island as inevitably causing problems, not least in the formal debates of Land Tribunal meetings. Sophie Nempan, from south Erromango, herself childless, rejected with scorn the idea that adoption could be an option nowadays. Erromango's population is low: people are needed to work it. Nempan commented that the adopting parents would invest in bringing up the child only to have the birth family take the child back when he or she was old enough to work. This is a substantial, shocking, inversion of *kastom* ideas of investment. It is, it appears, not so much that adoption worked when there was more land, but that ideas about biological descent are gaining more and more weight in people's thinking. This is enabling biological descent to represent a stronger claim than investment.

The traction of the idea of biological descent is marked by a new word in Bislama, Vanuatu's lingua franca.[16] This is the term *bladlaen*, bloodline, a term which seems to have entered the language somewhere in the last decade.[17] It apparently entered Bislama through the deliberations of Malvatumauri, the Vanuatu National Council of Chiefs. Malvatumauri has for a long time struggled with questions of descent in establishing how chiefs can be identified (see Bolton 1998). The term was introduced into the workshop discussions by Chief Jacob Kapere, who is Head of the National Film and Sound Unit, and who happened to be audio-recording the proceedings at the time. Kapere made a distinction between family and *bladlaen*, a distinction which I had never heard before and which I understood to distinguish traditional forms of descent reckoning from more strictly biological ones. *Bladlaen* can refer to descent on both the mother's and the father's side, but has a primarily patrilineal emphasis. In the discussion that followed I asked about terms for descent in Vanuatu languages. The fieldworkers mentioned terms meaning rope, road, roots (specifically breadfruit roots), vein and name. Although vein (*string*) might suggest biological connection, most of these terms evoke lines of connection without emphasizing conception or birth.

The meanings referenced by the Bislama *bladlaen* do something which is rarely done in indigenous systems: the term essentializes a person, fixes their identity in a way that that closes off other options. In indigenous knowledge and practice people's options are always open: people use identity flexibly. An individual is not so much a man or a woman as a series of kinship locations: a woman is not so much a woman as a mother, a sister, a father's sister, a brother's daughter and so on. At key moments, for example in exchanges at marriages and funerals, individuals act in relation to the key parties by selecting from a range of possible kinship positions – perhaps sister to a bride, or grandparent/grandchild to the groom.

Margaret Rodman says that 'Land tenure ... is not a system of rights expressed in action but a process in which actions are selectively validated by rights' (1984:64), but in fact, one could equally say that identity is not a fixed location expressed in action, but a process in which actions are selectively validated by emphasizing a particular relationship or set of relationships.

This is not least because in indigenous Melanesian contexts gender does not operate independently of kinship. There are few rules for what all women can and cannot do, or for that matter, what all men can and cannot do, in relation to land. Rather, there are principles for what daughters, or elder brothers, or sister's sons or wives can do.

The new emphasis on biological descent seems to be entering ni-Vanuatu reckonings of kinship to a greater and greater extent, weakening traditional strategies like adoption. Although this might be seen to strengthen the importance of women's capacity to bear children, the emphasis on biological descent destabilises women's relationship to land. If investing in a child no longer makes that child one's own, if investment is a less powerful strategy, then investing in land is no longer a way to connect oneself to it. More significantly, if living on land and eating the food it produces no longer makes one a member of a descent group, but instead it is necessary to have a biological descent connection to it, then women no longer belong to the land they have married to in the way they once did. The change in emphasis turns such women into strangers. And it alienates a woman who cannot bear children, weakening the value of her nurturance of adopted children. It also weakens the importance of a woman's contribution to land by investing her labour into it.

Talking about land

One thing was clear from the discussions at the workshop: everybody recognizes that disputes about land will go on forever. There will always be rows, even where there is still a significant amount of *dakbus*, un-cultivated forest. If in the past those disputes might have been resolved by violence, they are now often brought before courts, frequently at village level. The 2001 Customary Land Tribunal Act was passed to establish a system of land-dispute resolution 'in accordance with the custom of those involved in the dispute', which could resolve disputes not amenable to local forms of resolution. But no amount of legislation will ever resolve all land disputes.

The issue of disputes and the constitution of the Land Tribunal raise the question of who may speak about land. This is often a key question framing research into customary land tenure (e.g. Naupa and Simo 2008:86). It arises from a European preoccupation with speaking as an expression of authority. It was nominated as one of the research questions for the workshop, and all the fieldworkers addressed it in their reports. All of them suggested that while women do not generally speak in the men's house or on the meeting ground, they do speak in the house, that is to say, they influence the men who speak in meetings. At the 2009 workshop I summarized to the women fieldworkers my sense of what they had been saying in their 2008 discussions about the right to speak about land. They agreed, making additions, so that we arrived at a summation along these lines: 'women bear children to the land, we raise pigs, we make mats, we work in the gardens. If we don't do these things, then we don't have any right to talk about land. But because we do these things we do have the right to talk about land.' Women can speak, and be listened to – in the house or at a meeting – because of what they contribute, invest, in the land and the community.

In general, the fieldworkers did not perceive the fact that they do not usually speak in the men's house meetings as a problem. The route of influence seemed adequate to them. Several fieldworkers pointed out that it is often senior women who hold the detailed knowledge about land boundaries and kinship connections for their community, which means that men turn to them for information and advice about issues relating to land. But the Customary Land Tribunal Act disadvantages women, by formalizing the processes that take place in men's house meetings, without allowing for the negotiations that often take place with women before those meetings. Practically, the legislation reinforces the idea that only men can speak about land. More significantly, the legislation moves the locus of information about land and boundaries from individuals and places it in court records: senior women are no longer able to be the source for detailed knowledge about land transactions. People must go to an office in Port Vila to obtain information about past decisions.

Making women's land-holding visible

It seems to me that the significant problem in the documentation of the 'rules of custom' about land tenure is the introduction of new and different concepts into the process. This happens at two levels. One level is the absorption of such concepts into ni-Vanuatu knowledge and practice, a process that is often subtle and undocumented. The incorporation of ideas about land *ownership* is the most critical example of this process, the new emphasis on *bladlaen* is another. The second level is that the documentation process itself is being framed by expatriate land-tenure thinking. Documentation becomes a process of making customary systems conform to Western models by analysing them in terms of key Western concepts such as ownership, rights and decision-making.

Research into customary land tenure that emphasises ownership already misses the key characteristic of land-tenure models in Vanuatu. This is investment. A group's tenure of land is expressed and validated by their investment in it. Equally, as anyone living in town knows, an individual's capacity to access and use their descent group's land is sustained by his or her ongoing investment of support to that group. Both women and men invest in land by gardening, by building houses, by taking care of forest, riverine and marine resources. Both invest in their descent group by contributing to exchanges and community fund-raising, and by participating in events. Investment demonstrates, sustains and effects land tenure.

The difficulty of documenting women's place in customary land-tenure systems in terms of ownership, rights and decision-making is quite considerable. If relationships to land are framed in these terms, then it can appear that women have nothing to do with land. But in fact, as for men, the relationship women have to land derives from their investment in that land. In *kastom*, marriage did and does not always move a woman to land with which she already has kinship connections, although this is a regular objective in making marriage arrangements. But by living on and investing in the land to which she marries, by eating the food of that land, a woman becomes part of it, and part of the kin-group that lives on it. Women bear children to the land, or raise adopted children to the land, providing people for it. Both men and women have a mutually interdependent relationship in their reliance upon and their investment in, their land.

The problem for those ni-Vanuatu who seek indigenous models of development, is to find a way to draw ideas of investment and affiliation into models of customary tenure, and to recognize in them the crucial contribution of women to land management. Models that focus only on ownership entirely miss the point. Of course, it is not always in everyone's interests to recognize the indigenous models by which both men and women are deeply part of their descent group's land: it is not in the interests of those men who want to sell their land. The challenge is to recognize how introduced concepts like land ownership and *bladlaen* are affecting ni-Vanuatu understandings of land ownership, to disentangle them from descriptions of indigenous models, and to resolve the contradictions they introduce.

Notes

1   Ni-Vanuatu is the term used in Vanuatu to refer to all those people who are descended from the pre-colonial population. Naturalized citizens and other expatriates are not normally covered by the term. Formulations such as 'Vanuatuan' are not used.

2   Rachel said '*Sipos yu swapem mama blong yu, yu save mekim karen long ples blong stret mama blong yu.*' (Fieldworker workshop proceedings 28 October 2008).

3   With the exception of the 2012 workshop.

4   I obtained permission from the workshop participants and the VKS director, Marcellin Abong, to write about the proceedings of that workshop in this chapter, a version of which has been published by the VKS (Bolton 2009).

5   In the Land Reform Act, Cap. 123 'improvements' are defined as including 'the reclaiming of land from the sea, clearing levelling or grading of land, drainage

or irrigation of land, reclamation of swamps, surveying and making boundaries, erection of fences of any description, landscaping of land, planting of long-lived crops, trees or shrubs, laying-out and cultivation of nurseries, buildings and structures of all descriptions which are in the nature of fixtures, fixed plant and machinery, roads, yards, gates, bridges, culverts, ditches, drains, soakaways, cesspits, septic tanks, water tanks, water, power and other reticulation systems, dips and spray races for livestock' (Laws of the Republic of Vanuatu Chapter 163 part I Preliminary).

6   Regenvanu was the Director of the Vanuatu Cultural Centre from 1995–2007. He became a Member of Parliament in March 2008, and has subsequently held the positions of Minister for Lands (in 2011) and Minister for Lands and Natural Resources (from March 2013). See also Regenvanu (this volume).

7   Joel Simo was initially funded as a 'host-national (ni-Vanuatu) volunteer' by CUSO, a Canadian international aid organisation which works through volunteers. Simo was later supported, through the Kaljoral Senta, by the Christensen Fund, a USA-based charitable foundation.

8   Simo observes 'when customary land laws are incorporated into an external legal framework, this establishes an attitude of exclusive right holding of the land and creates conflict within *kastom*' (2005:20–1).

9   There are also about 70 men fieldworkers, who meet at a separate workshop. The two groups generally pursue different research topics each year: the men's group discussed the topic of customary landholding (*Kastom fasin blong holem graon*) in 1996.

10   See Bolton (2003) for a discussion of this process.

11   In 1992 a chief on Ambae recalled for me an occasion on which, missing some of his cows, he went to the place he knew to be the *nasara*, the meeting ground, of the invisible community co-resident with people in his district, Longana (a group known as *mwai*). He made a speech on the *nasara* asking the *mwai* to return his cows, and the cows then reappeared.

12   Sophie Nempan reports for south Erromango that a woman must marry to her grandmother's descent group '*oltaem woman i mus mared i go long laen blong bubu woman*'. (Fieldworker workshop procedings Oct 2008).

13   However, the fieldworkers from Tanna explained that everyone who has a name from a land-holding group focused on a *nakamal* (a clearing where men meet and drink kava) has rights to access land there. This news was greeted with astonishment by fieldworkers from other islands.

14   The expression is '*apan akaja umaja*' (Simo 2005:3).

15   See also Demian 2004 for a discussion of adoption in Suau, Papua New Guinea.

16   Bislama is Vanuatu's lingua franca. All the debates discussed in this paper (at the National Land Summit, the women and land workshop and elsewhere) took place in Bislama.

17   Crowley's 1995 Bislama dictionary does not include *bladlaen* among the terms and
     phrases he lists related to blood. He translates clan as *laen, nakamal* or *smolnem*
     (1995:48, 298, 314).

References

Bolton, L. 1998. Chief Willie Bongmatur Maldo and the role of Chiefs in Vanuatu.
     The Journal of Pacific History 33(2):179–95.
——— 1999. Fieldwork, fieldworkers: developments in Vanuatu research. *Oceania*
     (Special Issue) 70(1):67–78.
——— 2003. *Unfolding the Moon: Enacting Women's Kastom in Vanuatu*. Honolulu:
     University of Hawai'i Press.
——— 2007. Resourcing change: fieldworkers, the Women's Culture Project and the
     Vanuatu Cultural Centre. In *The Future of Indigenous Museum: Perspectives
     from the Southwest Pacific*, N. Stanley (ed.), 23–37. Oxford: Berghahn
     Books.
——— 2009. *Women and Customary Land Tenure in Vanuatu: The Influence of
     Expatriate Thinking*. Port Vila Vanuatu: Vanuatu National Cultural Council.
Cox, M. 2007. *The Unfinished State: Drivers of Change in Vanuatu*. Canberra:
     Australian Agency for International Development.
Crowley, T. 1995. *A New Bislama Dictionary*. Suva, Fiji: Institute of Pacific Studies,
     University of the South Pacific and Port Vila Vanuatu: Pacific Languages
     Unit, University of the South Pacific.
Daley, L. 2009. Hijacking Development Futures: 'Land Development' and Reform in
     Vanuatu. Report produced by AID/WATCH Action on Aid Trade and Debt.
     Australia: Search Foundation.
Deacon, A.B. 1934. *Malekula: A Vanishing People in the New Hebrides* (ed. C.H.
     Wedgwood). London: George Routledge and Sons.
Demian, M. 2004. Transactions in rights, transactions in children: a view of adoption
     from Papua New Guinea. In *Cross-Cultural Approaches to Adoption*, F.
     Bowie (ed.), 97–110. London: Routledge.
Douglas, N. and N. Douglas 1990. *Vanuatu: A Guide* (revised edition). Alstonville,
     NSW: Pacific Profiles.
Fingleton, J. (ed.) 2005. *Privatising Land in the Pacific: A Defense of Customary
     Tenures* (Discussion Paper No. 8). Canberra: The Australia Institute.
[South Pacific] Forum Secretariat 2001. *Land Issues in the Pacific*. Briefing paper for
     the Forum Economic Ministers Meeting, Rarotonga, Cook Islands 19–20
     June 2001 [PIFS(01)FEMC.03].
Jolly, M. 1994. *Women of the Place: Kastom, Colonialism and Gender in Vanuatu*.
     Chur, Switzerland: Harwood Academic Publishers.
Lane, R.B. 1971. Land tenure without land policy. In *Land Tenure in the Pacific*, R.G.
     Crocombe (ed.), 248–72. Melbourne: Oxford University Press.

Larcom, J. 1983. Following Deacon: the Problem of ethnographic reanalysis, 1926–1981. In *Observers Observed: Essays on Ethnographic Fieldwork* (History of Anthropology, Vol. 1), G.W. Stocking (ed.), 175–95. Madison: University of Wisconsin Press.

Laws of the Republic of Vanuatu, Revised Edition 1988. Chapter 163 part I Preliminary. http://faolex.fao.org/docs/html/van38130.htm, accessed 4 February 2014.

Lunnay, C., M. Mangawai, E. Nalyal and J. Simo 2007. Vanuatu: Review of National Land Legislation, Policy and Land Administration. http://www.ausaid.gov.au/publications/

Naupa, A. n.d. . *Kastom*, women and land in Vanuatu. Paper presented to the World Bank, Justice for the Poor Symposium 4–5 June 2009 Jakarta, Indonesia.

Naupa, A. and J. Simo 2008. Matrilineal land tenure in Vanuatu 'Hu i kakae long basket?' Case studies of Raga and Mele. In *Land and women: The Matrilineal Factor: The Cases of the Republic of Marshall Islands, Solomon Islands and Vanuatu*, E. Huffer (ed.), 73–117. Suva: Pacific Islands Forum Secretariat. Also http://www.forumsec.org.fj/

Regenvanu, R. 2008. Issues with land reform in Vanuatu. *Journal of South Pacific Law* 12(1):63–7.

Rodman, M.C. 1984. Masters of tradition: customary land tenure and new forms of social inequality in a Vanuatu peasantry. *American Ethnologist* 11(1):61–80.

Simo, J. 2005. *Report of the National Review of the Customary Land Tribunal Program in Vanuatu*. Port Vila: Vanuatu National Cultural Council.

——— 2008. *Melanesian Philosophy of Land Faces Challenges*. Port Vila: Vanuatu National Cultural Council.

Taylor, J.P. 2008. *The Other Side: Ways of Being and Place in Vanuatu* (Pacific Islands Monograph Series 22). Honolulu: University of Hawai'i Press

Van Trease, H. 1987. *The Politics of Land in Vanuatu: from Colony to Independence*. Suva: Institute of Pacific Studies, University of the South Pacific.

Lissant Bolton is Keeper of the Department of Africa, Oceania and the Americas at The British Museum.

III

Heritage as political discourse

CHAPTER 7

Port Vila mi lavem yu

Visualizing the urban experience in Vanuatu

✳

HAIDY GEISMAR

In May 2011, the exhibition Port Vila Mi Lavem Yu (Port Vila I Love You) opened at the East-West Center in Honolulu, Hawai'i. The culmination of a three-year research project the exhibition was curated by Haidy Geismar (NYU/UCL) and Eric Wittersheim (École des Hautes Études en Sciences Sociales, Paris) in collaboration with the Hon. Ralph Regenvanu (Member of Parliament for Port Vila, and current Minister of Lands and Natural Resources) and Viviane Obed (formerly of the Vanuatu Cultural Centre's Young People's Project) with contributions from numerous other local assistants and anthropologists.

Urban life in Melanesia has attracted scholarly attention for some time with anthropologists and others examining the intersections of church, new social movements, land rights, urban settlements, gender relations, money, tourism and globalization (e.g. Brookfield 1973; Gewertz and Errington 1999; Goddard 2005; Rawlings 1999) and their impact on traditional lifeways. In turn, museums have also been trying to collect and document the new artefacts and aesthetics of Melanesian urban life. O'Hanlon's book and exhibition, *Paradise: Portraying the New Guinea Highlands* (held at the Museum of Mankind, see O'Hanlon 1993; Clifford 1997) explored the Wahgi recycling of consumer goods to produce war shields in the Highlands of Papua New Guinea. Large exhibitions in the 1990s at the Chicago Field Museum and the Tropenmuseum in Amsterdam collected and exhibited the aesthetics of imported (largely Chinese manufactured) commodities by presenting urban marketplaces in their exhibition halls (both of which were criticized for lack of connection to Pacific Islanders, despite their contemporary focus, see Kahn 1995, 2000). By expanding the usual exhibition conventions of timeless and exotic ritual cultures in Melanesia, these projects, notwithstanding their limitations, presented the roles that globalization, commodity consumption and urbanization play in the aesthetic life of Melanesians, and exhibited urbanization in largely positive ways as a process of cultural intermingling, innovation and creativity. Indeed, it is certainly true that for many Pacific Islanders, patterns of circular migration ensure that both town and village are vital parts of everyday life, as is the consumption of global commodities, which have had a powerful presence in the region since the start of colonialism, but especially since the Second World War (see Foster 2002; Lindstrom and White 1994; Schneider 2012). Yet for many, living in urban Melanesia is an experience tainted with ambivalence. People come to town seeking to earn money, desiring to participate in a sense of global modernity, but they also quickly become aware of the losses (of language, traditional practice and intergenerational knowledge) that this can incur. Towns such as Honiara and Port Moresby have become synonymous with ethnic tension, and the large numbers of unemployed youth provoke a public discourse around out-of-control teenagers, gangs and violence.

Our exhibition wanted to both explore the aesthetics of urban life in Vanuatu and provide a space for ni-Vanuatu to present their celebrations and ambivalences about life in town. We built on the collaborative research process developed by the Vanuatu Cultural Centre, VCC (Taylor and Thieberger 2009) and used extensively by Geismar in a number of other museum projects (Geismar 2003; Geismar, Herle and Longga 2007) in which the process of making a collection and developing a display was open to local interlocutors who would have the opportunity to create objects, texts and display strategies to convey their particular experiences of town. With funding from Le Fonds Pacifique of the French Overseas Ministry, and the support of two private collectors, we were able to commission six contemporary ni-Vanuatu artists to create new pieces specifically engaging with the theme of 'Life in Town'. In discussion with these artists and our local curators, we divided the exhibition into a number of themes that directed the collection of a host of other items: contemporary photography, everyday consumables, personal possessions. The final exhibition was divided into sections focused on: Port Vila's 'history' (comprised of historical images from the archives of the Vanuatu Cultural Centre); the urban kava bar or '*nakamal*' (an installation of a kava bar which was also the screening room for a specially produced film by Eric Wittersheim, *Man Vila*); 'home' (an installation evoking a domestic interior in an urban settlement, which contained locally collected clothing including a policeman's uniform, a school uniform, local t-shirts and calico, a bible, posters and photographs taken by a youth photography project organized by Wan Smol Bag theatre company); and the 'marketplace' (an installation of a local handicrafts market and the interior of a trade store selling good predominantly imported from China), around which were interspersed contemporary artworks and artist's commentaries.

It quickly became clear that there was a critical tension between our desires to generate an aesthetic field for the experience of everyday life in Port Vila and our hope to engender a critical commentary about the process of rapid urbanization that the small city has experienced. Out of a total population of just over 250,000, nearly 50,000 live in Vanuatu's capital, many of them in informal settlements without adequate facilities in makeshift houses (Wittersheim 2011; cf. Goddard 2005 for Papua New Guinea). Port Vila is a place of many paradoxes. It is a town in which nearly every island is represented by a settlement of people who work hard to maintain their local language and cultural traditions, developing new urban rituals around marriage, initiation and reconciliation. Whilst people maintain as much as possible of their cultural traditions in town, lack of access to traditional resources (pigs, yams, ceremonial mats) has resulted in an increased entanglement of money within ceremonial spheres and a growing debate upon the appropriateness of money as bride-wealth or compensation. Port Vila is also where intermarriage between different island communities has resulted in Bislama, the national creole, becoming an increasingly vibrant and dynamic language, often the first language of urban children.

Perhaps the most pressing concern in town is access to land, both to live on and to cultivate gardens upon. The market in Port Vila has expanded to provide international produce such as coriander and red onions, but is increasingly too expensive for local people. Eric Wittersheim's film, *Man Vila*, specially made for the exhibition, highlighted the concerns of Tannese settlers in Port Vila who find it increasingly difficult to access the coast for swimming or fishing, as beach-front properties are developed by foreign investors or siloed by local land claims. Similarly, the influx of mass-produced commodities has opened up new sound worlds of reggae and hip-hop, and the cultural space of evangelical Christianity, yet it has also precipitated much local discussion about the effects of pornography and violent films on young people (Lindstrom 2007). The Vanuatu Cultural Centre has for many years focused research on the pressing questions of gender, youth and land, with projects that have, for instance, explored and validated the experience of women, examined young people's experience of justice in town (Mitchell 2004), or documented the ways in which land ownership was traditionally managed (Simo 2007). Alongside the VCC, Wan Smol Bag – a theatre company focused on social justice and local empowerment – has run a Youth Photography Project over several years, giving cameras to young people living all around Port Vila and asking them to document their own lives. Their images, several of which were presented in our exhibition, show a world in which life is undoubtedly hard, but in which young people remain focused on family, and try to maintain themselves as active members of their communities.

This ambivalent aesthetic resonated in Honolulu, where the exhibition opened in the art gallery of the East-West Center. Although relatively small in space, the East-West Center gallery is known for its interest in innovative Pacific work, including the first show of contemporary Native Hawaiian art in the exhibition 'Ho'okū'ē (Resistance)' in 1997. Honolulu, like Port Vila, has become increasingly too expensive for its native population, many of whom have been pushed to live in informal settlements along the beaches leading out of town, and do not have the prospect of regular employment or access to healthcare. Instead, many indigenous Hawaiians are either marginalized or pressured into performing a version of their traditional culture for tourists. Many of the staple foods of urban ni-Vanuatu – tinned tuna, corned beef, white rice imported from China or Australia – are also staples in Honolulu, and bring with them the associated lifestyle diseases of diabetes, high blood pressure and heart disease. In both Honolulu and Port Vila the long-standing presence of Asian merchants has contributed profoundly to the daily fabric of economic life, in particular, and has precipitated a very specific dialogue on globalization that intersects with the political and economic interests that emanate from North America, Australia and Europe.

The questions regarding how to present these topical issues, primarily through visual means, and how to engender challenging discussion on the benefits and the troubles of urban development became part of the curatorial strategy of the exhibition itself. Creating both the collection and the display engendered a dialogue about the role of town in contemporary ni-Vanuatu life and raised many provocative questions, as Joseph John, one of the participating artists commented:

> Today's generation is losing their customary identity. The Western system is influencing them and making them have no interest in their traditional ways. We can see many changes in their clothing and other activities. The children of today no longer have much physical activity – they spend all their time in front of a computer, television or mobile phone. The quality of produce in our store has gone down and makes us sick. DVDs show us many bad habits and practices, and today our crime rate is rising, there is less respect for elders, chiefs, teachers and neighbours…. Today we are struggling to find a way to solve all of these problems. We need to find a way to solve these problems before we ruin our paradise nation of the South Pacific, Vanuatu.

In the following photo essay we present several of the artworks made for the exhibition, alongside some installation shots and other objects that were collected that resonate with these themes. We are grateful for the opportunity to memorialize, and catalogue, the exhibition.

Figure 1   Main Road, now Kumul Highway, Port Vila in 1920. Image courtesy of the Vanuatu Cultural Centre archive.

Figure 2   Main Road, Kumul Highway, 1970. Image courtesy of the Vanuatu Cultural Centre.

Figure 3   Nakamal Installation, East West Gallery, 2011. Photograph by Haidy Geismar.

Figure 4   Installation of a domestic interior, East West Gallery, 2011. Photograph by Haidy Geismar.

Figure 5   Land Disputing, *David Ambong, 2011. Acrylic on canvas.*

Artist statement: This artwork shows what is happening in Port Vila today. As shown on the picture, some land has been sold to one of the investors while its customary ownership is still under dispute. In Port Vila today investors are buying land and developing it with shops and office rentals. In the picture the land has been sold by a Ni-Vanuatu to an investor; the money has been paid to him in full. Frequently, when disputers are made aware that the land has already been sold by their opponent, conflict arises that at times causes them to be fighting against each other, even though they may be brothers. In the picture the brothers are fighting over the payment while the investor has already develop[ed] the land freely... This artwork also tells us that people are going for money and [are] not thinking of developing their own land for their future generations.

Figure 6   Port Vila Everyday, *Emmanuel Watt, 2011. Multimedia installation.*

Artist statement: Vanuatu is still one of the civilizations on the planet where man is born rich, thanks to its customary system. In Vanuatu it is the human being who belongs to the earth, but if we detach from it without reflection, we become poor. In other societies, people must buy land. In Vanuatu, 80 per cent of the population lives with the rhythm of nature. Port Vila, the capital of Vanuatu, is like any other city in the world of 50,000 inhabitants, with its advantages and disadvantages. For example, the market is open daily and there are all sorts of local products such as laplap, a typical dish of Vanuatu cooked with manioc, banana, taro or yam, an ancestral way of cooking.

Kava is a traditional beverage made from the 'false pepper plant', it is served every day in the evening at the nakamal or kava bar in all areas in Port Vila. The nakamal is an extraordinary meeting point through which one can get a general idea of the way of life of its inhabitants. Thus the market and nakamals are meeting places for everyday talk. Nevertheless, behind this peaceful touch of paradise, lies a reality that casts a shadow over the future of this city and becomes more and more alarming: Efate is the island of Vanuatu that is selling most land to foreigners. Therefore the landmark with a question mark in my piece indicates a danger with respect to the earth if ni-Vanuatu sell land without thinking wisely. For my work I have chosen the market, Kava and the landmark to address the issue of land that is the real wealth and the future of a human being, city, nation, ni-Vanuatu.

Figure 7   The market, *Juliette Pita, 2011. Acrylic paint on canvas.*

Artist statement: My original design is mainly based on what we call here in Vanuatu the 'custom economy'. Custom and cultural practices are always transformed in our traditional lifestyles, and ways of trading become a form of business for cash, especially in Port Vila. Some examples are: women weaving mats and baskets etc. for sale; other arts and crafts (women's artefact shops); selling kava roots and juice – there are kava bars all over Port Vila; and the selling of food at the Port Vila Market House. The Market House sells the products of women and men from all over the island of Efate. You can see the island of Efate as the background to the picture. It is mainly women who sell things at the market. The Port Vila market is mainly a women's place.

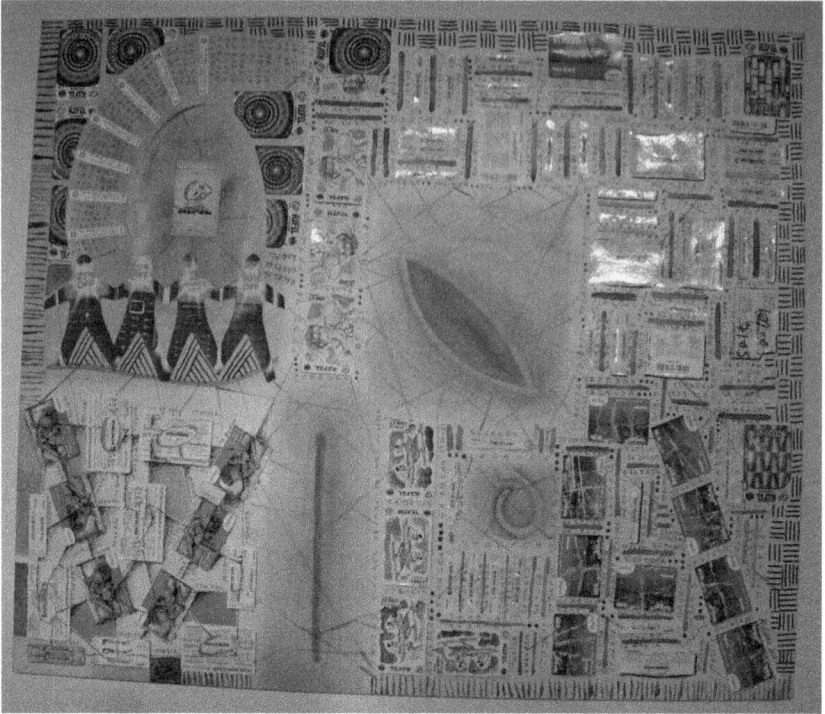

Figure 8   The Virus in the City, *Sero Kuautonga, 2011. Acrylic paint and phone cards on canvas.*

Artist statement: Cell phones have been introduced since the beginning of this century in Port Vila and now almost everyone has one. In the beginning, it was considered as a luxury object for only well-paid people living in town. Today it is just like a toy that anybody can access. Whether or not it is necessary for everyone to get one, today everybody is contaminated by the system. Yes, the system that facilitates life for some people, on the other hand brings problem to others. Everywhere in Port Vila today, people walk over empty telephone refill cards. Our environment is polluted by throwing empty cards everywhere and by the exposure of radio waves to people living in town, and by the telecommunication towers built in town to facilitate the network system. women's place.

Figure 9 Store keeper, *Fres Wota, Prisca, 24 July 2009. Wan Smol Bag Youth Photography Project.*

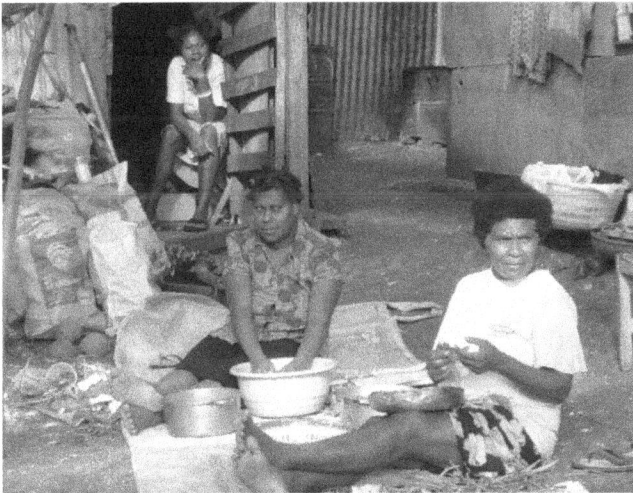

Figure 10 Women prepare a meal at their home in Ohlen, *Wilma, 16 July 2009. Wan Smol Bag Youth Photography Project.*

Figure 11   Efram Iapwatu at his computer, Ohlen Nabanga settlement. Efram is a student at Malapoa College, July 2010. Photograph by Lamont Lindstrom.

Acknowledgements:

The exhibition was curated by Haidy Geismar and Eric Wittersheim, with assistance in Port Vila from The Honourable Ralph Regenvanu, Jacob Kapere and Abong Thompson (Vanuatu Cultural Centre) and Viviane Obed; and in Honolulu from Michael Schuster, Eric Change and Bill Felz. Benedicta Rousseau, Catriona and Armstrong Malau, Leslie Vandeputte and Monika Stern all contributed to the content. Additional images were provided by Lamont Lindstrom and the National Film, Photo and Sound Archive. We wish to acknowledge the financial support of the East-West Center Gallery, Le Fonds Pacifique, Ministère des Affaires Etrangères (Paris), IRIS (EHESS-CNRS, France), Wan Smol Bag Theatre Company (Port Vila), New York University, Blacksands Association (Paris), Nicholas Berlanga and Kylie Maloney.

References

Brookfield, H.C. 1973. *The Pacific in Transition: Geographical Perspectives on Adaptation and Change*. Edward Arnold.

Clifford, J. 1997. Paradise. In *Routes : Travel and Translation in the Late Twentieth Century*, 147–86. Cambridge, Mass.: Harvard University Press.

Foster, R.J. 2002. *Materializing the Nation: Commodities, Consumption, and Media in Papua New Guinea*. Bloomington: Indiana University Press.

Geismar, H. 2003. *Vanuatu Stael: Kastom and Creativity*. Cambridge: Cambridge University Museum of Archaeology and Anthropology.

Geismar, H., A. Herle and N.F. Longga 2007. *John Layard Long Malakula 1914–1915*. Cambridge: Cambridge University Museum of Archaeology and Anthropology.

Gewertz, D. and F. Errington 1999. *Emerging Class in Papua New Guinea: the Telling of Difference*. Cambridge: Cambridge University Press.

Goddard, M. 2005. *The Unseen City: Anthropological Perspectives on Port Moresby, Papua New Guinea*. Canberra, A.C.T.: Pandanus Books.

Kahn, M. 1995. Heterotopic dissonance in the museum representation of Pacific Island Cultures. *American Anthropologist*, 97(2): 324–38.

——— 2000. Applying anthropology: another view of museum exhibit development. *Anthropologica* 42(1):91–4.

Lindstrom, L. 2007. Survivor Vanuatu: myths of matriarchy revisited. *The Contemporary Pacific*, 19(1):162–74.

Lindstrom, L. and G.M. White (eds) 1994. *Culture-Kastom-Tradition: Developing Cultural Policy in Melanesia*. Suva: Institute of Pacific Studies, University of the South Pacific.

Mitchell, J. 2004. Kilem taem (killing time) in a postcolonial town: young people and settlements in Port Vila, Vanuatu. In *Globalization and Culture Change in the Pacific Islands*, V.S. Lockwood (ed.), 358–74. Upper Saddle Rivers, NJ: Prentice Hall.

O'Hanlon, M. 1993. *Paradise: Portraying the New Guinea Highlands*. London: British Museum Press for the Trustees of the British Museum.

Rawlings, G.E. 1999. Foundations of urbanisation: Port Vila Town and Pango Village, Vanuatu. *Oceania* 70(1):72.

Schneider, K. 2012. *Saltwater Sociality: A Melanesian Island Ethnography*. Oxford: Berghahn Books.

Simo, J. 2005. Report of the National Review of the Customary Land Tribunal Program in Vanuatu. Port Vila: Vanuatu National Cultural Council.

Taylor, J. and N. Thieberger 2011. *Working Together in Vanuatu: Research Histories, Collaborations, Projects and Reflections*. Acton, A.C.T.: ANU E Press. epress.anu.edu.au/vanuatu_citation.html, accessed 23 December 2013.

Wittersheim, É. 2011. Paradise for sale. the sweet illusions of economic growth in Vanuatu. *Journal de la Société Des Océanistes* 133:323–32.

Haidy Geismar is Reader in Anthropology at University College London.

CHAPTER 8

Culture, politics and tourism on Tanna

✳

LAMONT LINDSTROM

A tourist brochure boasts that 'Tanna Island is renowned for its active volcano, custom villages, potent kava, cargo cultists, strong traditions, exciting festivals, gigantic banyan trees, magnificent wild horses, long black and white beaches, velvet nights, and much more' (Tanna Beach Resort n.d.). Another promises that tourists will 'learn about the fascinating John Frum cult', in addition to seeing 'the island's top spectacle, the volcano after dark', as well as 'penis-sheathed and grass-skirted custom dancers [and] age old festivals' (Go Pacific Holidays n.d.:9). These advertisements do not exaggerate. Tanna really is a beautiful and fascinating island – a place that more and more tourists are visiting.

Vanuatu's National Tourism Office, along with independent promoters, features Tanna as a main island 'getaway' from the country's major tourist hotels, located in the capital town Port Vila. Vanuatu's tourism planners have posed Tanna as a principal outer island destination for the more adventurous. An enlarged airport on the island provides infrastructure, and local entrepreneurs now cultivate tourists as a new form of cash crop, building bush vacation 'bungalows' and inventing or repackaging local events and experiences for tourists to purchase. Few Tannese, in recent years, have earned much money from their coconut or coffee plantations, and tourists have become an important source of cash. Although life, today, demands money, most islanders remain focused on cultivating their local exchange relationships and political allegiances. These affairs remain at the heart of island daily life even while tourism is reshaping it.

Vanuatu (the New Hebrides before its independence in 1980) ranks with Fiji, French Polynesia, the Cook Islands and New Caledonia as a leading regional tourist target. Its popularity has grown as other south-west Pacific venues have experienced coups, urban riots and miscellaneous social unrest. In 1995, 82,019 tourists arrived in the country. By 2011 visitor numbers had surged to 225,493, including 124,818 day-visitors from cruise ships (Vanuatu National Statistics Office n.d.). Tourism and related services (trade, finance, real estate, hotels and restaurants, and government) have become Vanuatu's most significant economic sector, providing (by 2011) 34 per cent of the country's GDP (United Nations Economic and Social Commission for Asia and the Pacific 2013).

Vanuatu prioritizes tourism within its national development planning (de Burlo 1996, 2003; Hall 1994). 'Traditional villages', natural scenery, local culture and 'folk life' are featured attractions (Tourism Council of the South Pacific 1991; see Regenvanu, this volume, for an alternative vision of Vanuatu's future). Major constraints limiting the growth of tourism, according to Vanuatu's Third National Development Plan (1992–6), included getting ni-Vanuatu (citizens) to appreciate and accept its benefits, and effectively advertising the diversity 'of certain social and cultural traditions and practices of local communities' (Vanuatu, Republic of n.d.:102). Efforts to boost Vanuatu's marketability within global tourist networks, however, have been increasingly successful. The islands, for example, in 2004 served as the backdrop for one of American television's popular *Survivor* series, which happily played up the archipelago's tropical beauty, primitive culture and exotic natives (Lindstrom 2007b).

The increasingly entwined relationship between tourism and tradition, old and new, in Vanuatu, is particularly notable on Tanna. Tourists come here to climb Iasur, a small, continuously erupting cinder-cone volcano, which spits up lava bombs and spreads volcanic ash across the island. Some also arrive as cultural tourists. The Tannese's remarkable success in preserving (and transforming) certain spectacular aspects of tradition attracts visitors who want to experience 'untouched' island life at the same time as they potentially undermine it. Islanders continue to exchange goods to celebrate birth, naming, a boy's circumcision, a girl's first menses, marriage and death, and tourists in recent years often wander into these ceremonies, their cameras clicking (Figure 1). The tourist business has also latched onto the first-fruit exchanges (*nieri* or *niel*) that occasionally take place as families in several villages celebrate their taro or yam harvests. Domestic and some international tourist packagers especially keep their ears to the ground for upcoming *nakwiari* festivals (which tourist publications call Toka), the island's most spectacular dance fest. Hundreds of people from two regions exchange pigs and kava after a night and a day of rousing song and dance, nowadays also performing for audiences that include growing numbers of tourists.

Figure 1   Tourists wander at a circumcision exchange, 2010. Photo by L. Lindstrom.

Islanders have added newer sorts of performance to traditional spectacle (see Debord 1994). Since the nineteenth century, they have created new ideological organizations that have melded indigenous with foreign knowledge systems (Bonnemaison 1994; de Burlo 1984; Guiart 1956, 1975; Lindstrom 1990; Lindstrom and White 1994). Notably, they have innovated vibrant rituals in association with the John Frum movement – a local syncretic religion sometimes described as a 'cargo cult'. Another group in the south-west combines an appreciation of John Frum with a symbolic allegiance to Prince Philip of Great Britain (Baylis 2013). In the home villages of Prince Philip's supporters, visitors encounter islanders who (when tourists are in sight) sport traditional bark skirts and penis wrappers.

Tourist brochures typically feature John Frum as the epitome of the Pacific cargo cult. Since 1945, anthropologists, journalists and others have used this term to describe a variety of South Pacific social movements, especially those that erupted during and after the Pacific War (Lindstrom 1993). According to the story, cultists turned to religious ritual in order to obtain 'cargo'. Sometimes cargo meant money or various sorts of trade goods (vehicles, refrigerators, guns, tools and the like). And sometimes, metaphorically, cargo represented the establishment of a better, more moral society that would follow reassertion of local sovereignty and the withdrawal of colonial rulers.

Back on Tanna, some of John Frum's predictions concerned the impending arrival of American troops and cargo, and this prophecy proved correct in

1942. Island men and boys joined Labor Corps organized by the US Army and Navy and shipped north to military installations established on Efate Island. This wartime experience deepened people's original commitment to John Frum and has since strongly coloured his followers' rituals and symbols (Lindstrom 1993). Although the movement, in 2000, split into three factions, core John Frum supporters continue to gather every Friday evening and dance until daybreak at Ipikil village (Sulphur Bay) (Tabani 2008:21). In addition, since 1957, every 15 February people celebrate the founding of the movement and leaders appear in antique US military uniforms (Tabani 2010).

To investigate the transformation of Tanna into a tourist target, and of local ceremony and culture into spectacle, I draw on a growing body of travel narratives, touristic brochures and Internet websites that makes the island visible and available for global consumption, advertising its charms, cultural and otherwise. These various touristic accounts and advertisements create a certain sort of Tannese 'other', or rather a series of others. At the same time, they drown out many of the island's own stories about itself and, perhaps more insidiously, make certain local stories easier to hear while muting others.

Cultural tourism

Globalization, as has been frequently observed, remakes the local. Far-reaching political and economic projects (and we can count among these old-fashioned colonialism, modernity, development and the like) do indeed erode and occasionally even erase local cultures and social forms. More commonly, however, globalization sparks transformation in localism, as people respond creatively to resist and co-opt extrinsic forces. Marshall Sahlins, for one, has called this sort of creative hybridity 'culturalism' or 'the differencing of growing similarities by contrastive structures' (1999:411; see also Herzfeld 2004). John and Jean Comaroff (2009:51) describe 'ethno-preneurs' busy everywhere turning local culture into global product. British sociologist Roland Robertson (1995) popularized a stylish term for such remade localism: *glocalization*. Globalization works both sides of the cultural street. Insofar as people's lives become increasingly homogenized, the value of the exotic increases. Starbucks is good, perhaps, but not as good as some stand-alone coffee shop that exudes its unique locality – one that is not available anywhere else. As people's lives become increasingly globalized, home takes on new meaning and increased value as a refuge from an unsettled world. This sort of hyper-valuation of home is one of the main engines that drive today's diverse fundamentalisms, whether of religion, language or slow food diet (Appadurai 2006:7).

Cultural tourism (sometimes also called indigenous or ethnic tourism) is increasingly popular within today's global marketplace (Kirshenblatt-Gimblett

1998). Cultural tourism competes with, but often supplements, other kinds of travel, insofar as tourists spread their attention on their holidays to consume adventure tourism, ecotourism, extreme tourism, destination tourism, disaster tourism, heritage tourism, leisure/relaxation tourism, medical tourism, sex tourism, sustainable tourism, and also volunteer vacations, safaris, pilgrimages and various sorts of travelling self-consciously defined not to be tourism. Each side of these binomials (e.g. cultural tourism) implicates the other. Sex workers attract tourists whose demands and desires then reshape whatever local sexual practices are on offer. Beaches lure tourists and an industry that promotes or at least retails more seashore. In the case of cultural tourism, likewise, spectacular traditions that are amenable to a certain sort of packaging draw tourists whose hopes and expectations feedback to transform, if often sometimes also sustain, those traditions.

Both sides of the globalization/glocalization nexus spur cultural tourism. Back home, people throughout much of the world elaborate local cultural products to set them apart from the world, differencing growing similarity by creating contrastive structures, as Sahlins put it. Such elaboration may create richer cultural spectacles and fodder for tourists to consume. Simultaneously, people are driven to seek out contrastive structural difference elsewhere, insofar as home, now, looks like just about everywhere else. These desires for contrastive structure, at home and abroad, boost the numbers of those of us who seek variety in travel. We go on tour in search of cultural difference partly in order to work on our understandings of ourselves (MacCannell 1976). Touring someone else's culture can reveal common humanity beneath cultural variation or, conversely, it can evoke refreshing awareness of difference between self and other. Tourists travel for these cross-cultural experiences and sensations that clarify boundaries of identity that globalization increasingly erodes and blurs. The tourist industry caters to these interests to experience the other, or the self by means of the other, by packaging up bite-sized episodes of cultural difference: customary dances in hotel bars and airports; tours of villages; suitcase-sized carvings in gift shops; local foods in restaurants, or tame versions of these at least; and so forth. Pacific islanders are well positioned in this marketplace. Cultural diversity, particularly in its most easily packaged forms of song and dance, carvings, artwork, food and architecture, is readily available throughout Vanuatu.

Just as the developed world produces the majority of consumer goods, so does it command and shape the global tourist marketplace and its narratives – or perhaps we might better say its currencies. Touristic narratives are orchestrated according to Western expectation and experience. They 'report back from the local to the transnational' (Hutnyk 1999:95), setting the value of Tanna, or Thailand, or Tulsa within a global marketplace. One can deny the validity of those currencies, but one has to use them if the goal is to sell oneself to tourists. Outside the global marketplace, people may set their own value on their traditions. But once within the marketplace, a culture's exchange value slips away from local control to be assessed instead in terms of what Herzfeld has called a 'global hierarchy of value' (2004:2–3). The global market, notably, demands that Pacific tourist venues such as Vanuatu advertise their beaches and reefs, but also their different, unique and even bizarre cultures. Vanuatu's National Tourism Office, no surprise, once featured on its website a smiling young Tannese girl, bedecked in traditional leaves and face-paint, under the slogan 'the friendly face of the Pacific' (http://vanuatu.travel). Vanuatu's smiling faces and exotic bodies, alongside its exotic cultures, are what draw thousands of tourists a year into the archipelago (Lindstrom 2007a; see Desmond 1999 for comparative discussion of feminized Polynesian bodies vis-à-vis a more masculine Melanesia in tourism discourse).

Many cultural tourists coming into the Pacific carry in their baggage evolutionary dogma either of the romantic eighteenth- or primitivist nineteenth-century sort. These expectations situate two kinds of native – the ignoble and the noble. Since Bougainville, Rousseau and John Williams, the Pacific has furnished both varieties of savage to the European imagination. At least some cultural tourists arrive seeking dangerous primitive thrills, while others will be on pilgrimage to discover the noble wisdom of human ancestors (see Kanemase 2008:120–2; Stanley 1998:102). Some of us, happy in our modernity, seek occasionally to dally in what we hope to be eerie wilderness inhabited by primordial natives before we return, refreshed, to our comfortable, orderly suburbs, perhaps with some primitive carving for our living-room wall. Others of us, less happy in our modernity, seek through touring to uncover a truer, more essentially human past, where people lived in harmony with nature, uncorrupted by the pollutants of modern civilization.

Tourism's currencies now powerfully define and confine Tanna as other. Island lifeways and products are rewritten and transformed by these demands as particular themes come to identify the island within the global market (see Tabani 1999). The relationship between tourism and identity works both ways. When visitors come to gaze, people learn something about who they are – or what they are within global circuits, at least. And *which* cultural differences in particular tourists choose to focus on become part of island identity. The 'tourist gaze' (Debord 1994; Hollinshead 1999; Urry 1990) is a form of surveillance – one that transforms life into spectacle. Culture is no longer a lifeway, but a product. A dance is no longer just a dance, it is a performance (Adams 1997; de Burlo 1996). Houses become typical examples of local style; kava becomes the local beverage; *lavalavas* (men's waist cloths) and hibiscus bark skirts symbolize simple island life. And the tourist gaze is infectious.

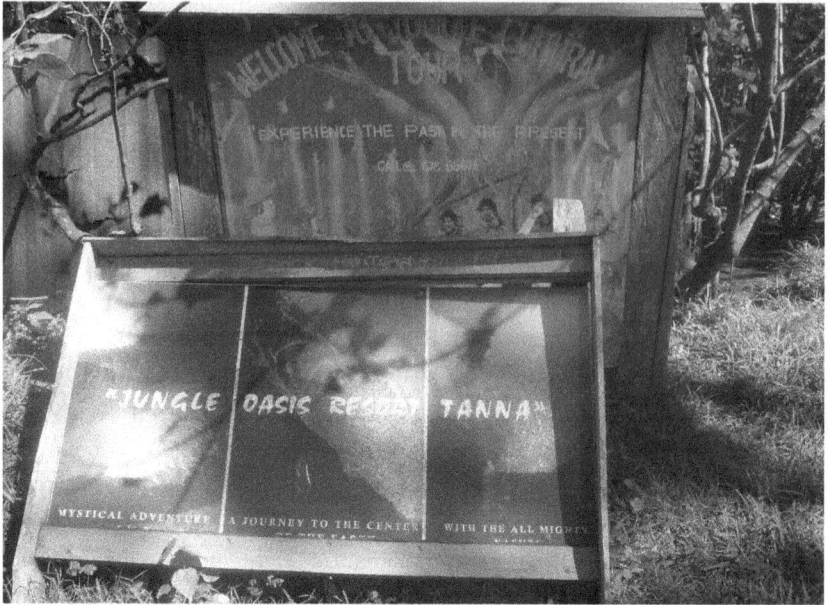

*Figure 2   Bungalow signboards – 'Experience the Past in the Present', 2013. Photo
by L. Lindstrom.*

Those underneath the gaze learn to look back at themselves according to how
tourists see them. People live, and they watch themselves live, in ways that
are shaped according to tourist expectations. Tourism remakes identity as
islanders now sell themselves to a growing flood of visitors as living primitives,
as jungle natives, as cargo cultists and even as erstwhile cannibals (Figure 2).

Tanna's traditional/neo-traditional 'culture' that tourists consume is
both real and manufactured in the sense that people nourish and protect
traditions partly because these can be sold to visitors hungry for the sensation
of difference. Islanders dance for reasons more important than money; dance
still functions as it always has to bring together people from two regions. But
tourism, too, promotes and motivates cultural performance, and islanders
have, for today's touristic reasons, become careful to manage their cultural
resources, whether these are dance, religious ceremony, art style or a cuisine.
They know that tourists will pay to see their *nakwiari* or to call in at Sulphur
Bay's John Frum rites. People manage culture both because it is theirs but also
because it can be sold.

Tourist Tanna

Modern tourism on Tanna began in the 1960s when Robert Paul, an
Australian trader working at Lenakel on the west coast of the island, built a
few bungalows to house visitors (Dunn 1997). At the time, a newly established

domestic air service – New Hebrides Airways – had begun to fly day-trippers to Tanna from Port Vila (de Burlo 1984, 1996; Douglas 1996). This service (later renamed Air Melanesie, which subsequently became the domestic carrier Vanair and then Air Vanuatu) was successful enough that an associated local tour company, Tanna Tours, was created to transport and guide visitors to selected spots around the island (de Burlo 1984:243).

Today, planes fly twice daily from Port Vila to Tanna. Air service occasionally also links Tanna with New Caledonia to the south. Most tourists fly down from Port Vila in the morning, take a tour of the volcano and perhaps visit a village or beach, and then fly back up to Vila that evening. Some, however, stay longer in one of an increasing number of small tourist bungalows that island entrepreneurs have established. Most of these have fitful piped water supplies and erratic generator-produced electricity. They attract only the most adventuresome traveller. Some, however, are tied into a developing electricity grid centred around Lenakel (Black Man Town), the island centre on East Tanna, or have otherwise improved the amenities they offer to tourists.

Island women and men earn a little cash in roadside marketplaces by selling passing tourists food and handicrafts such as baskets, mats and ritual feather plumes. In addition, some men work as taxi drivers and tour guides, driving visitors from the airfield in the west across the central mountains and down to Iasur volcano and Port Resolution on the east coast. Local entrepreneurs have quickly caught on to tourist expectation – where the cameras tend to point – and they sell to this interest in experiencing true culture and primitive nature. Alongside charging entrance fees to volcano and beach, they know they can make money with 'traditional' dress. Visitors, for example, purchase day tours of so-called *kastom* communities in south-west Tanna, notably the traditionalist supporters of Prince Philip (Connell 2007; Robinson and Connell 2008). In this area people make a point of their fidelity to tradition by donning bark skirts and penis wrappers. They returned to such *kastom* dress, so local stories go, in 1970, when encouraged to do so by freelance photographer Kal Muller, who was seeking more picaresque subject matter to sell to the *National Geographic Magazine* (Muller 1974; see Lutz and Collins 1993).

Bungalow keepers, recently, have also tapped into a tourist appreciation for sleeping in tree houses – a penchant that animates sightseeing elsewhere in Melanesia, notably among the Korowai and Kombai communities of Indonesian Papua. Tree houses, as Stasch (2011:80–1) notes, intertwine 'with the utopian otherness of childhood and of reintegration with nature, including wildness, animality, primitive archaicness, construction skill, and the dystopian nightmare of war of all against all'. Tanna bungalow keepers

Figure 3   Iapwatu in front of a tourist tree house, 2013. Photo by L. Lindstrom.

recently have thrown up a half dozen of these houses near the volcano, a style unknown in island custom (Figure 3). If they sometimes find it difficult to meet tourist demand for hot water, electricity or familiar foods, they can at least provide a bit of natural communion in the tree tops.

In addition to the attractions of seemingly authentic culture and unspoiled nature, some visitors come to Tanna specifically seeking cargo cultists. Most probably learn about John Frum after they arrive. Connell (2007) and Robinson (Robinson and Connell 2008), who surveyed visitors to several touristic *kastom* villages, found that few of them knew anything at all about Tanna, having arrived only with plans to visit Iasur volcano and to experience life on a generic Pacific Island. Those who consulted tourist guidebooks, however, would have read of John Frum, as these guides always feature the movement as an attraction. They mention in particular the movement's 15 February celebrations and its sacred red crosses. Savvy tourists learn, from these texts, a potted version of the cargo cult story: that the Tannese are waiting for the return of John Frum and the American military with its cargo ships. Like Toraja or Alor, Indonesia (see Adams 2006), where tourists also seek exotic religious spectacle, travellers to Tanna are coached to look especially for 'the rather bizarre "cargo cults" whose adherents await the return of a legendary leader bearing huge amounts of Western goods' (Ted Cook Tours 1988).

After 2000, when the movement split into several factions, John Frum events and sites became less amenable and attractive to outsiders. Tourism boosters moved along to refocus their marketing on Iasur volcano, the island's tropical beauty, and its *kastom* lifeways although they still continue to promote John Frum as a sideline. Air Vanuatu's July–September 2010 in-flight magazine, for example, alongside celebrating the island's 'ancient culture' and 'untouched waterfalls', promised tourists that:

> There are also cult tribes to learn about, including the Prince Philip cult
> and the John Frum cargo cult. If you visit on a Friday, you will be privy to
> the weekly ceremony when John Frum members conduct rituals such as
> raising flags and marching in unison, holding the belief that mimicking these
> American acts will lead to the delivery of magical cargo like radios, jeeps,
> fridges and other manufactured items owned by American visitors during
> WWII.
>
> (Air Vanuatu 2010:19)

The original cargo-cult tourist on Tanna was English naturalist and broadcaster David Attenborough. Attenborough went to Tanna in the late 1950s in search of a strange cargo cult (de Burlo 1984:252; Lindstrom 1990:116). He was after 'the chance of witnessing if not the birth, then the very early stages in the development of a new religion' (Attenborough 1960:49). In his associated BBC television documentary, *People of Paradise*, and assorted writings, Attenborough introduced two of the principal tropes of cargo-cult tourism: discovery and mystery. His popular narratives were among the first of many to imagine a mysteriously cultic Tanna (Lindstrom 1993). They rehearsed themes of simple natives who wait forlornly for wealth to arrive, rather than educating and applying themselves; of rascal cult leaders; of spirits, mystery and veiled cult truths; and of anti-mission and anti-government politics.

Such stories of strange Tanna continue to circulate widely in international tourist media, which have become the main purveyor of island information within global circuits. Tourist literature portrays the island's attractions as both strange and beautiful: Tanna is packaged up as natural paradise and exotic adventure. In this discourse, Tanna has become the 'Island of John Frum Myth'. And John Frum is the essential cargo cult; he is even a classic: 'a classic example of cargo cultism in Melanesia' (Trompf 1984:43). Tanna itself, when known abroad at all, is known as the home of John Frum. Its culture is now cargo culture. These stories are told in visitor guides and in articles penned by itinerant travel writers. An early handbook to independent Vanuatu, for example, boosted the cargoistic features of a quick trip to Tanna: 'Here one can climb an active volcano, visit villages whose adherence to non-Christian customs ways is devotedly maintained, observe the behaviour and paraphernalia of one of the longest lived "cargo cults", among other attractions.' (Douglas 1986:85). Similarly, *Harper's* writer Will Bourne described Tanna as a place:

> without money, without hunger, without work, beyond a little casual
> cultivation; a place where guava and the coconut fall ripe into the
> outstretched hand... Who John was – and whether he ever walked the earth
> under this or any other name – no one can say.
>
> (Bourne 1995:61)

It is a tricky business when one's culture goes on sale in the global tourism marketplace as primitive and peculiar. A New Zealand tourist brochure boosting Vanuatu's attractions, for example, elevates Tanna into 'one of the most remarkable islands in the Pacific Ocean' and 'an attractive add-on' to a Vanuatu holiday. It promises tourists an experience of Tanna's fascinating volcano and its 'mysterious cargo cults', concluding 'overnight stay or longer gives you the opportunity of seeing the splendour of Yasur Volcano at night, and to experience the primitive nature of Tanna' (Go Pacific Holidays n.d.).

Tanna is packaged as primitive experience. This island possesses the 'world's most accessible volcano' and also the world's most accessible cargo cult. Tourist literature uses the volcano to frame John Frum, and John Frum to frame the volcano. Each magnifies the spectacle of the other. Iasur is thrilling because it is the home of the mysterious John Frum; and cargo-cult mystery is heightened by eruptions of black volcanic plumes of ash lowering over the cultic red crosses and flagpoles of Sulphur Bay. Lonely Planet's *Travel Survival Guide to Vanuatu* enumerates Tanna's John Frum attractions:

> From Lenakel one can tramp around the island and encounter John Frum
> sights along the way – John Frum dances, Saturday nights at Imanaka,
> John Frum supporters at Lamnatu, the John Frum church at Yaneumakel,
> more John Frum people at White Sands, and at Sulphur Bay, the centre of

the John Frum cult, red crosses, Friday night dances, bamboo rifles, and
American insignia.

    (Harcombe 1991:141–3; see also Gourguechon 1977:316; Theroux
1992:192–201)

Happily for trekkers on a budget, Sulphur Bay is adjacent to the volcano:
'Since the John Frum movement emerged, Sulphur Bay people have often
said that John Frum is living in the volcano.' (Harcombe 1991:144). Abundant
Internet sites have come to supplement printed tourist handbooks and stories.
A former Tafea tourism website, for instance, offered a typical summary of
what a tourist might expect:

> The John Frum Cargo Cult. It's certainly an eye opener, seeing an entire
> culture base its belief system around the Gods living in the U.S.A. who are
> responsible for the 'magical' manufacturing of such goods as radios and
> jeeps, fridges and just about every other manufactured item that cannot be
> fashioned from the jungle or the sea.
>
>   (www.tafea-tourism.com [no longer extant])

These partial, often repeated stories about John Frum have become
'authenticating visible markers' of otherness (in MacCannell's terms (1976)).
Most are cartoonish narratives of evil colonialism, repressive missionaries and
romantically primitive islanders who march with American insignia and pray
to red crosses. John Frum survives due to 'the charismatic specter at its center'
(Bourne 1995:61), but 'the final irony' is that 'America isn't coming. Isaak [a
third generation movement leader] will learn eventually that he must scratch
his Toyota from the very soil he grew up on' (Bourne 1995:61).

    Luckily for tourist promoters, islanders most likely will not learn this
lesson very soon. Enacting cargo cults will continue to be a remunerative
tourist spectacle, useful for attracting touristic interest and dollars. Tourists
are invited to gaze at John Frum leaders and followers as a 'fascinating
cult' adhered to by 'deprived' Tannese endlessly waiting for Western cargo
(Crowley and Crowley 1996). Tourism stresses the visual. It packages up
culture and landscape as spectacle. John Frum is boiled down into its
most familiar and essential objects – red crosses, American flags and Iasur
volcano. No longer a suspect anti-colonial social movement feared by
colonial officials as dangerous rebellion, the movement has been now safely
domesticated, repackaged, reduced to a few essentials, and put on display
(cf. Kirshenblatt-Gimblett 1998:7). These narratives parallel other discourses
of international development that also create universalizing and stereotyped
representations of exotic peoples as passive, ahistorical subjects in need of

Western technology, education and monetary aid (Escobar 1995:8–9). Finally, the tourist narrative has remarked the serendipitous and pleasing effect of John Frum Americophilia. A BBC report, for instance, quoted American tourist Marty Meth, 'a retired businessman from New York, who had travelled to Tanna to see the festivities. "It's really nice to see Americans welcome here since in so many places in the world we're not so welcome these days", he added' (Mercer 2007:2).

Though the majority of Tannese today deny following John Frum, despite these protests their home is now well known as the land of cargo cult. The tourist industry has positioned the island within the global marketplace, minting its currency as remote, authentic, simple, bizarre, wild and savage (both noble and ignoble). Visitors today cannot help but read Tanna except in terms of John Frum, and John Frum except in terms of cargo cult.

Cargo cult(ural) tourism

Touristic othering is choosy. Not everyone or everything on Tanna succeeds equally as a money-making representative of either cultic exotica or primitive beauty. Tourism thus benefits some people and groups while belittling others. It privileges or threatens islanders differentially depending on their local position and interests. Tourism brings people, money, goods, ideas and sometimes disease into a region, and many of these imports can be seized upon as new resources. Some families benefit if they manage to capture revenue from passing tourists. Others, who live away from scenic areas, are thereby relatively impoverished. Tourism benefits certain artists over others if one particular art style comes to be known as characteristic of a particular place. It privileges the more cosmopolitan young over their elders, who then may complain bitterly about cultural erosion. It may empower men over women, or sometimes women over men, depending on the access of each gender to the tourist economy.

As visitor numbers increase, so often do political dispute and argument. Tourists' purchasing power may imbalance a local economy so that, for example, the slipper lobster catch once enjoyed by everyone now all goes into visitor bellies. But fisherman profit. Tourists in search of sexual encounters threaten existing social relations. But young men and women may be advantaged, experientially if not also monetarily. Tourist demands often unsettle the timing and staging of local festivals and ceremonies (Jolly 1994; see chapters by Henry and White, this volume). But local hotels, guest houses and tour guides benefit from these rearrangements, however troublesome. Visitors swallow strange stories about Tanna's cargo cultists, but John Frum and Prince Philip devotees profit by turning themselves into exotic tourist spectacles.

The history of Pacific tourism is replete with examples of industry-caused conflict (cf. Butler and Hinch 1996; de Burlo 1984, 1996; Hall and Page 1996; Silverman 2013). Tourism on Tanna has similarly sparked sharp clashes, particularly over money, between competing families and villages (Tabani 2010:322; see also Jay 2002). Islanders dispute rights to guide tourists; they argue about what tourists ought to be free to see; and they disagree over how visitor revenues should be shared. Most of island culture is not part of some public domain but rather belongs to specific families, and people quarrel over rights to make money from this (see Harrison 2000:676). John Frum supporters and their rivals, notably, have regularly fought over access to income from Iasur volcano. Visitors pay a fee (currently around US$35) to ascend the volcano and often also hire local guides. People from villages surrounding Iasur have argued since the 1960s about how this revenue should be shared, who should guide, and also about which families actually own the volcano. Numerous times over the past 50 years these disputes have turned violent as rival villagers attacked one another. Local leaders have ordered the volcano closed to tourists until tempers cooled enough so that a redivision of volcano income could be negotiated. Tannese have also argued about the propriety of charging tourists to attend *nakwiari* festivals. Tourists who merely watched a *nakwiari* festival in 1995 paid 3,000 vatu, but those who wanted to photograph dancers paid 5,000 vatu (about US$55). Some insist that *kastom* demands that everyone be admitted free to these feasts. Others counter-claim that tourist payments are necessary to support families and 'development' of the island's economy.

Iasur volcano and Sulphur Bay village, main cargo-cult stations on visitor itineraries (cf. Harcombe 1991; Stanley 1996), attract significant tourist income, which they generate significant conflict over. The *South Pacific Handbook*, for example, informs its readers to 'have exact change' when visiting Sulphur Bay (Stanley 1996:761; see also Crowley and Crowley 1996:155). A competing tourist handbook provides similar advice about how to compensate cargo cultists for one's visit and also some rough souvenir price guides: 'Wait at the entrance to Sulphur Bay village. Someone will invite you in and show you around... Grass skirts sell here for about 400 VT.' (Harcombe 1991:142). Touristic Tanna thus combines primitive adventure with bargain-basement exotic-shopping opportunities. This is all to the good, except when tourist flows set off local conflicts over money and over the objects and spectacles, including John Frum ritual, that tourists wish to consume.

John Frum and *kastom* have been at the centre of this sort of local conflict since the 1960s, when visitors became a regular aspect of life on Tanna (de Burlo 1984; Douglas 1996; Tabani 2010). Although local entrepreneurs have developed tourist bungalows and tour-guide businesses, other islanders refuse to cooperate with their efforts. Lonely Planet's *Travel Survival Kit* for Vanuatu, for example, warns that 'Camping is banned in Tanna. However, there are some leaf houses used by villagers at Sulphur Bay and Ireupuow [Port Resolution] where local people may let you stay.' It goes on to note:

> There's a fair amount of rivalry between different villages as to who gets the tourist dollar. Accordingly, 'unescorted' tours by foreign visitors are strictly prohibited by the Tafea [local government] Council. So you may need to be rather discrete on Tanna, if independent travel is more your style.
>
> (Harcombe 1991:137)

Tourists, and their cash, are unevenly distributed and this produces new sorts of inequality. People who live in many parts of the island have tried to develop tourist attractions with variable success. More and more visitors have begun to make their way to Port Resolution on the east coast, where they stay in local guesthouses and, previously, swam with a tame dugong when this was alive. Nearer the volcano, however, other entrepreneurs failed to attract tourists to visit a lava tube and bat cave on their land. On the south-eastern coast, one local entrepreneur erected a sign offering to show unique rock formations to the very occasional tourist who might pass down that road. Hardly any visitors, however, paid the 200 vatu fee requested to see these remarkable stones, as few venture much beyond the airport and government centre (Black Man Town or Lenakel) in the west, or the volcano, Sulphur Bay and Port Resolution in the east.

Global tourist currencies set the value of this or that locality or village (Comaroff and Comaroff 2009:18–21). While Tannese people presume that visitors ought to be interested in places that are locally important – such as where the spirit Mwatiktiki left his petrified remains or a mythically significant waterfall – tourists, in fact, may be bored by these unspectacular sights. Instead, they seek out venues associated with the sort of exotic other they desire – places such as Sulphur Bay, cargo-cult headquarters and Iasur volcano, an epitome of primitive, mysterious, dangerous, although beautiful nature.

Nowadays, tourism is a ubiquitous aspect of the cultural landscape of Tanna. It is an increasingly significant part of the island economy and everyday life. Previously, travel to foreign places was the main means by which islanders accessed external information; today, tourists carry ideas and images directly onto the island. Tourism challenges and rebalances the island's political arena. People perceive increasing flows of visitors as both an economic opportunity and a growing social problem. They welcome tourists but, like any of us might, demand to preserve a cultural and social space in which they may live their lives away from the touristic gaze. Tourism, like economic development at large, generates alternate and often opposing responses (see Sahlins 1992). Some, including both customary and John Frum partisans, reason that although tourism brings resources, information and connections to their island, it is far less important than their everyday exchange relationships and local political allegiances. Others, who sense that their economic futures will depend significantly on cash, are more willing to welcome and profit from the island's growing numbers of visitors. Those Tannese who reject or withdraw from touristic dealings, however, still must deal with their local impacts and ultimately with the new global imaginings about their island that tourism is promoting.

Tannese culture and landscape are on sale in the tourist marketplace as the 'cargo cult island', the home of John Frum myth. Visitors arrive and point their cameras at what they see as strange and exotic cargo cultists or ancient, unchanging *kastom*. The currencies of the global marketplace have fixed Tanna's exchange value. Tanna has touristic value principally as the home of an active volcano, *kastom* lifeways and active cargo cultists. Tourist narratives which define and broadcast the truth of Tanna as other will not entirely silence island notions of self. But the Tannese, including *soi-disant* John Frum cargo cultists, are increasingly subject to a powerful, global tourism discourse that hijacks local understandings of self.

Acknowledgements

I worked on an early draft of this chapter with Charles (Chuck) de Burlo before his untimely death in 2005, and I acknowledge his enthusiasm and his input. The chapter also draws partly on several previous publications, including Lindstrom 1997 and 2001. I thank Kun-hui Ku and the participants of the May 2008 Austronesian Workshop at National Tsinghua University, Taiwan, for comments on the paper, and also several anonymous reviewers.

References

Adams, K.M. 1997. Ethnic tourism and the renegotiation of tradition in Tana Toraja (Sulawesi, Indonesia). *Ethnology* 36:309–20.

——— 2006. *Art as Politics: Re-crafting Identities, Tourism, and Power in Tana Toraja, Indonesia.* Honolulu: University of Hawai'i Press.

Air Vanuatu 2010. Around + about. *Island Spirit* 51 (July–September):18–19.

Appadurai, A. 2006. *Fear of Small Numbers: An Essay on the Geography of Anger.* Durham: Duke University Press.

Attenborough, D. 1960. *People of Paradise.* New York: Harper Brothers.

Baylis, M. 2013. *Man Belong Mrs Queen: My South Sea Adventures with the Philip Worshippers.* Brecon, UK: Old Street Publishing.

Bonnemaison, J. 1994. *The Tree and the Canoe: History and Ethnogeography of Tanna.* Honolulu: University of Hawai'i Press.

Bourne, W. 1995. The gospel according to Prum: a curious tale of power, prophecy, and cargo in the South Pacific. *Harper's Magazine* (January):60–71.

Butler R. and T. Hinch 1996. *Tourism and Indigenous Peoples.* London: International Thomson Business Press.

Comaroff, J.L. and J. Comaroff 2009. *Ethnicity, Inc.* Chicago: University of Chicago Press.

Connell, J. 2007. The continuity of custom? Tourist perceptions of authenticity in Yakel Village, Tanna, Vanuatu. *Journal of Tourism and Cultural Change* 5:71–86.

Crowley, D.J. and M.L. Crowley 1996. Religion and politics in the John Frum festival of Tanna Island, Vanuatu. *Journal of Folklore Research* 33:155–64.

de Burlo, C. 1984. Indigenous response and participation in tourism in a Southwest Pacific Island nation, Vanuatu, Ph.D. dissertation, Syracuse University.

——— 1996. Vanuatu. In *Tourism in the Pacific: Issues and Cases,* C. Michael Hall and S.J. Page (eds), 235–55. London: International Thomson Business Press.

——— 2003. Tourism, conservation, and the cultural environment in rural Vanuatu. In *Pacific Island Tourism,* David Harrison (ed.), 65–81. Elmsford, NY: Cognizant Communications Corporation.

Debord, G. 1994. *Society of the Spectacle.* New York: Zone Books.

Desmond, J.C. 1999. *Staging Tourism: Bodies on Display from Waikiki to Sea World.* Chicago: University of Chicago Press.

Douglas, N. 1996. *They Came for Savages: 100 Years of Tourism in Melanesia.* Australia: Southern Cross University Press.

Douglas, N. 1986. *Vanuatu: A Guide.* Sydney: Pacific Publications.

Dunn, M. 1997. *Pandemonium or Paradise? Kath and Bob Paul in the New Hebrides 1946–1980.* Bathurst, NSW: Crawford House.

Escobar, A. 1995. *Encountering Development: The Making and Unmaking of the Third World.* Princeton: Princeton University Press.

Go Pacific Holidays n.d. Go Vanuatu (brochure). Auckland: Go Pacific Holidays.

Gourguechon, C. 1977. *Journey to the End of the World: A Three Year Adventure in the New Hebrides.* New York: Scribner.

Guiart, J. 1956. *Un siècle et demi de contacts culturels à Tanna, Nouvelles-Hébrides.* Paris: Musée de l'Homme.

——— 1975. Le Mouvement 'Four Corner' à Tanna (1974). *Journal de la Société des Océanistes* 46:107–11.

Hall, C. M. 1994. Tourism in Pacific Island microstates: a case study of Vanuatu. *Tourism Recreation Research* 19(1):49–58.

Hall, C.M. and S.J. Page (eds.) 1996. *Tourism in the Pacific: Issues and Cases.* London: International Thomson Business Press.

Harcombe, D. 1991. *Vanuatu: A Travel Survival Guide.* Hawthorne (Australia): Lonely Planet Publications.

Harrison, S. 2000. Prestige goods to legacies: property and the objectification of culture in Melanesia. *Comparative Studies in Society and History* 42:662–79.

Herzfeld, M. 2004. *The Body Impolitic: Artisans and Artifice in the Global Hierarchy of Value.* Chicago: University of Chicago Press.

Hollinshead, K. 1999. Surveillance of the worlds of tourism: Foucault and the eye-of-power. *Tourism Management* 20:7–23.

Hutnyk, J. 1999. Magical mystical tourism. In *Travel Worlds: Journeys in Contemporary Cultural Politics*, R. Kaur and J. Hutnyk (eds), 94–119. London: Zed Books.

Jay, M. 2002. The last cargo cult. *Nthposition* (blog), http://www.nthposition.com/thelastcargo.php (accessed 2 November 2013).

Jolly, M. 1994. Kastom as commodity: the land dive as indigenous rite and tourist spectacle in Vanuatu. In *Culture, Kastom, Tradition: Developing Cultural Policy in Melanesia*, L. Lindstrom and G.M. White (eds.), 131–46. Suva: Institute of Pacific Studies, University of the South Pacific.

Kanemasu, Y. 2008. Weapons of the workers: employees in the Fiji Hotel Scene'. In *Tourism at the Grassroots: Villagers and Visitors in the Asia-Pacific*, J. Connell and B. Rugendyke (eds), 114–30. London and New York: Routledge.

Kirshenblatt-Gimblett, B. 1998. *Destination Culture. Tourism, Museums and Heritage.* Berkeley, CA: University of California Press.

Lindstrom, L. 1990. *Knowledge and Power in a South Pacific Society.* Washington, DC: Smithsonian Institution Press.

——— 1993. *Cargo Cult: Strange Stories of Desire from Melanesia and Beyond.* Honolulu: University of Hawai'i Press.

——— 1997. Cultural tourism in the Pacific. *South Pacific Study*, 18(1): 33–45.

——— 2001. The Tannese. In *Endangered Peoples of Oceania: Struggles to Survive and Thrive*, J. Fitzpatrick (ed.), 183–96. Westport, CT: Greenwood Press.

——— 2004. Cargo Cult at the third millennium. In *Cargo Cult & Culture Critique*, H. Jebens (ed.), 15–35. Honolulu: University of Hawaii Press.

——— 2007a. A body of postcards from Vanuatu. In *Embodying Modernity and Postmodernity in Melanesia*, S. Bamford (ed.), 257–82. Durham: Carolina University Press.

——— 2007b. Survivor Vanuatu: myths of matriarchy revisited. *The Contemporary Pacific* 19:162–74.

Lindstrom, L. and G.M. White (eds) 1994. *Culture, Kastom, Tradition: Developing Cultural Policy in Melanesia.* Suva: Institute of Pacific Studies, University of the South Pacific.

Lutz, C.A. and J.L. Collins 1993. *Reading National Geographic.* Chicago: University of Chicago Press.

MacCannell, D. 1976. *The Tourist: A New Theory of the Leisure Class.* New York: Schocken Books.

Mercer, P. 2007. Cargo cult lives on in the South Pacific. BBC News, 17 February, http://news.bbc.co.uk/2/hi/asia-pacific/6370991.stm (accessed 2 November 2013).

Müller, K. 1974. Tanna awaits the coming of John Frum, *National Geographic Magazine* 145:706–15.

Robertson, R. 1995. Glocalization: time-space and homogeneity-heterogeneity'. In *Global Modernities,* M. Featherstone, S. Lash and R. Robertson (eds.), 25–44. London: Sage.

Robinson, P. and J. Connell 2008. 'Everything is truthful here': custom village tourism in Tanna, Vanuatu'. In *Tourism at the Grassroots: Villagers and Visitors in the Asia-Pacific,* J. Connell and B. Rugendyke (eds.), 77–97. London and New York: Routledge.

Sahlins, M. 1992. The economics of develop-man in the Pacific. *Res* 21:13–25.

——— 1999. Two or three things I know about culture. *Journal of the Royal Anthropological Institute* 5:399–421.

Silverman, E.K. 2013. After *Cannibal Tours*: cargoism and marginality in a post-touristic Sepik River society. *The Contemporary Pacific* 25:221–57.

Stanley, D. 1996. *South Pacific Handbook.* Chico, CA: Moon Publications.

Stanley, N. 1998. *Being Ourselves for You: The Global Display of Cultures.* London: Middlesex University Press.

Stasch, R. 2011. The camera and the house: the semiotics of New Guinea 'tree houses'. *Comparative Studies in Society and History* 53(1):75–112.

Tabani, M. 1999. *Kastom* et traditionalisme: quelles inventions pour quelles traditions à Tanna (Vanuatu). *Journal de la Société des Océanistes* 109(2):121–31.

——— 2008. *Une pirogue pour le paradis: le culte de John Frum á Tanna (Vanuatu).* Paris: Éditions de la Maison des Sciences de l'Homme.

——— 2010. The carnival of custom: land dives, millenarian parades and other spectacular ritualizations in Vanuatu. *Oceania* 80:309–28.

Tanna Beach Resort n.d.. Tanna Island: Republic of Vanuatu (brochure). Tanna: Tanna Beach Resort.

Ted Cook Tours 1988. *Tanna tours* (brochure). Port Vila: Ted Cook Tours.

Theroux, P. 1992. *The Happy Isles of Oceania: Paddling the Pacific.* New York: G. P. Putnam's Sons.

Tourism Council of the South Pacific 1991. *Study of Travel Trade Perception of the South Pacific in Germany, UK and France.* Suva: Fiji.

Trompf, G. 1984. What has happened to Melanesian 'cargo cults'?. In *Religious Movements in Melanesia Today (3)*, Wendy Flannery (ed.), 29–51. Goroka: Melanesian Institute for Pastoral and Socio-Economic Service.

United Nations Economic and Social Commission for Asia and the Pacific 2013. Annual core indicators online database, www.unescap.org/stat/data/statdb/DataExplorer.aspx (accessed 23 October 2013).

Urry, J. 1990. *The Tourist Gaze: Leisure and Travel in Contemporary Societies.* London: Sage.

Vanuatu National Statistics Office n.d. Tourism summary (online). www.vnso.gov.vu/index.php/tourism-stats (accessed 21 August 2013).

Vanuatu, Republic of, n.d. *Third National Development Plan, 1992–1996.* National Planning and Statistics Office, Office of the Prime Minister. Port Vila: Vanuatu.

Lamont Lindstrom is Kendall Professor of Anthropology at the University of Tulsa.

CHAPTER 9

Coming together

Kastom, religiosity and scale-making in
New Ireland, Papua New Guinea

✳

GRAEME WERE

The term *kastom* has been widely discussed by anthropologists working in
Melanesia from the 1980s onwards (Foster 1992; Jolly 1982; Keesing 1982;
Lindstrom 1993; Otto 1992; Tonkinson 1982; White 1993, amongst others). In
general, the term refers in a quite abstract way to traditional practices that are
understood to derive from the pre-colonial past, whether invented, idealized,
imagined or revised. *Kastom* activities are often politically orchestrated, a
response to processes of mission Christianity, colonialism and modernity.
People may live their lives according to *kastom*, but they also reflect upon,
evaluate, discuss, modify and dispute it, and these interactions are taking
increasingly politicized forms (Harrison 2000:663). For this reason, White
(1993:478) contends that the term *kastom* should not be used in any abstract
sense, but instead applied to specific contexts to refer to pragmatically defined
forms of customary knowledge and practice.

In this chapter, I do not wish to engage with the general literature on
kastom. Rather, I am interested to show how, in northern New Ireland (Papua
New Guinea), *kastom* is a resource that not only underpins social, political
and religious identities as a form of what we might call indigenized heritage
(see Butler 2006; Rowlands 2002); but also how groups of religious adherents
perform *kastom* to conjure an image of connectedness to other religious
communities, on different scales, that allows for a flow of resources on a
local and translocal basis. This chapter – like others in this volume – will
highlight how Melanesians are authoring creative responses to social and
political challenges that emerge in the world, and thereby provides a regional
perspective on the types of religious transformations taking place.

I will demonstrate how different scales of mobilization and connectedness are revealed and made visible in ritual performance in northern New Ireland. Scale is important because, as Anna Tsing has argued, it is not a neutral frame for viewing the world, but must be brought into being and made visible (Tsing 2005:58). She states that to focus on the making of scale is to draw attention to key interests and alliances that this process mobilizes, as scale-making provides a space for asserting claims and contestations.

Recently, Hirsch has fruitfully drawn on Tsing's work in his analysis of the connections between national scale-making projects of the Papua New Guinea nation-state and the local projects of Fuyuge speakers of the Papuan highlands (Hirsch 2007). Framed within a discussion of forms of epochal thinking, his analysis focuses on the different perceptions of time involved in unique scale-making projects and the links between such projects. These projects are expressed in the form of connections between state development projects in the 1980s (e.g. roads, cash cropping, urban development) and the flow of Fuyuge resources (the appropriation of law and the flow of betel-nut). These connections, Hirsch states, are influenced by Fuyuge speakers and disclosed in various mythical narratives and ritual events, which also highlight how the Fuyuge speakers perceive time as epochal (Hirsch 2007:136). Projects of scale-making, in this context, rely on the Fuyuge orchestrating ritual events in order to magnify themselves and create a translocal presence.

Indeed, Hviding (this volume) demonstrates how a similar process of mobilization is orchestrated through the organization of maritime festivals in New Georgia, Solomon Islands. He argues how the spectacular display of a fleet of war canoes – which are raced at the festivals – captures not only the maritime heritage of the region; but also the ambition and political will of the Christian Fellowship Church – a rural social movement – to magnify its influence across Solomon Islands.

In the Nalik area of northern New Ireland, on which my discussion centres, the channels of connection between local and global forms differ to those of the Fuyuge. The visibility of the nation-state is weak compared to that of overseas missionaries, who have exerted a huge and highly visible influence on people's lives on the island, and continue to do so to the present day. I will describe how these missionaries have left visible traces on the social landscape, both in terms of sectarian tensions and a perceived cultural loss amongst Nalik people. In particular, I will demonstrate how *kastom* is a powerful frame for reworking the past through a political mobilization of identity and difference. But I will also argue that *kastom* mobilizes a social and political presence on multiple scales that is focused on 'coming together'. 'Coming together', I will demonstrate, is a local expression for the unification of mission activities alongside *kastom*.[1] It is steeped in the language of unification, with Papua New Guinea pidgin terms such as *'bung wantaim'* and *'kam insait'* being used to express this form of unity. 'Coming together', moreover, is expressed most potently through highly visible performances of *kastom* that draw on a combination of ancestral images, objects and dances. One aim of this dramatization, as I will show, is to attract exclusive rights to resources on a local, regional or global scale. Thus, 'coming together', as I will demonstrate, can be seen to be rooted in an ideology that visibly connects people in New Ireland to networks of religious followers (and their resources) beyond the immediate locality.

The first part of this chapter will briefly outline the history of the Christian mission in New Ireland and the advent of the Methodists and Catholics in the period from the 1880s until the 1950s. It deals with Christian missionaries division of the landscape along sectarian lines and the consequences of this on local forms of sociality. The second part explores the conditions that led to the emergence of the Baha'i faith in the post-Second World War era of the 1950s. It shows how the faith destabilized sectarian allegiances by offering an alternative to Christianity and the opportunity for Naliks to restore ancestral performances alongside Baha'i activities, a form of 'coming together'. It traces the history of the faith until the present day, and how it embraced *kastom*. Beginning with reforms within the Catholic Church in the 1960s, the third part of the chapter shows how Catholics responded with their own competing modes of 'coming together' through ancestral performances and ritual object production. These restorative activities, I will argue, fostered competitive claims to what Naliks perceived as an authentic past and fuelled tensions between the Methodists, Catholics and the Baha'is in the region. This chapter ends by asserting how 'coming together' can be understood as a potent form of political and social mobilization, a dynamic scale-making device that provides the space for establishing the possibility of collective action if the promises of the future are not met.

Mission Christianity in New Ireland

The late nineteenth century to early twentieth century saw the onset of sustained missionary activity in New Ireland, with Methodists and Catholics vying to convert communities to Christianity. First the Methodists arrived, in 1875, lead by the English missionary George Brown. Shortly after, the Catholics followed, establishing their bases in 1881 and in 1901. The scramble to convert people led to intense rivalries between the two denominations, so much so that the German administration governing New Ireland instated a policy of zoning missionary activity on the island and on neighbouring New Britain. This policy of zoning – applied also to British New Guinea and the Solomon Islands – meant that missionary efforts were confined to certain areas (Hassall

1990; Langmore 1989). The result was a landscape divided along sectarian lines, with entire villages either supporting the Catholic mission or its rival, the Methodists. Allegiance to the mission was sustained through incentives. This granted access to benefits controlled by the missionaries, such as schools and health clinics, as well as labour opportunities on mission plantations. Thus, belief was prescribed by geographic location, in effect, creating a religious map made up of clusters of Methodist and Catholic villages.

The arrival of missionaries heralded the beginnings of religious transformation in the region, as they introduced and imposed a new moral order, often in punitive or heavy-handed fashion (Were 2005). Ritual practices associated with the dead, particularly the production and display of carved wooden funerary figures (*malanggan*) together with seemingly erotic, or considered distasteful, dance performances, were singled out by missionaries for censure as they were deemed antithetical to Christian ideals and sensibilities.[2] Carved objects, such as the wooden *malanggan* figures and the clam- and turtle-shell breastplate *kapkap*, both revealed during ritual events, appeared to fit missionary preconceptions of idol worship or warfare (when *kapkap* were worn), and were confiscated, to be shipped back to England and Germany, or to other centres of missionary activity where they served both as illustrations of pagan life and to reinvigorate the missionary process (see Küchler 1997). The absence of traditional objects and dance performances could thus be seen as a conspicuous sign of the strength of the missionary organization in controlling the production of traditional cultural forms and of the faith New Irelanders placed in Christianity.[3]

The disruption by missionaries of the traditional ritual economy also affected customary exchange networks, as the two were intertwined. For instance, missionary stipulations regulating marriage had a significant impact on historical clan alliances across northern New Ireland. Missionaries imposed the regulation that Methodists could marry only Methodists; and Catholics only Catholics. The outcome was while Naliks practised exogamous relations and patrilocal residency, many people wishing to marry outside their natal village found it difficult when their prospective marriage partner lived in a village under the control of the rival mission. Sectarian divisions meant that the reciprocations of traditional social networks could only be continued when allied villages or clan lineages fell under the same mission control, or when one of the marriage partners converted to the rival denomination.

This initial period of intense missionary activity made a huge and highly visible impact on Nalik people's lives. Some missionary centres based in villages earned a reputation for severely disrupting the traditional lives of Nalik people. For example, the Nalik villages of Lugagun and Fissoa both fell under the control of Catholic missionaries who earned a fearsome reputation for upholding a ban on *malanggan*. Missionaries outlawed all carving practices, so that during mortuary feasts carvings could no longer be displayed. This prohibition disrupted the traditional exchanges that were centred around *malanggan* and led to an inevitable weakening of the carving tradition. Many Naliks recall the names of carvers who fled the harsh control of the missionaries; others recount stories of those who faced recrimination or who resisted the prohibitions. So it appears, somewhat paradoxically, that while the Nalik people are some of the strongest adherents to Christianity, Naliks also blame the Christian mission for its destructive influence on Nalik culture and identity. By the 1950s, the Baha'i faith offered a solution to Nalik people's concerns over their perceived loss of cultural identity.

The arrival of the Baha'is in the post-war era and coming together

In the 1950s the Baha'i faith established a foothold in the Nalik village of Madina. Thereafter, the village became known as the birthplace of the faith in Papua New Guinea.[4] To understand why the Baha'i faith emerged in New Ireland, it is important to consider the social conditions that led to its emergence. Like elsewhere in Melanesia, the post-Second World War era in New Ireland was marked by social and political unrest (e.g. Brunton 1981). Dissent was directed primarily towards the Christian missionaries because, as Young (1997) observes, the missions made such inroads into the rural areas of the region that they acted as quasi-governmental bodies. To exemplify these feelings of dissent, Rodney Hancock, a Baha'i working in the Nalik area during this period, narrates how Madina's resident Methodist pastor left his post after unsuccessful attempts to coerce locals to conform to missionary stipulations (Hancock 2002). The resistance of the Madina people towards missionary control reveals feelings of resentment on the part of the Nalik population towards the missionaries who controlled the region, often with uncompromising zeal.

Further events were to unfold when a Nalik teacher Apelis Mazakmat returned to the Nalik area proclaiming the merits of Baha'i teachings to some Nalik *maimai* (knowledgeable men who orchestrate *kastom* on behalf of a clan they represent). Their immediate response was to invite Baha'i pioneer Rodney Hancock, who Mazakmat had met, to discuss the faith: its core teachings and its one-world philosophy. The senior people of Madina quickly recognized the potential of the faith to act as a modern alternative to Christianity; its tolerance towards Nalik culture meant that it offered them a chance to overcome their feelings of loss by creating a space for the revitalization of their own cultural traditions.[5]

By 1957, the village of Madina became the first place in Papua New Guinea to host mass conversions to the Baha'i faith. It had also established the first local spiritual assembly, a self-elected governing body that oversaw the running of the faith amongst local people. This local spiritual assembly offered a new form of religious self-representation and self-organization. Through the actions of this elected collectivity, Naliks could begin to imagine a future where unity between all the peoples in the world existed – the joining of Naliks with Europeans and people from other world cultures – a place free from fragmentation and rivalry, where traditional cultures could flourish. As a unification of world religions, it is easy to see how locals saw the faith as 'coming together'. The Baha'i one-world philosophy meant that there would be none of the schisms of Christianity or Islam; the Baha'i faith simultaneously endorsed the Christian god, the Nalik creation god Nakmai (as well as Nakmai's malevolent twin Marauli as the Devil) and the Baha'i prophet Baha'u'llah, as well as other divine figures referred to in world religions that the Naliks had heard about. Naliks could therefore embrace the Baha'i faith and build on their existing knowledge of the Bible. Moreover, the 'one world' teachings of the Baha'i prophet Baha'u'llah confirmed Nalik people's suspicions that the Christian missionaries had acted wrongly in proscribing traditional cultural practices.

The first local spiritual assembly resulted in the election of predominately senior Naliks – *maimai* and ritual experts – who, as the first convenors of the faith, were responsible for administration and religious guidance. Their role as religious leaders became intertwined with their political role in the village as arbiters of customary law (Were 2007). As the Baha'i faith was tolerant of religious expressions, the members of the local spiritual assembly were ably equipped to create a space to reinvigorate Nalik traditions through their expert knowledge of dealings in the ancestral realm.[6]

'Coming together' thus became a political frame for expressing the right to practice one's own cultural tradition while at the same time fashioning the self as a model follower of the Baha'i faith through the learning of texts of its most important prophet, Baha'u'llah. By invoking ancestral performances as a form of worship which Baha'is themselves possessed as memories, Baha'is created an identity of themselves as a religious community that thrived on integrating *kastom* into their religious activities. Baha'is expressed their own capacity to unite *kastom* with the teachings of Baha'u'llah through the image of a bird. The bird is a highly significant symbol in Nalik society, as clans – the principal element of kinship and social organization – are named after local birds. Two wings support a bird in flight: one wing denotes *kastom* and the other, the teachings of Baha'u'llah. To Naliks they also express a notion of unity and harmony.

'Coming together' manifests itself potently through Baha'i forms of worship. Baha'is consider the restoration of ancestral images such as *malanggan* figures and dance performances – which Naliks believe to be under threat of loss – to be a form of worship. This form of worship not only acts as a powerful expression of the Baha'i faith's capacity to enact *kastom*, it also underlines a shared understanding of beliefs concerning death and the afterlife. This is demonstrated in the way Naliks share with the Baha'is a concept that the body separates from the soul at death. Naliks believe the soul leaves the body at death and roams the places familiar to the deceased, such as hamlets and gardens, sometimes performing malevolent deeds. It is not until the carving of a *malanggan* figure for a mortuary feast that the soul can be arrested, contained and then released to begin its journey towards the ancestral world (Küchler 1987). *Malanggan* carvings thus act as tangible expressions of the Baha'i faith's handling of the ancestral realm. It is through the organization of *kastom* activities – considered by Baha'is as a form of worship – that Baha'i followers believe they are safeguarding their culture and identity against loss; but they also believe they are safeguarding the prosperity of their own soul and its place in the afterlife. This is explained by the Baha'i belief that God remembers each act and that it is God's judgement that can bring about the speedy progression of the soul into the afterlife. Through acts of worship, the Baha'i faithful are consciously caring for their individual souls and preparing its journey to the afterlife when they die. At death, Naliks imagine that they will reap the benefits of their ancestors in a paradisiacal afterlife; but crucially, in engaging in the worldwide community of the Baha'i faith, they are also reunited with the Baha'i dead from across the world. These benefits are exclusive to the faithful.

The faithful's intention to appear connected to the outside world is dramatized through the Baha'i New Year celebration, held every year in March in the village of Madina outside the Baha'i Centre built on the side of the Boluminski Highway. The spectacular event involves Baha'i prayer meetings and offerings carried out alongside ancestral performances. Baha'is from all over Papua New Guinea and Australia are invited to attend, as well as *maimai* and local people from across New Ireland. The event is extremely popular, and during the day, an aura of ritual intensity is evoked through the orchestration of dance performances and the display of *malanggan* carvings. Baha'is say that the ritual events – referred to as 'coming together' – are intended to draw people to Madina, to demonstrate to them the Nalik Baha'i's knowledge of the ancestral past and to transmit the message of the faith as a tolerant institution.

This has much the same effect as tourism in Tanna, Vanuatu, in Lindstrom's (this volume) analysis, in which he explains how local culture is packaged as a primitive experience, domesticated and put on display to the world. Lindstrom goes on to describe how tourism planners have positioned the island within the global marketplace by utilizing the ancestral as a source of economic innovation.

The Baha'i New Year event can be seen as a type of scale-making project because it is a way for Baha'is to present themselves on a translocal basis. The convergence of people and their subsequent dispersal magnifies the reputation of the Baha'is beyond their immediate locality and the Nalik region, to Port Moresby, Australia and beyond, to their centre in Haifa. Moreover, news of the event is also widely disseminated through newsletters and publications amongst the Baha'i worldwide community. This is a process that lies at the heart of their capacity to enact *kastom* to wider levels of visibility. This form of mobility on the part of the Nalik Baha'i faithful conjures up an image of connectedness to the outside world, intensifies their cosmopolitanism, and draws new converts in.

In order to further enhance this possibility of a spiritual afterlife with economic rewards, Naliks regularly make monetary donations towards the Ark Fund, a project Naliks believe will lead to the display of individual names of converts in a special temple in Haifa, the faith's administrative centre in Israel.[7] Baha'is imagine that once the world becomes unified under their leadership, the names in the temple will be remembered, ultimately enabling them to claim possession over any future spiritual and economic benefits that will accrue to the faithful. Many of these donations are made publicly at *kastom* activities organized by the Baha'is. Their actions are intended to make visible the faithful's connectedness to the outside world, by staking a claim to Haifa as a religious centre, and also to transmit the faith's message amongst those present. The act of donation (*lalaxau*) is denied to their Christian counterparts and onlookers – who would normally be expected to participate in mortuary feasts held in village hamlets (and not in the space outside the Baha'i Centre). The New Year celebrations therefore demonstrate the scale-making projects of the Baha'i faithful: the conjuring up of exclusive global networks so as to attract possible spiritual assets and resources open to those that have converted. It serves to demonstrate how the Baha'is had to imagine global networks before they developed the possibility of acquiring exclusive rights and privileges that are denied to their Christian counterparts.

Liberalization of the mission and transformation of sectarian rivalries

The height of support amongst Nalik people towards the Baha'i faith coincided with an era of change within the Catholic Church. The Vatican II reforms in the 1960s ushered in a more tolerant and liberal approach to traditional practices by the missionaries. These changes had a widespread impact on the people of northern New Ireland, and led to a more sympathetic attitude by

Catholic priests towards the production and display of *malanggan* carvings and *kapkaps* as well as to performances at mortuary feasts.[8]

An outcome of this liberal policy amongst Christian followers has been the redefining of the old rivalry between the Catholic and Methodist missions. Whereas a century earlier, the two rival factions had fought over the land and the people, the new era of tolerance and understanding established a new form of sectarian rivalry between Catholics and Methodists, this time over competing claims to harness *kastom* effectively. Amongst the Nalik, rival Methodists and Catholics each assert that their denomination has 'more *kastom*' than their rivals. By this, I mean that each attempts to perform *kastom* activities conspicuously during public events orchestrated in the vicinity of the mission building. Each declares the authenticity of their activities, its likeness to what they imagine the ancestral past to be, and how it manifests a new spirit of understanding between the mission and Nalik people. Such competition exists on the village level, as each village tends to fall under the auspices of one mission. Hence people in one village may refer to other people in a nearby village (and under the auspices of a different mission) as a place where 'no one knows how to practise *kastom*'. In occurrences where village loyalties are split between the two missions, then one finds sectarian rivalries played out along hamlet lines. Sectarian rivalries are also played out on a personal level. This commonly arises during ritual events that involve rival *maimais*. *Maimais* from a neighbouring village and under the control of a rival mission face derision from others who claim that they show a lack of customary knowledge. 'How would a Catholic know about *kastom*?' was a familiar comment that can be heard at ritual events when Naliks scrutinize *kastom*. By this, they were inferring that Catholics are brought up lacking knowledge of *kastom* because the mission hindered access in the past.

This new era has led to the assimilation of Nalik funerary objects alongside Christian burial practices as an expression of 'coming together'. For example, in the Nalik village of Fissoa in 2000, a place with a local reputation for harshly repressing the practice of *malanggan* carving due to the establishment of a well-organized Catholic mission there, a mortuary feast was held in which *malanggan* carvings were displayed on top of cement gravestones. One Catholic follower, after commissioning the carving of a *malanggan* carving, proclaimed: 'we too now have *kastom*', the carving thus acting as a metonym for *kastom* as a whole. Whilst heralding a more tolerant attitude on the part of the Catholic mission, the incorporation of Nalik forms alongside Christian gravestones raises important questions about how converts accept and integrate both new and old forms alongside each other into ritual events, and how these objects are perceived to achieve the desired ritual effect.

Figure 1   Catholic malanggan carving on display in the Catholic Church, Kavieng, 2000. Photograph by Graeme Were.

Catholic and Methodist reworking of the past is visibly expressed through the production of funerary objects in the form of carvings, pillars and shell breastplates. The three following examples illustrate how such forms typically incorporate traditional symbols and motifs alongside Christian iconography in novel ways.[9] My first example examines three *malanggan* wooden carvings on display in the Catholic Church in Kavieng, the provincial capital of New Ireland. The three carvings stand vertically, and incorporate traditional symbols such as animal, bird and spirit figures, as well as incised geometric designs. Two are painted in the traditional *malanggan* colours of earthy red, yellow, white and black, whilst the third remains unpainted (perhaps

*Figure 2   Pol Mandau wearing his kapkap with crucifix incorporated, 2000.
Photograph by Graeme Were.*

unfinished). Yet, when one draws closer, the carvings also incorporate human
representations. According to the Bishop of Kavieng, who I interviewed in
2000, these images were carved to represent the Holy Trinity: the Father, Son
and the Holy Spirit. To enhance the biblical feeling, the carving incorporates a
shining sun radiating downwards, reminiscent of a Christian icon.

While the Catholic '*malanggan*' carvings subtly incorporate Christian
elements into the overall design, other forms of Christian funerary art
offer more obvious transformations. This is no more evident than in my
second example, a clam- and turtle-shell breastplate, *kapkap*, belonging to
Pol Mandau from Lemusmus village on the west coast of New Ireland. The
kapkap is a traditional emblem of rank of a *maimai*, worn suspended from the
neck during mortuary-feasting activities. It is composed of giant clam-shell
ground into a disc, on top of which is suspended an intricately carved plate
of turtle-shell. The two pieces are joined together with a length of cordage

Figure 3   Carved wooden pillars in the Libba Methodist Church, 2000. Photograph by Graeme Were.

or shell money. The turtle-shell is carved into a pattern composed of a series of radiating concentric circles, each filled with geometric designs (see Were 2006). This example is significant because Pol Mandau's *kapkap* differs in one respect. Whilst the centre of a *kapkap* traditionally has a large central motif designed in the form of cross, Mandau's has a white crucifix of Jesus nailed to the cross attached to the centre. He explained his *kapkap* had originated from '*taim bilong tumbuna*' (the ancestral past). His justification demonstrates just how the past is reworked so that Christianity and Nalik *kastom* appear to come together harmoniously.

My final example draws on the design of churches in northern New Ireland. Many are built from brick and mortar, whilst others rely on traditional materials such as timber, thatch and bamboo. Like the previous examples, the interior design of many churches expresses ideas of unity. For example, the Methodist church in the Notsi village of Libba looks like any other well-funded church built in New Ireland. It is constructed of bricks and mortar with a corrugated iron roof. Inside one finds a series of wooden pillars, each with their own designs carved into the surface. The carved pillars are innovations of the interior design of a traditional men's house: decorative pillars would be carved with symbols and designs belonging to respective clans. The Libba church pillars also incorporate traditional designs: geometric shapes found on *malanggan* carvings run horizontally and vertically, framing large frescoes of depictions of Christ with adorations alongside.

Libba has a reputation in northern New Ireland as a place to find skilled craftsmen who can cut house posts such as these. Indeed, a number of men from the village carved the posts that support the ceiling of the airport in the provincial town of Kavieng. These posts are considered to be controversial as they display *malanggan* designs that are owned by various clans. Many of the carvers who cut the posts have died, and local stories claim that because the carvers received payment for their work without compensating their respective clans, the spirit of the carvings devoured them. This tale demonstrates how New Irelanders are not entirely certain of the potency of carvings, even when transformed into Christian forms.

These three examples of innovative forms of material culture are regarded by Christian followers in northern New Ireland as tangible signs of the tolerance and understanding that now exists between the mission and *kastom*. Many are sceptical of recognizing these forms as '*kastom*', however, though these examples clearly show the religious transformations taking place and how the past is reworked in ways that incorporate Christianity alongside traditional symbols and forms.

Nowhere are these innovative forms more conspicuously displayed than during church-opening ceremonies by rival missions, when mission and *kastom* now meet. Organized by the mission faithful, these spectacular ceremonies are modelled on mortuary feasts. Like the Baha'i New Year celebrations and the canoe-racing festival described by Hviding (this volume), these colourful events involve large gatherings on a plot of land surrounding the new church building over the course of the day. Local MPs, VIPs and dignitaries deliver speeches, and conspicuous amounts of pig, taro and sago are consumed by all, an index of the mission's status and wealth. The event is also a visible sign of 'coming together', as the activities incorporate traditional dance performances alongside a Christian service. The highlight of any opening celebration is a sequence of colourful dance performances, or what followers call *kastom*. Mission organizations hire dancers especially for the event. Particular credit is given to the mission for organizing dance performances that are rarely performed or once thought forgotten (as they heighten the status of the mission). Even though Naliks may treat these performances with scepticism (as they have not forgotten how missionaries once opposed traditional dances), the competitive nature of the church celebration is a reminder of the importance of *kastom* activities at such events, and the activities serve as a powerful visual and material sign for transmitting the faith as a tolerant institution committed to righting the wrongs of the past through 'coming together'.

While 'coming together' amongst the Baha'i faithful is a project aimed at securing connections and resources on a worldwide scale with its centre in the Israeli city of Haifa, the *kastom* activities organized by the Catholic and Methodist missions appear to be orientated on a different level. This is demonstrated by the informal exchanges that take place during church-opening celebrations and other activities organized by the Christian faithful. It is common to find 'bring and buy' and 'exchange a basket' activities amongst Nalik women intended to raise cash and resources for the church. These activities involve the pooling of familial resources (cash, food, consumer goods etc.) which are placed in a coconut-leaf basket and publicly exchanged in front of the mission building at a pre-arranged date. While the emphasis is on the corporate production of wealth through the pooling of familial resources, the exchange also stresses the production of new reciprocal exchange relations outside of clan networks as a consolidation of the Christian community in northern New Ireland. Hence it is common for Nalik women belonging to the Methodist church to exchange with other Methodist women from other villages in the region. These networks sustain a new form of belonging, whereby new collectives can be imagined on a localized scale.

This expanding localism helps sustain sectarian rivalries through the tethering of village, clan and personal identities to the shared history of missionization in the region. The significance placed on invoking the past thus places emphasis on *kastom* as a form of possession that has to be acquired and held on to, much like an object. It is through the visible expression of 'coming together' that the Christian faithful can assert their modern identity, which allows space for a renewed emphasis on revitalization, unity and sustainability. In this sense, as Hirsch (2007) states in relation to projects of scale-making by the Fuyuge, scale is both spatial and temporal in its dimensions. The projects conjured up by the Christian faithful are framed by the process of making visible connections to an imagined ancestral past (temporal) in order to imagine new localized economies (spatial) and thereby attract new resources.

Concluding comments: towards a just future

I have suggested that, on the one hand, mission Christianity is seen as disruptive to local sociality and antithetical to the ancestral past; whilst on the other, it offers a space for belonging through the tethering of identity to an imagined past that incorporates Christianity alongside *kastom*. I have also discussed how the Baha'i faithful seek to assert exclusive rights to economic assets and rewards through their harnessing of the ancestral past as a form of worship. However, in each case, we find that these actions are predicated on the need to redress the memory of past prohibitions on traditional practices through processes of selective remembering, and that these actions have redefined the sectarian landscape.

The point I wish to come to is that the cultural performances objectified as *kastom* and integrated into mission activities tend to serve as competing scale-making devices for defining a just future, a powerful metaphor for reworking the past through political mobilization in order to present sets of religious followers as networked, locally, regionally and globally. As Anna Tsing states: 'The scales they conjure come into being in part through the contingent articulations into which they are pushed or stumble.' (2005:57–8). Indeed, the fact that the Nalik people's past reveals a long and difficult series of social, political and religious upheavals suggests that 'coming together' may be a more deeply engrained and socially integrated strategy than I have outlined above. But what is just as clear is how these competing and intersecting projects of scale-making preserve a space for renewed episodes of collective action if the promises of the future are not kept. As Comaroff and Comaroff (2009) aptly comment in relation to marketing of the Shipibo community in Peru as a tourist destination, the ancestral is used as a source of innovation, a view that is at odds with conventional understandings of heritage, tradition and culture. This creative response on the part of Melanesians that I have described demonstrates how societies deal with events such as colonialism, missionization and global market forces through religious and political transformation. In this sense, 'coming together' is a metaphor both for belonging, connectedness and stability, as well as a vehicle for further transformation and change.

As a Pacific alternative to the relation between mission and *kastom*, I hope I have shown how 'coming together' not only offers a potent insight into emerging political identities but presents a more critical, subtle line in representation and mediation centred around redemption, the future and return, in the form of spiritual and economic wealth.

Acknowledgements
This paper has benefited from the insightful comments of Annelin Eriksen, Eric Hirsch and Geoffrey White.

Notes

1   This unification of *kastom* with Christianity contrasts markedly with the notion of 'break from the past' as described by Robbins (2004) in his study of Christianity amongst the Urapmin of the western Highlands of Papua New Guinea.

2   The diaries of Reverend Ira Mann (1919–41) and W.C. Groves (1932–4) reveal the often harsh actions of missionaries towards traditional activities in New Ireland.

3   Harrison (2000: 670) suggests that Melanesians may have initially treated mission Christianity as a powerful new cultic ritual or system of magic that had to be acquired in order to be possessed.

4   Peter Smith's introduction to the Baha'i faith describes its emergence out of the Babi movement in the 1860s, establishing itself throughout the world with several million followers. He claims the multi-ethnic background of followers is an endorsement of the faith's claims to unite all the peoples of the world (Smith 2008:xv).

5   There are similarities in the story of Tom Kabu, the Papuan Gulf movement leader, who converted to the Baha'i faith in the 1960s. See Hassall (1991).

6   It is interesting how those indigenous groups that have converted to the Baha'i faith, worldwide, often express their belief in traditional performances.

7   The Ark Fund appears to be a project initiated locally by the Nalik people.

8   From the 1970s, cultural revivalism is widespread across the Pacific region, especially in the context of political independence.

9   There are many examples of these forms of material religion throughout New Ireland that suggest the integration of Christian imagery alongside New Ireland traditional forms.

References

Brunton, R. 1981. The origins of the John Frum movement: a sociological explanation. In *Vanuatu: Politics, Economics, and Ritual in Island Melanesia*, M.R. Allen (ed.), 357–77. London and Sydney: Academic Press.

Butler, B. 2006. Heritage and the present past. In *Handbook of Material Culture*, C.Tilley *et al.* (eds), 463–79. London: Sage.

Comaroff, J.L. and J. Comaroff 2009. *Ethnicity, Inc.* Chicago: University of Chicago Press.

Foster, R.J. 1992. Commoditization and the emergence of *kastam* as a cultural category: a New Ireland case in comparative perspective. *Oceania* 62(4):284–94.

Groves, W.C. 1932–4. Records of anthropological research. PMB 611, Pacific Manuscripts Bureau, Canberra: Australia National University.

Hancock, R. 2002. *Longpela Bun Nating: My Life as a Baha'i Pioneer in Papua New Guinea*. Boroko, Papua New Guinea: National Spiritual Assembly.

Harrison, S. 2000. From prestige goods to legacies: property and the objectification of culture in Melanesia. *Comparative Studies in Society and History* 42(3):662–79.

Hassall, G.H. 1990. Religion and Nation State Formation in Melanesia: 1945 to Independence. Unpublished Ph.D. thesis, Australian National University.

1991. The failure of the Tommy Kabu Movement: a reassessment of the evidence. *Pacific Studies* 14(2):29–52.

Hirsch, E. 2007. Epochs of scale-making in Papua'. In *Holding Worlds Together: Ethnographies of Knowing and Belonging*, M.E. Lien and M. Melhuus (eds), 121–41. Oxford: Berghahn Books.

Jolly, M. 1982. Birds and kastom banyans of South Pentecost: kastom in anti-colonial struggle. *The Australian Journal of Anthropology* 13(4):338–56.

Keesing, R.M. 1982. *Kastom* and anti-colonialism on Malaita: 'culture' as political symbol. *Mankind* 13:357–73.

Küchler, S. 1987. *Malangan*: Art and memory in a Melanesian society. *Man* 22:238–55.

——— 1997. Sacrificial economy and its objects: rethinking colonial collecting in Oceania. *Journal of Material Culture* 2(1):39–60.

Langmore, D. 1989. *Missionary Lives: Papua, 1874–1914*. Honolulu: University of Hawai'i Press.

Lindstrom, L. 1993. Cargo cult culture: toward a genealogy of Melanesian 'kastom'. *Anthropological Forum* 6 (4):495–513.

Mann, Rev I.J. 1919 – 1941 Diaries and papers. PMB 630, Pacific Manuscripts Bureau, Australian National University, Canberra.

Rowlands, M. 2002. Heritage and cultural property. In *The Material Culture Reader*, Victor Buchli (ed.), 105–14. Oxford: Berg.

Otto, T. 1992. The ways of *kastam*: tradition as category and practice in a Manus village. *Oceania* 62:263–83.

Robbins, J. 2004. *Becoming Sinners: Christianity and Moral Torment in a Papua New Guinea Society*. Berkeley: University of California Press.

Smith, P. 2008. *An Introduction to the Baha'i Faith*. Cambridge: University of Cambridge Press.

Tsing, A.L. 2005. *Friction: an Ethnography of Global Connection* Princeton, NJ: Princeton University Press.

Tonkinson, R. 1982. Kastom in Melanesia: introduction. *The Australian Journal of Anthropology* 13(4):302–5.

Were, G. 2005. Thinking through images: *kastom* and the coming of the Baha'is to northern New Ireland, Papua New Guinea. *Journal of the Royal Anthropological Institute* 11(4):659–76.

——— 2006. *Kapkap*: the art of connecting in island Melanesia. *Journal of Pacific Art* (NS) 1:27–35.

——— 2007. Fashioning belief: the case of the Baha'i faith in northern New Ireland
   Anthropological Forum 17:239–53.

White, G.M. 1993. Three discourses of custom. *Anthropological Forum* 6:475–94.

Young, M.W. 1997. Commemorating missionaries heroes: local Christianity and
   narratives of nationalism in the South Pacific. In *Narratives of Nation in the
   South Pacific,* T. Otto and N. Thomas (eds), 91–132. Amsterdam: Harwood
   Academic Publishers.

Graeme Were is Senior Lecturer in Anthropology and Museum Studies,
University of Queensland.

CHAPTER 10

Gauging perceptions of heritage in Palau

$*$

STEPHEN WICKLER

The fact that Western concepts of 'preservation' and 'conservation' can prove inappropriate, ineffective and counterproductive when imposed unilaterally on other societies or cultures has been acknowledged and discussed for decades within the realms of both cultural (Byrne 1991; King 2004; Mathers *et al.* 2005; Phillips and Allen 2010; Smith 2006) and natural (Adams and Mulligan 2003; Chapin 2004; Meskell 2012) heritage. There remains, however, a need for more widespread recognition of interrelated issues that also includes the Pacific region (Allen and Phillips 2010; Torrence and Clarke 2000; van Meijl 2009). The imposition of Euro-American political and socio-economic control, and of projects conceived and funded by non-indigenous agents, has often been oblivious to local ideas about what should be preserved or conserved and how. The issues and problems raised by these disjunctions are widespread and symptomatic of situations in which foreigners and elite 'experts' set the agenda for cultural heritage and environmental conservation in non-Western states and communities.

Western-imposed divides between cultural and natural heritage have also been problematic, with perceptions that the two are incompatible, two sides in an unwinnable battle (Chapin 2004; Colchester 2004). This has sometimes led to exclusion of local people and their views from the conception and operation of environmental projects, which, again, can doom them to failure. These issues have been subject to international discussion since the 1990s, when they were key to the arguments between advocates of people-free and local-people-as-stewards approaches to African game parks (e.g. debates between Terborgh, Western and Leakey) and narratives of *terra nullius* or 'empty lands' (see Meskell 2009a, 2012). Similar problems have emerged in the Pacific region, as evidenced by the decline of many colonial-era museums (Stanley 2007), nature reserves and other institutions due to a lack of post-colonial public interest or support. Many places have seen a chronic failure of cultural heritage projects (see White, Regenvanu in this volume), and of many environmental projects, for lack of local agency within them. Ironically, many projects that outsiders fund and conceive as being for 'cultural preservation' fail due to their inability to culturally connect with local people. The role of archaeology in imposing non-indigenous scientific tenets embedded in the Western intellectual tradition for the 'management' and 'preservation' of indigenous cultural heritage has been particularly divisive within the context of ongoing decolonization (Lilley 2009; Meskell 2009b, 2012; Smith 1999).

In this chapter I explore and examine heritage issues in the Republic of Palau in western Micronesia from an archaeological perspective in which linking cultural practice to material culture is emphasized. My previous experience as a field archaeologist in Palau provided the background for field research conducted in 2009 on Palauan perceptions of heritage as part of the Pacific Alternatives project. The results of my interview-based research in turn provide a point of departure for an assessment of themes within Palauan cultural and natural heritage.

The initial section of the chapter addresses the theme of cultural heritage and the framework for what is known as 'historic preservation' (heritage preservation) in Micronesia and Palau. The role played by the Palauan Bureau of Arts and Culture as 'authorized' agents and 'experts' within heritage management is discussed and evaluated and is followed by an assessment of potential alternative models for cultural heritage management. The second theme to be discussed is the current state of natural-heritage conservation in Palau, where I attempt to understand why the conservation of natural heritage is of central importance in Palau while the safeguarding of cultural heritage is generally neglected and rarely integrated into conservation measures. Following the discussion of themes reflecting cultural and natural heritage, I highlight the perceived need among Palauans for increased awareness of cultural heritage, particularly material/archaeological heritage. Some of the heritage issues that the Palauans whom I interviewed perceived as having the greatest importance are briefly presented along with potential explanations for the general lack of emphasis placed on archaeological remains and material culture in general. The final section presents three case studies of ongoing community-based approaches in Palau that explicitly seek to increase the awareness of heritage and can contribute to finding more meaningful alternatives to the existing system of heritage management and control at the state level.

Background and research approach

My archaeological field experience in Palau includes archaeological mitigation work for several years following independence in 1994 and a project conducted as an independent researcher in 2000. During this time spent in Palau, my interaction with the local population and appreciation of Palauan definitions of, and concerns for, cultural heritage were limited. I felt it was therefore necessary to adopt a more introspective stance and critically assess my role as an outside expert 'manager' of Palauan cultural heritage. My intention was to reverse roles and spend time listening to what Palauans had to say about this topic, rather than dictating what should be done to interpret and safeguard the Palauan past. This is akin to the process described by Lilley (2009) as the transformation of archaeologists from visiting strangers to resident guests in the indigenous communities in which they work. A correlate of this approach was to examine the role played by actors within the heritage-preservation community in Palau, who can be viewed as the officially sanctioned indigenous experts on the theme of cultural heritage. Another related topic of interest, which had perplexed me for some time and I planned to address, is the paradoxical contrast between the high level of public awareness in Palau of the importance of natural heritage and far less developed appreciation of cultural heritage as expressed through material culture and the archaeological record in particular.

Despite its small size and a population of only about 20,000, Palau has a complex political infrastructure with a total of sixteen states, each electing a governor and legislature. This complexity is reflected in an affinity for bureaucracy and it is estimated that native-born Palauans account for less than ten per cent of those working in non-government related jobs. The population of Palau is undergoing a steady decline in the average growth rate, accompanied by an increase in median age and a migration from rural to urban settings, where seventy-seven per cent of those over the age of twenty now live. A transition from extended to nuclear family units with a smaller household size and fewer children is also ongoing (Government of Palau, 2005 census data). All of these factors are symptomatic of a steadily increasing pace of change that has had an appreciable impact on how Palauans define themselves and their view of cultural heritage.

During the course of my field research over a period of one and a half months in 2009, I attempted to undertake a broad assessment of how cultural heritage is defined, perceived and valued by listening to Palauan voices through formal interviews and numerous informal conversations. My primary focus was on conducting interviews with individuals representing a cross section of Palauan society, reflecting age, gender, ethnicity, occupation, education and socio-economic status. A total of twenty-seven videotaped interviews were conducted in addition to a number of less formal conversations. A slight majority of the interviewed subjects were men (n=15), of which most were between thirty-five and sixty years of age (n=12), followed by individuals under thirty-five (n=8) and over sixty (n=7). There were seven females in each of the first two age categories and two females in the third. Although a broadly based group of individuals was sought, circumstances dictated that a majority of those interviewed were Palauans with college level education living in the population centre of Koror. A number of those interviewed were chosen through contacts I had established during my previous fieldwork in Palau, but most were contacted through word of mouth during the course of my stay in 2009. Although individuals recognized for their traditional knowledge were intentionally sought out, Palauans with diverse backgrounds within politics, governmental agencies, NGOs, heritage management, education, business, health and culture were also included. Topics addressed in the interviews and other conversations included the importance of both tangible and intangible cultural heritage and the role of natural and cultural resources in preservation/ conservation. My intention was to explore and gauge the meaning and importance of concepts such as 'cultural heritage' and 'tradition' for each individual.

I found that a substantial number of the Palauans I was in contact with had a limited awareness of the range of material culture represented by the archaeological record. The perception of archaeological objects and sites as witnesses to the past and the importance of their role as cultural representations in contemporary Palauan society also appeared to be lacking or poorly developed. This was particularly evident for remains that are detached from oral traditions due to greater age or other attributes. During the course of the interviews, the themes that I had selected to focus upon were substantially modified and a variety of subthemes and related topics emerged. This meant that the questions that were asked in interviews varied to some degree over time and between individuals, making for a less systematic approach but also offering greater depth and additional insights.

The heritage-preservation framework in Micronesia and Palau

As was the case for most of Micronesia, Palau was placed under the care of the United States following the Second World War as part of the Trust Territory of the Pacific Islands. During the 1980s the people of the Trust Territory began to organize themselves into three new nations in 'free association' with the United States – the Republic of Palau, the Federated States of Micronesia and the Republic of the Marshall Islands. Palau entered a Compact of Free Association with the United States in 1994, when it achieved full independence. An American model of heritage preservation was initially imposed as part of a package for the Trust Territory during the 1970s. Although not specifically addressing cultural-heritage preservation, Kiste and Marshall (1999) provide a reasonably balanced assessment of the role played by American anthropologists in Micronesia and the legacy of American colonial rule.

Although preservationists within the system may argue to the contrary (e.g. King 2006), I and many others (see Hanlon's critique in this volume) would assert that this took place with limited recognition of, and input from, indigenous Micronesian perceptions of cultural heritage. The United States Historic Preservation Act of 1966, as amended in 1974, provides the framework for heritage preservation throughout Micronesia today and was the basis for Micronesian national and state programmes that evolved out of the Trust Territory system. Important adopted elements include the National Register of Historic Places and the Historical and Cultural Advisory Board. Actions undertaken, assisted, or permitted by the United States government are subject to Section 106 review in Micronesia. This review process includes the identification of properties that might be eligible for inclusion in the National Register, their evaluation against specified criteria, determining whether adverse effects will occur, and developing ways to avoid, reduce or mitigate such effects. As Hanlon (this volume) points out, the registration of archaeological sites such as Nan Madol in Pohnpei on the US National Register of Historic Places can be considered 'the ultimate colonial act'.

Funding for heritage preservation in Micronesia is administered through heritage preservation grants from the US National Park Service (NPS). One can question the appropriateness of a system in which the US Department of the Interior Office of Insular Affairs, a branch of the federal government that deals with domestic affairs, has responsibility for the administration of Micronesian affairs. The role of the NPS in implanting an Americanized version of the 'proper' way to deal with the past through supplying policy and training to indigenous actors is also a valid concern that has been raised in Micronesia (e.g. Rainbird 2000:159). The problematic role of Americans as experts and advisors incapable of understanding or respecting indigenous values and traditions has long been recognized, as Katharine Kesolei (1977) pointed out in her important paper on the features of Palauan heritage.

The Palau Historic Preservation Act of 1978 (Title 19 of the Palau National Code) upheld the basic framework for heritage preservation as administered through the Division of Cultural Affairs (now Bureau of Arts and Culture), within the Ministry of Community and Cultural Affairs, as part of the executive branch of the national government. Title 19 does incorporate some noteworthy modifications of the US Historic Preservation Act, including 'a strong program of support for intangible cultural properties and activities ...

to preserve Palauan culture and tradition in the face of *inevitable increasing foreign contact and interaction*' (emphasis added) and the importance of 'living national treasures' defined as 'individuals especially skilled or knowledgeable in the arts, customs, traditions, folklore or history of the Republic'. Despite these departures, Title 19 is still true to its original US blueprint and the funding structure for the Bureau of Arts and Culture (BAC) remains heavily dependent on financing from the Historic Preservation Fund administered by the NPS. Continuing dependence on US funding to maintain a programme whose existing structure is a precondition for continued financing makes it difficult to implement changes that reflect indigenous values and concerns.

Assessing heritage preservation in Palau and alternative models

> Considerable, widespread dissatisfaction with current levels and practices of historic preservation is apparent right across Micronesia and is consistent regardless of ethnicity, culture, gender and age. Organizations and groups that currently have responsibilities for preserving elements of Micronesian culture (whether by tradition or appointment) are perceived to be failing those responsibilities.
>
> (O'Neill and Spennemann 2006:540)

The assertion above is based on results from a project in which questionnaires were distributed to secondary level students and adults throughout Micronesia, asking respondents to rate the performance of those responsible in preserving tangible and intangible heritage. The authors also claim that the level of dissatisfaction with the performance of governments and their departments appears to be particularly strong, and that they are failing to support local traditional culture. My personal observations of the heritage-preservation system in Palau support the general conclusions of this study.

A brief review of the heritage-preservation programme in Palau under the auspices of the Palau Bureau of Arts and Culture (BAC) and Historic Preservation Office (HPO), illustrates some of the challenges facing heritage preservation not only in Palau, but Micronesia as a whole. One way of gauging the success of the Palau HPO is to examine recommendations presented in the *Palau Five Year Historical and Cultural Preservation Plan for 1998–2003* (Fitzpatrick and Kanai 1997). It is noteworthy that the senior author of the plan was an American technical assistant and that no follow-up plan has been produced, although a draft for a new plan was more recently formulated by an American on the BAC staff (Knecht and Kanai 2006). There has been only limited progress towards meeting the proposed goals of the plan, including increased training and education for staff, publication of draft reports from fieldwork, and expansion of the range and type of investigations being undertaken. The training problem is illustrated by the fact that there are currently no Palauans with a postgraduate degree in archaeology. Training programmes funded primarily by the NPS have had a limited effect on increasing the professional qualifications of the staff, and training often focuses on methods that are difficult to fund or support locally. Yearly site nominations to the National Register have shown no appreciable increase and few of the sites recorded by archaeological mitigation work linked to infrastructure improvement projects such as the extensive Compact Road project have been added to the register.

A variety of programmes to improve heritage preservation and the BAC have been implemented over the years with external funding. Apart from regular training programmes through the NPS, a significant number of technical assistance projects were funded through the University of Oregon Micronesia and South Pacific Program from 1990 to 1999. A review of the programme by Gale and Fitzpatrick (2001) concludes that projects dealing with heritage preservation, including the five-year plan for Palau, were the most successful and led to increased public awareness and involvement with cultural resource management. Fitzpatrick and Kanai (2001) also point to the numerous cooperative archaeological research projects to provide training for HPO staff. One of the most extensive efforts, the Palau Stone Money Project, contributed directly to an American Ph.D. dissertation (Fitzpatrick 2003).

Although there have been benefits from externally funded training and support projects, the guidelines and objectives of such projects are determined to a large extent by the outside agencies providing the funding in consultation with the BAC. The role of local communities in this process is minimal and reflects the heavily politicized nature of the BAC and their distance from Palauans at the grassroots level. Historic Preservation Officer Vicki Kanai (2001) warns of the danger of thinking that priorities set by the HPO should lead the thinking of the community, and acknowledges the dichotomy between expert-led and community-led preservation. Palauan BAC archaeologist Rita Olsudong (2006) identifies population increase and foreign influence in Palau as major threats to cultural heritage, and which the BAC is struggling to address with a limited staff and budget. She also admits that the BAC has an image problem and claims it is due to the dissemination of misleading information by outside parties, while admitting that community outreach could be improved.

Alternative models of cultural-heritage preservation

The gulf that often separates Euro-American and indigenous models remains an underlying problem in attempts to find a more appropriate and culturally sensitive approach to heritage preservation in Micronesia. It is also important to recognize that distinctions between Western and indigenous approaches must be nuanced as communities often select and meld elements from both sources (see Geismar 2005). Problematic issues include the importation of cultural-resource management concepts such as 'significance' that determine the value assigned to cultural heritage (Smith 2004, 2006). Although heritage preservation in the United States has made some strides towards accommodating alternative ways of seeing, such as the recognition of 'traditional cultural properties' (King 2004), it remains an essentially elitist enterprise run by experts grounded in a long-standing Western scientific tradition.

As preservationist Thomas King (2006:511) acknowledges:

... what made historic places historic in Micronesian terms was not – or was in only a minor way – what Euroamerican history said about them, or what Euroamerican archaeology could learn from them. It was how they worked in traditional culture, how they informed and maintained traditional identity. Historic places could not be dealt with in isolation; they had to be understood, interpreted, and managed as integral parts of ongoing cultural life.

Although this statement reflects a broad consensus of opinion, it remains antithetical for much of what Euro-American heritage preservation still represents in Micronesia. There is clearly a need for more locally grounded indigenous perspectives in which terms such as 'significance' as currently defined by American bureaucrats are transformed into appropriate concepts that are linked to cultural practice at the local level. On the other hand, traditional concepts of cultural significance that have become embedded in the ethnographic literature, such as Parmentier's interpretation of traditional Palauan 'signs of history' as 'physically manifested vehicles that bear culturally endowed meaning' (1987:11), are not necessarily relevant in contemporary Palauan society.

Safeguarding expressions of traditional knowledge through legislation can be one means of increasing the awareness of these resources. This has being attempted with a Palauan bill for 'Protecting and Promoting of Traditional Knowledge and Expression of Culture' (Senate Bill No. 7-3, SD3). This legislation proposes comprehensive safeguarding of traditional ownership and intellectual copyright for both tangible and intangible cultural property. Issues of cultural property and traditional ownership have proved to be complex and divisive both elsewhere in the Pacific and on a global scale (Geismar 2008; Smith and Akagawa 2009; van Meijl 2009), but the fact that Palau is grappling with such problems suggests an increased awareness of the need for an indigenous platform for cultural heritage and heritage preservation.

Natural heritage and conservation in Palau

Public awareness of natural heritage in Palau has been actively cultivated for several decades by environmentalists and local non-governmental organizations such as the Palau Conservation Society (PCS) founded in 1994. The Palauan conservation movement represents an internal, locally based approach that has enjoyed considerable success in obtaining international funding, and which has served as a model for conservation elsewhere in Micronesia. Unfortunately, a number of both foreign and indigenous conservation efforts in Palau have taken a narrow 'people-free' approach in which local inhabitants are viewed as an intrusive, disruptive element within the ecosystem and a threat to sustaining biodiversity. This approach eliminates the potential for a more holistic perspective in which concerns for both natural and cultural heritage are given equal priority. As mentioned, the privileging of nature over culture reflects a global conservation issue that has also been criticized in the Pacific (Bayliss-Smith *et al.* 2003; Hviding 2003). The global desires of powerful international conservation bodies such as the WWF and IUCN have been criticized for viewing 'community-based conservation schemes as inherently contrary to the goals of biodiversity conservation, which should be based on rigorous biological science' (Chapin 2004:20, see also Chapin and Flavin 2005).

One reason for this situation may be the necessity of catering to the agendas of the multinational conservation organizations in order to secure funding for community-based conservation. Conservation in Palau has also increasingly focused on large scale projects such as the Ecosystem-Based Management (EBM) initiative that commenced in 2006 as a response to infrastructure development, and construction of the Compact Road on Babeldaob. A proposal for a second EBM initiative cycle was submitted in 2009 (Babeldaob EBM Partnership 2009). The initiative was developed in large part by PCS with funding from the Packard Foundation and has been criticized for a lack of emphasis on cultural aspects of management.

The Protected Areas Network (PAN) was established by legislation in 2003 as an attempt to coordinate and administrate conservation areas in Palau. Although a 2008 revision of the PAN legislation (RPPL No.7-42) states that 'historical sites and cultural properties as recognized by the Historical and Cultural Preservation Act' *may* be included in the networks, the importance of cultural heritage is clearly secondary to natural heritage. There is also growing concern that the original intention of assisting and implementing the plans of state governments and community organizations has been transformed into a top-down political model which enables the national government to control the funding of conservation areas. The imposition of a 'Green Fee' on visitors earmarked for the management and enforcement of protected areas is one of the steps that have been taken.

The Micronesia Challenge is a political initiative launched by Palau in 2006 and signed by all the governments of Micronesia with a goal of protecting thirty per cent of near-shore marine and twenty per cent of terrestrial resources in Micronesia by 2020. Palau is well on its way to achieving this goal with a total of thirty-four conservation areas as of 2009, including eight areas added since 2006. This illustrates the pride and prestige attached to environmental conservation at the highest levels in Palau, in contrast to more limited efforts to integrate concerns for cultural heritage into existing conservation practices and the preservation of cultural heritage in general.

Recent legislation in Palau concerned with conservation has raised a number of issues revolving around traditional use of environmental resources and how this can be reconciled with a strict conservation approach in which cultural values and heritage are secondary to biodiversity. One example is an amendment of the Marine Protection Act of 1994 that was signed into law in 2006 (RPPL No. 7-18). This legislation enacts a complete ban on export, fishing, purchase or sales, receipt or possession of two highly valued and culturally important fish species, the Humphead Wrasse (*maml*) and Bumphead Parrotfish (*kemedukl*). The impact of this legislation was a topic of considerable concern among individuals that I interviewed and was viewed by some as an example of a lack of sensitivity to traditionally based conservation practices, of which Johannes (1981) provides a detailed description. In his comments on the legislation, the President of Palau also expressed concern that the measures might be too drastic.

Another illustrative example of conflicting interests between strict expert-led scientific conservation and traditional conservation is the approach taken to conserving mangroves in Palau. Although limited use of mangroves is permitted, harvesting or impacting mangroves in a number of conservation areas, including the Ngerikiil Watershed in Airai State and all of Koror State, is prohibited. At least four conservation areas are specifically designated for mangroves. This has led to objections by some Palauans, including residents of Ngerusar Hamlet in Airai State, that the mangroves are expanding at a rapid rate, as confirmed by monitoring since the early 1980s, and are threatening other resources such as breeding areas for fish on shallow reef flats. Paradoxically, one of the principle arguments by conservationists for the importance of mangroves is their role as nursery areas for fish (Babeldaob EBM Partnership 2009:10; Palau International Coral Reef Center 2008). Some individuals within this community advocate cutting back the mangroves to re-establish the situation as it was several decades ago.

Conservationists argue that increased run-off leading to siltation rather than strict conservation has created the situation that allows mangroves to expand along the coast. They also emphasize the important role of mangroves as filters. Another problem is that traditional use of mangroves, including clearing and maintaining mangrove channels and harvesting mangroves for firewood (charcoal) and building material, is no longer being practised to any extent. Mangroves were traditionally controlled and managed, but are now free to expand unchecked. There are also situations where mangroves have impacted archaeological sites and are damaging traditional structures, such as the stone causeway to Orrak Island, but are difficult to remove due to strict conservation regulations. This is a complex situation with no straightforward solution, but does illustrate the existence of differing perceptions of how natural and cultural heritage should be viewed and integrated within Palauan communities.

Palauan myths, legends and other oral traditions are often cited as a source of traditional environmental management practices (Gordon n.d.; Palau Community Action Agency 1975). Palau had a well-developed traditional conservation ethic that included use of a moratorium (*bul*) and taboos enforced by traditional leaders, as Johannes (1981) describes with regard to marine resources. This ethic is actively referenced by contemporary conservationists to illustrate and support their own agendas for protecting natural heritage. At the same time, it is pointed out that traditional customs were based on titled elitism contrary to modern democratic ideals enshrined in the Constitution. In my view the ambivalence to traditional cultural practices on the part of the conservation community reflects an internal conflict between privileging nature and culture.

Addressing the need for increased awareness of cultural heritage in Palau

The discussion above serves to illustrate the complex issues involved in balancing the concerns for cultural and natural heritage in Palau, and provides a fitting backdrop to the evaluation of what can and should be done to improve the awareness of, and concern for, cultural heritage in Palau. My overall impression of the current situation in Palau suggests a significant need for raising consciousness about, and awareness of, cultural heritage in its broadest sense. The greatest need for increased awareness applies to archaeological heritage and other tangible cultural resources, although intangible cultural heritage is equally important and vulnerable. The rapid pace of development and increasing outside influence is frequently cited as a principal source of conflict in the preservation of Palauan traditions and the implementation of heritage preservation (Kanai 2001, Olsudong 2006). This awareness is also reflected in the Historical and Cultural Preservation Act of 1978, which specifically mentions the threat of 'inevitably increasing foreign contact and interaction'. There was a general recognition among those interviewed that Palau has witnessed an increasingly materialistic focus in which personal gain is placed above a concern for traditional values. The pervasive influence of cash has had a detrimental influence on cultural heritage and traditional rituals such as the first birth ceremony and funerals. The importance of community and kinship links with reciprocal exchange and obligations are being replaced by market values and escalating expenditures. This trend cannot be blamed entirely on outside influences, as it also reflects attitudes increasingly accepted and internalized within Palauan society.

Potential loss of the Palauan language was viewed as one of the most significant threats to intangible cultural heritage by a majority of those interviewed. Reasons for this threat include rapid social change with a shift in focus from the extended to nuclear family, the influence of non-Palauan domestic helpers in raising Palauan children, the high status of English in the workplace, and increasingly pervasive role of television in promoting a non-Palauan lifestyle and use of English. A number of individuals also remarked that the influence of grandparents and other elders in passing on language skills has been diminished by the introduction of retirement homes that further isolate family members.

Although there was disagreement and uncertainty about how to reverse this trend, education was mentioned as a priority, as was the need for families to make a concerted effort to ensure active use of the Palauan language by their children in the home. Concern with the threat of language loss was especially prevalent among younger women with children in primary school. Legislation enacted in 2009 (Senate Bill 7-79, SD2) requiring the use of Palauan Orthography in the classroom reflects a widespread concern for preserving and strengthening the Palauan language, although political actions need to be socially accepted and reinforced. A lack of clarity and ambivalence regarding language use is also reflected in the government, where proceedings are conducted in Palauan but the written record is in English.

When asked why aspects of cultural heritage are not prioritized in a more explicit manner, Palauans I spoke with often replied that traditions are kept alive through internalized daily use and thus need not be portrayed as something in need of safeguarding or preservation. This is a deeply embedded reflection of the importance of social practice in which a traditional lifestyle is maintained through links to the land and a sense of place or belonging. The importance of sense of place in maintaining local identity and heritage is a hallmark of traditional Palauan society, and has received increasing attention on a global scale (Schofield and Szymanski 2011). However, the increasing distance between contemporary Palauan society and traditional culture requires greater objectification of what is valued and should be retained.

Some older Palauans expressed a concern that Palau is losing touch with traditions, which are being replaced by imported cultural models espoused by short-term consultants with no vested interest in the future of Palau. Some degree of scepticism was also evident concerning the influence of younger Palauan professionals born and/or raised abroad who have returned to the country and hold key positions. The term 'born-again Palauan' has been coined to express a feeling of ambivalence towards individuals who have not been born and raised in the country, but who feel that they have the right to instruct others on appropriate cultural behaviour. On the other hand, it is acknowledged that there is a need for highly skilled and competent Palauans with outside knowledge that make a conscious decision to live and invest their future in Palau.

The importance of local-community approaches to cultural heritage

A majority of the Palauans interviewed were convinced that attempts to increase awareness of cultural heritage had to be initiated at the local-community level with a focus on the cultural values perceived as relevant by the individuals involved. Political initiatives focusing on cultural heritage are viewed as largely ineffectual, misplaced and inappropriate. This is due in part to the greater social distance between politicians, particularly at the national government level, and people at the village and hamlet level. This criticism is also directed towards government departments such as the BAC.

There is a growing body of cultural-heritage literature concerned with the role of communities, and this includes diverse perspectives from within archaeology (Atalay 2012, Moshenska and Dhanjal 2012) and museum studies (Peers and Brown 2003). Smith and Waterton's (2009) critical analysis condemns the comfortably self-evident notion of 'community' that has become 'near-mandatory' or 'borders on a pathological compulsion' and is used to make heritage professionals feel good about the work they do (ibid.:12–13). In their eyes, this 'feel-good' rhetoric has masked the fact that communities are often split by dissent and bear the burden of uncomfortable histories. Although this perspective can be seen as both reductionist and rhetorical in its own right, it does address a valid concern and highlights the necessity of addressing dissonant heritage within communities. The complexity and multivocality of communities has been recognized and articulated within the realm of post-colonial archaeology (Gosden 2001) and also acknowledged by some members of the heritage-preservation community in the Pacific (Spennemann 2006).

In the case of Palau, Kanai (2001) presents an astute assessment of the plurality of views represented at the community level and of the need for a constant rethinking of the role played by archaeology and ethnography in responding to community needs. She also points out the ease with which one can fall into the trap of assuming that there is a single monolithic community within Palau. Plurality is the key to understanding Palauan communities that reflect a multiplicity of voices actively vying for attention. These include people from the outer islands of Sonsorol and Tobi, individuals with cultural ties elsewhere in Micronesia, especially Yap and the Marianas, and groups reflecting the colonial past such as Japanese and Americans. There are also major differences between cosmopolitan, educated Palauans and their more insular, rural counterparts. With these caveats in mind, I will explore the potential for community-based approaches to cultural heritage in Palau as an alternative to the current top-down politicized model in which experts representing authorized heritage are placed in a privileged position. Three recently initiated and ongoing examples of community-based action are presented as potential sources of inspiration for the construction of alternative models through which the awareness and perceived importance of cultural heritage in Palau can be augmented.

The baseball-field project at Tabelmeduu, Ngaraard State

In 2006, Governor Laurentino Ulechong of Ngaraard State proposed construction of a baseball field along the western side of the central ridgeline adjacent to the Compact Road in the vicinity of Ulimang Hamlet. A unique prehistoric site complex (Site B:NA-4:15) dating to around 500 BC had been identified at this location during archaeological mitigation for the Palau Compact Road in 2000. In response to the application for Historic Clearance from Ngaraard State, the Palau Historic Preservation Office, Bureau of Arts and Culture (BAC) initially recommended an alternative location for the development. Subsequently, a Memorandum of Agreement (MOA) was signed between BAC and Ngaraard State in which the governor stated that no alternative site was available. BAC then agreed that the project could proceed providing that archaeological data-recovery mitigation was carried out. Archaeological mitigation excavations conducted within the proposed development area in 2007 revealed numerous additional features associated with early ritual, domestic and specialized use between 500 BC and AD 500 and preservation of the site was recommended (Liston 2008). Despite

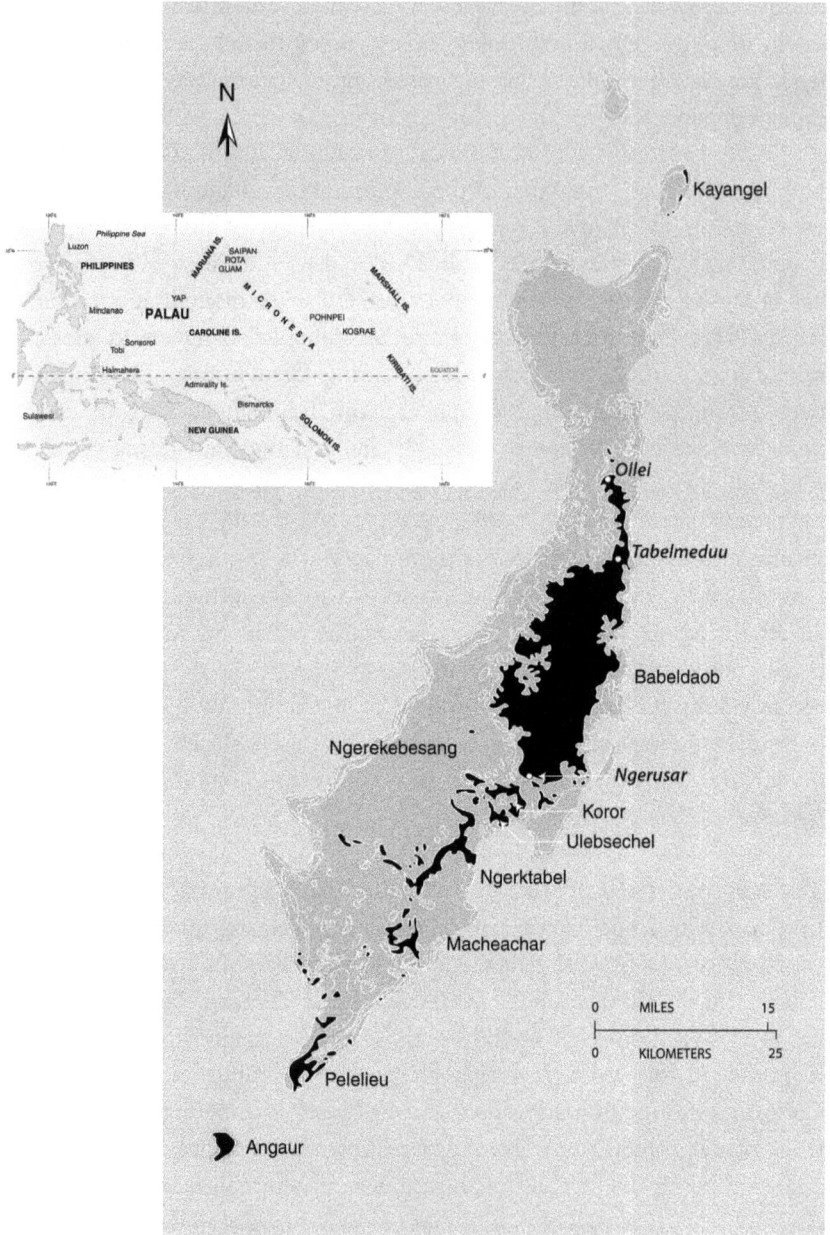

*Figure 1   Map of Palau showing the case-study locations mentioned in the text.
Illustration: Ernst Høgtun, Tromsø Museum.*

these recommendations, BAC approved the project, although archaeological monitoring was required. During the course of excavation, site tours were conducted for local residents and many others from throughout Palau that in turn attracted considerable media attention and raised public awareness to the threatened destruction of an irreplaceable archaeological resource.

A final draft of the environmental assessment for the proposed development was submitted by a local consulting firm (7N Consulting Services 2007) to the Environmental Quality Protection Board (EQPB) in which it is stated that the benefits of the project far outweighed any negative impacts. Interestingly, there is no mention of negative impacts to cultural resources in the document. A letter from EQPB was then sent to Governor Ulechong reviewing the environmental assessment and requesting additional information to substantiate the claim of 'negligible and insignificant impacts' and requiring that alternative project sites be provided.

A petition by local residents to stop the development provided the basis for a joint resolution by the state legislature to preserve the archaeological site at Tabelmeduu and force the governor to find an alternative location. Subsequently, a second petition was submitted to EQPB signed by a number of individuals who had signed the original petition in which the undersigned 'acknowledge our misunderstanding and signing of a petition opposing construction of the Ngaraard baseball field' and provide full support for the project. The accompanying letter states that it is hoped the petition will help speed the process of approval for the earth-moving permit. The question of whether this new petition was coerced by the governor is a matter of debate.

In November 2008 EQPB sent a notice of determination that an Environmental Impact Statement (EIS) was required for the project. They concluded that the project would have 'very significant adverse environmental impacts' with 'destruction of a cultural resource' of greatest importance. Changes in drainage patterns threatening the Compact Road are also mentioned. Given the considerable time and resources required to complete an EIS, it appeared most likely that the project would be stopped as of March 2009.

This rather long and convoluted sequence of events is presented in part to illustrate the manner in which heritage preservation operates in Palau. This case reveals the politicized nature of heritage preservation and the difficulty in providing and enforcing independent professional assessments. It is ironic that the EQPB, an agency whose mandate is to address environmental concerns, appears to be ultimately responsible for preserving a unique cultural resource. More importantly, this is a powerful example of how community action driven by heightened awareness can have make an appreciable contribution to stopping the destruction of archaeological heritage. A decisive element in

this situation was the efforts of the independent, locally based archaeologist
Jolie Liston, who excavated the site and successfully informed the public
of its importance through site tours and other community-based activity.
This case also highlights the widespread lack of knowledge and awareness
among Palauans regarding prehistoric archaeological sites in general, and
monumental earthworks such as those in the vicinity of Tabelmeduu in
particular. Due in part to their antiquity, the massive sculpted earthworks
that dominate the landscape of Babeldaob are excluded from the oral history
narratives and are therefore detached from Palauan cultural knowledge and
identity (Liston and Miko 2011; Wickler 2002a and b).

Ngerusar Hamlet sustainable ecotourism and aqua-farming project, Airai State

This is an ongoing project in the Rock Islands run by the non-profit
community organization Ngaraklasekl, based in Ngerusar Hamlet within
Airai State along the southern coast of Babeldaob Island. The project obtained
initial financing from the United States Department of Agriculture (USDA) in
2007 for ecotourism development (Ngaraklasekl 2007). The original USDA
funding was for $50,000 and an additional $70,000 had been solicited from
the Taiwanese government as of March 2009. Key project personnel include a
former staff archaeologist for the BAC, a local businessman, and an EQPB staff
member. The main objective of the project is to generate jobs for members of
the organization and other residents of Ngerusar Hamlet (population c. 200)
through the development of ecotourism and aqua-farming. The entire project
area, including two larger rock islands and a number of smaller islets, is
protected by Airai State with a ban on hunting and restrictions on commercial
fishing, and also includes the Ngeream Conservation Area which is focused on
the protection of mangroves. The project is also incorporated into the master
plan for Airai State (Airai State Planning Commission 2010).

A major component of the project is the development of a foot trail across
the island of Ngeream with interpretive information on archaeological sites,
flora and fauna. There is a wealth of archaeological resources in the project
area and at least fifty sites have been recorded in the Ngerusar region. These
include Yapese stone-money quarrying sites, burial caves, a pictograph cave, a
traditional village site, a stone dock and cave complex, and numerous Japanese
defensive installations from the Second World War. The second central
component of the project is an aqua-farm development for both clam and
finfish production, with allotments of land and marine areas to community
organization members. Small-scale ecotourism is planned in the future with
kayaking and interpretive tours. This project is a promising example of what
can be accomplished by competent local actors concerned with small-scale

development as a future investment for the community. It also attempts to actively incorporate both cultural and natural resources, which are given equal emphasis in the overall project framework.

The Ebiil Society, Ngarchelong State

The Ebiil Society is a community-based NGO established in 2005 that undertakes projects and activities promoting the protection and preservation of cultural and natural heritage from its base at Ollei in Ngarchelong State at the northern end of Babeldaob Island. The organization was founded by a community group that emerged through actions to establish a permanent conservation site in the Ebiil Channel, an important spawning area for grouper species. The principle focus of the organization has been on public education programmes teaching environmental protection through cultural practices. An annual summer camp was started in 2005 to develop ethnic pride through indigenous-knowledge training on the combined topics of culture and environment (Kloulechad-Singeo 2011a and b). Although the original focus was on local youth, it has since been expanded to include participants from throughout Palau and former campers are encouraged to become counsellors themselves. Since 2010, the camp has been divided into 'experience' (age 11–14) and 'research' (age 15–24) groups.

Archaeologists from the BAC have also been involved in the summer camp programme and directed the clearing of Kukau el Bad, a traditional stone platform, with the participation of the Ollei community (Olsudong 2006). Other activities included the identification of traditional village boundaries in Ngarchelong. The students and local young people participating in the camp had no knowledge of these boundaries or their clan platforms (*odesongel*), which also serve as traditional burial grounds, and were able to gain a greater awareness of their cultural identity through camp activities. As part of the focus on learning by doing, traditional activities such as fishing, designing and constructing stone structures, and taro cultivation have been emphasized. Although there was initial opposition from the Ngerchelong state government, who saw the society as a competing entity, there is an increasing recognition of shared goals for the local population.

Society membership is open to all and other states have expressed a growing interest in starting similar organizations and camp programmes. The society officers and board of directors include highly competent individuals from Ngarchelong with both natural and social-science backgrounds and a common interest in a holistic approach to protecting their local resources. The Ebiil Society represents another case of a grassroots initiated effort with a focus on local heritage issues and concerns and on educating local young people about their cultural identity. As with the Ngerusar project, it explicitly advocates an approach actively integrating a concern for both natural- and cultural-heritage resources.

Fostering dynamic approaches to cultural heritage in Palau

How can concepts of cultural heritage that reflect dynamic, living entities replace static reified vestiges of the past narrowly defined as something in need of preservation? As illustrated by the case studies presented above, it is necessity to situate attempts to increase awareness of cultural heritage at the local level in order to develop approaches that are relevant and useful. The plurality of voices in Palauan communities should also be viewed as an expression of strength rather than a negative factor reflecting dissonance. Archaeologists have an obligation to work towards involving local residents directly in field investigations and to inform them of their results. This has been sadly lacking in the essentially extractive domain of cultural-heritage management.

Despite its externally imposed Euro-American perspective and politicized nature, the 'authorized' cultural-heritage management system in Palau has contributed to protecting and preserving cultural resources and identity. However, much more could be achieved through increased legitimacy and influence at the local-community level. Locally based efforts within natural heritage conservation have achieved impressive results and could serve as a model for increasing awareness and engagement in cultural heritage. The incorporation of cultural heritage into existing conservation approaches would also provide a more holistic and dynamic perspective for preservation efforts.

Palau and most of what is currently defined as Micronesia have a unique history of cultural-heritage preservation practice dominated by an American model that can be traced back to the Trust Territory system (see Hanlon, this volume). Although this system contrasts markedly with the remainder of the Pacific beyond the American sphere of control, many of the same concerns have been raised, and the need for local communities to actively shape attitudes and actions regarding their cultural heritage is comparable to the situation in Palau. The importance of gauging attitudes towards cultural heritage locally has been forcefully articulated by my experiences in Palau and necessitated a re-evaluation of my role as an outside 'expert'. It is hoped that this chapter can serve as something more than a policy-based exercise and that the lessons I have learned may also be applicable to other parts of the Pacific and contribute to addressing some of the issues that are grappled with in this volume.

The Palauan case also offers lessons that can contribute to the broader heritage debates presented in the beginning of this chapter. The need for a more holistic integration of cultural and natural heritage concerns is apparent on a global scale. Palau represents an interesting variant of this issue in which indigenous actors within the conservation community must overcome ambivalence towards cultural heritage that has been dictated in part by a dependence on funding from powerful international NGOs and other bodies. Both cultural and natural heritage would also be better served by paying more attention to community-led approaches that are increasingly advocated in the international literature. The revival of cosmopolitism in a new guise that attempts to address multi-scalar engagements by integrating an overarching framework of global politics with the concerns of the individual and the community offers a potential alternate perspective to heritage (Appiah 2006; Vertovec and Cohen 2003). Cosmopolitan archaeologies (Meskell 2009b) are particularly relevant to heritage ethics and can provide a 'middle path' to addressing the issues presented in this chapter.

Acknowledgements

Firstly, I wish to thank Edvard Hviding and the Bergen Pacific Studies Research Group, Department of Social Anthropology, University of Bergen, for inviting me to participate in the 'Pacific Alternatives' project as well as the Research Council of Norway for their generous funding which made possible my research project in Palau. There are numerous organizations and individuals in Palau whose assistance was indispensable for my fieldwork in 2009. The Belau National Museum and its Director (now Minister) Faustina Rehuher-Marugg, the Bureau of Arts and Culture, and the Ministry of Community and Cultural Affairs were all instrumental in providing institutional support. My field research would not have been possible without the many Palauans who were willing to share their knowledge, insights and opinions with me in the form of interviews and more informal conversations. I owe a heartfelt thanks to all of you. I am particularly indebted to the tireless efforts of Julita Tellei, whose extensive network of contacts made it possible for me to gain a deeper understanding of Palauan culture. Finally, I wish to acknowledge constructive comments by Edvard Hviding and three anonymous reviewers that have improved the original version of this chapter.

References

Adams, W.M. and M. Mulligan (eds) 2003. *Decolonizing Nature: Strategies for Conservation in a Post-Colonial Era*. London: Earthscan.

Airai State Planning Commission 2010. *Airai Master Plan*. Airai State, Republic of Palau.

Allen, H. and C. Phillips 2010. Maintaining the dialogue: archaeology, cultural heritage and indigenous communities. In *Bridging the Divide: Indigenous Communities and Archaeology into the 21st Century*, C. Phillips and H. Allen (eds), 17–48. One World Archaeology 60. Walnut Creek, California: Left Coast Press.

Appiah, K.A. 2006. *Cosmopolitanism: Ethics in a World of Strangers*. New York: W.W. Norton.

Atalay, S. 2012. *Community-based Archaeology: Research with, by, and for Indigenous and Local Communities*. Berkeley: University of California Press.

Babeldaob EBM Partnership 2009. Utilizing an ecosystem-based management process to improve ridge-to-reef management of coastal resources of Babeldaob Island, Palau. Grant proposal submitted by the Palau Conservation Society.

Bayliss-Smith, T., E. Hviding and T. Whitmore 2003. Rainforest Composition and Histories of Human Disturbance in Solomon Islands. *Ambio* 32(5):346–52.

Bryne, D. 1991. Western hegemony in archaeological heritage management. *History and Anthropology* 5:269–76.

Chapin, M. 2004. A Challenge to Conservationists. *World Watch* (November/ December):17–31.

Chapin, M. and Flavin, C. 2005. Comments from readers and response from the author. A challenge to conservationists: phase ii. *World Watch* (January / February):5–20.

Colchester, M. 2004. *Salvaging Nature: Indigenous Peoples, Protected Areas and Biodiversity Conservation*. Montevideo: World Rainforest Movement and Forest Peoples Program.

Fitzpatrick, S.M. 2003. Stones of the Butterfly: An archaeological investigation of Yapese stone money quarries in Palau, Western Caroline Islands, Micronesia. Unpublished Ph.D. Dissertation. Eugene: University of Oregon.

Fitzpatrick, S.M. and V.N. Kanai 1997. Palau five-year historical and cultural preservation plan: 1998–2003. Unpublished report prepared by Division of Cultural Affairs and Historic Preservation Office, Ministry of Community and Cultural Affairs, Government of Palau.

——— 2001. An applied approach to archaeology in Palau. *Cultural Resource Management Journal (CRM)*, 24 (1): 41–3.

Gale, M.K. and S.M. Fitzpatrick 2001. The Micronesia and South Pacific Program – a decade of cultural resource preservation assistance. *Cultural Resource Management Journal (CRM)* 24(1):38–40.

Geismar, H. 2005. Copyright in context: carvings, carvers, and commodities in Vanuatu. *American Ethnologist* 32:437–59.

——— 2008. Cultural property, museums and the Pacific – re-framing the debates. *International Journal of Cultural Property* 15:109–22.

Gordon, M.M. n.d. *Conservation Practices and Ethics of Palau: Values and Practices Taught Through Oral Instructions, Legends and Proverbs.* Koror: Palau Resource Institute.

Gosden, C. 2001. Postcolonial archaeology: issues of culture, identity, and knowledge. In *Archaeological Theory Today,* I. Hodder (ed.), 241–61. Cambridge: Polity Press.

Hviding, E. 2003. Contested rainforests, NGOs and projects of desire in Solomon Islands. *International Social Science Journal* 55(4):439–53.

Johannes, R.E. 1981. *Words of the Lagoon: Fishing and Marine Lore in the Palau District of Micronesia.* Berkeley: University of California Press.

Kanai, V.N. 2001. Managing a plurality of views: historic preservation in Palau. In *Cultural Interpretation of Heritage Sites in the Pacific,* D.H.R. Spennemann and N. Putt (eds), 106–14. Suva, Fiji: Pacific Islands Museums Association.

Kesolei, K. 1977. Cultural conservation. Restrictions to freedom of inquiry: Palauan strains. Unpublished paper presented at a workshop on the role of anthropology in contemporary Micronesia (TTPI).

King, T.F. 2004. *Places That Count: Traditional Cultural Properties in Cultural Resource Management.* Walnut Creek, California: AltaMira Press.

2006. How Micronesia changed the U.S. historic preservation program and the importance of keeping it from changing back. *Micronesian Journal of the Humanities and Social Sciences* 5(1/2):505–16.

Kiste, R.C. and M. Marshall (eds) 1999. *American Anthropology in Micronesia: an Assessment.* Honolulu: University of Hawai'i Press.

Kloulechad-Singeo, A. 2011a. *Cultural Mapping – Republic of Palau.* Secretariat of the Pacific Community and Ministry of Culture and Community Affairs, Government of the Republic of Palau.

——— 2011b. *Teaching Indigenous Knowledge Towards Environmental Conservation: A Case Study of Camp Ebiil in Palau* (EIU Best Practices Series 22). Asia-Pacific Centre for Education for International Understanding (APCEIU), UNESCO.

Knecht, R. and V.N. Kanai 2006. Palau five year historical and cultural preservation plan: 2006–2011. Draft copy of report for department review, Palau Bureau of Arts and Culture and Historic Preservation Office, Ministry of Community and Cultural Affairs, Government of Palau.

Lilley, I. 2009. Strangers and brothers? Heritage, human rights, and cosmopolitan archaeology in Oceania. In *Cosmopolitan archaeologies. Material Worlds,* L. Meskell (ed.), 48–67. Durham, North Carolina: Duke University Press.

Liston, J. 2008. Archaeological data recovery at Tabelmeduu, Ngaraard Earthwork District, Republic of Palau. Unpublished report prepared for Ngaraard State. Ganda Report No. 2120–1. Kailua, Hawaii: Garcia and Associates (GANDA).

Liston, J. and M. Miko 2011. Oral tradition and archaeology. Palau's earth
     architecture. In *Pacific Island Heritage: Archaeology, Identity and
     Community* (Terra Australis 35), J. Liston, G.R. Clark and D. Alexander
     (eds), 181–204.. Canberra: ANU E-Press.

Mathers, C., T. Darvill and B.J. Little (eds) 2005. *Heritage of Value, Archaeology of
     Renown: Reshaping Archaeological Assessment and Significance.* Gainsville:
     University of Florida Press.

Meskell, L. 2009a. The nature of culture in Kruger National Park. In *Cosmopolitan
     Archaeologies. Material Worlds,* L. Meskell (ed.), 89–112. Durham: Duke
     University Press.

——— 2009b (ed.) *Cosmopolitan Archaeologies. Material Worlds.* Durham, North
     Carolina: Duke University Press.

——— 2012. *The Nature of Heritage: the New South Africa.* Malden, Massachusetts:
     Wiley-Blackwell.

Moshenska, G. and S. Dhanjal (eds) 2012. *Community Archaeology: Themes, Methods
     and Practices.* Oxford: Oxbow.

Ngaraklasekl 2007. Application for financial aid assistance for the Ngerusar Hamlet
     Sustainable Eco-tourism and Aqua Farming Project. Submitted to the
     United States Department of Agriculture.

Olsudong, R. 2006. Cultural heritage and communities in Palau. *Micronesian Journal
     of the Humanities and Social Sciences* 5 (1/2):547–55.

O'Neill, J. and D.H.R. Spennemann 2006. Perceptions of Micronesians on the
     effectiveness of the historic preservation programs. *Micronesian Journal of
     the Humanities and Social Sciences* 5(1/2):540–6.

Palau Community Action Agency 1975. *Palauan Legends.* Mangilao: University of
     Guam, Micronesian Area Research Center.

Palau International Coral Reef Center 2008. Mangroves. Brochure sponsored by the
     Japan International Cooperation Agency.

Parmentier, R.J. 1987. *The Sacred Remains: Myth, History, and Polity in Belau.*
     Chicago: University of Chicago Press.

Peers, L.L. and A.K. Brown (eds) 2003. *Museums and Source Communities: a
     Routledge Reader.* London and New York: Routledge.

Phillips, C. and H. Allen (eds) 2010. *Bridging the Divide: Indigenous Communities and
     Archaeology into the 21st Century* (One World Archaeology 60). Walnut
     Creek, California: Left Coast Press.

Rainbird, P. 2000. The non-use of archaeology in Chamorro land rights:
     a comparison with Aboriginal Australia. In *Native Title and the
     Transformation of Archaeology in the Postcolonial World* (Oceania
     Monographs 50), I. Lilley (ed.), 153–63. Oceania Publications, University of
     Sydney.

Schofield, J. and R. Szymanski (eds) 2011. *Local Heritage, Global Context: Cultural Perspectives on Sense of Place*. Farnham: Ashgate.

7N Consulting Services 2007. Environmental Assessment for construction and operation of the proposed baseball field park for the people of Ngaraard State, Republic of Palau. Final draft report submitted to the Palau Environmental Quality Protection Board.

Smith, L.T. 1999. *Decolonizing Methodologies: Research and Indigenous Peoples*. Dunedin: Otago University Press.

Smith, L. 2004. *Archaeological Theory and the Politics of Cultural Heritage*. London and New York: Routledge.

——— 2006. *Uses of Heritage*. London and New York: Routledge.

Smith, L. and N. Akagawa (eds) 2009. *Intangible Heritage* (Key Issues in Cultural Heritage Series). London and New York: Routledge.

Smith, L. and E. Waterton 2009. *Heritage, Communities and Archaeology* (Duckworth Debates in Archaeology Series). London: Duckworth.

Spennemann, D.H.R. 2006. Gauging community values in historic preservation. *CRM: The Journal of Heritage Stewardship* 3(2):6–20.

Stanley, N. (ed.) 2007. *The Future of Indigenous Museums: Perspectives from the Southwest Pacific*. New York and Oxford: Berghahn Books.

Torrence, R. and A. Clarke (eds) 2000. *The Archaeology of Difference: Negotiating Cross-Cultural Engagements in Oceania* (One World Archaeology 38). London: Routledge.

van Meijl, Toon (ed.) 2009. *Pacific Discourses about Cultural Heritage and its Protection*. Special Issue, *International Journal of Cultural Property* 16(3).

Vertovec, S. and R. Cohen (eds) 2003. *Conceiving Cosmopolitanism*. New York: Oxford University Press.

Wickler, S. 2002a. Terraces and villages: transformations of the cultural landscape in Palau. In *Pacific Landscapes: Archaeological Approaches*, T. Ladefoged and M.W. Graves (eds), 63–96. Easter Island Foundation. Los Osos, California: Bearsville Press.

2002b. Oral traditions and archaeology: modeling village settlement in Palau, Micronesia. *Micronesian Journal of the Humanities and Social Sciences* 1(1/2):39–47.

Stephen Wickler is Associate Professor of Archaeology at Tromsø University Museum.

CHAPTER 11

Re-presenting Melanesia
Ignoble savages and Melanesian alter-natives

*

Tarcisius Kabutaulaka

Introduction

In his statement to the nineteenth Melanesian Spearhead Group (MSG) leaders' summit in Noumea, New Caledonia, on 21 June 2013, the Solomon Islands Prime Minister, Gordon Darcy Lilo, couched his speech around the theme 'MSG: Our Place in the Sun in Oceania', and called on 'Melanesians to rise up to the challenges facing their region and find their place amongst the nations of the world' (Lilo 2013). This is a bold statement, especially given the enormity of the social, political and economic challenges that Melanesian countries face. Further, to claim 'our place in the sun' is daring in the light of over three centuries of generally negative representations of Melanesian peoples and societies in Western discourses; negative representations that have over time been internalized by Pacific Islanders – including Melanesians – and used to perpetuate relationships with Melanesia that have racist, essentialist and social-evolutionary elements. The challenges for re-presenting Melanesia are, therefore, not just socio-economic, but epistemological as well. But Prime Minister Lilo's call also illustrates the fact that Melanesians have adopted the term 'Melanesia', and are using it to challenge the negative representations; to 're-present' and 'alter' the images of Melanesia, vying for a 'place in the sun'. It is also an acknowledgement of the potential for economic developments in Melanesia because of its comparatively large population and land area, and rich terrestrial and marine resources.

Here, I examine the dominant representations of Melanesia as a place and Melanesians as peoples, how these influence understandings of and responses to contemporary developments in Melanesia, and how Melanesians are beginning to challenge, 're-present' and 'alter' these negative images and representations. I begin with an overview of the discourses about race in Europe in the seventeenth to nineteenth centuries that influenced the racial mapping of Oceania and framed representations of Melanesians, and examine their influence on contemporary relationships between Melanesians and others, including other Pacific Islanders. I also discuss how they influenced relationships amongst Melanesians themselves.

This is an issue that is not often discussed openly, for fear of offending others, which is why I use the conversation about 'Pacific alternatives' to highlight the issues, encourage dialogue, and hopefully create understanding and strengthen Oceanian connections. These conversations will sometimes be uncomfortable. However, they are important if we are to better understand and deal with our shared colonial experiences. This is not about blaming others for the negative representations of Melanesia. Rather, it is about understanding how Western colonial discourses influence relationships in Oceania, and between Oceanians and others. This is also an attempt to view 'our sea of islands' (Hau'ofa 2008) from the vantage point of Melanesia. While I do not claim to represent Melanesians, I contribute a Melanesian's perspective to the discourse.[1] This is important, as I examine how Melanesians have responded to the negative representations, and argue that they have appropriated the term 'Melanesia' and used it in positive, empowering and progressive ways to mobilize, redefine and re-present themselves. It is a process of altering the image of the native to vie for a 'place in the sun in Oceania.'

Black islands

Oceania is often presented as comprising three sub-regions: Polynesia, Micronesia and Melanesia.[2] Nowadays, Pacific Islanders and others use this tripartite division, even those ardently opposed to this mapping of the region and the meanings and relationships they represent. Pacific Islanders use these categories to frame their identities within Oceania and often express themselves proudly as Polynesians, Micronesians and Melanesians, as well as Oceanians, or Pacific Islanders. These identities are expressed and celebrated through tattoos and popular culture – dance and music – as well as intergovernmental organizations such as the Melanesian Spearhead Group (MSG), the Polynesian Leaders Group (PLG) and the Micronesian Chief Executives. They are marked by cultural gatherings such as the Melanesian Arts Festival and Polyfest. But, how did this tripartite division of Oceania come about, and what were the historical, geographical and epistemological discourses and issues that underlie this mapping of Oceania?

The origin of these terms and the mapping of Oceania have been discussed in detail elsewhere (Douglas 1998; Dumont d'Urville 2003). However, for the sake of those not familiar with that story, let me briefly outline the discourses that informed and gave meaning to the tripartite division of Oceania into Melanesia, Polynesia and Micronesia. The person who is most often credited for the mapping of Oceania was the French botanist, explorer and naval officer, Rear Admiral Jules-Sébastien-César Dumont d'Urville, whose 1832 paper, 'Sur les Îles du Grand Océan' (Dumont d'Urville 2003) popularized the terms. However, while Dumont d'Urville might have popularized the terms, variations of these words and the ideas that informed them existed amongst Europeans – especially aristocrats, scholars, navigators and explorers – for over two centuries prior to the presentation and publication of his paper. This was not just a cartographical mapping of the region. It was also a racial one that reflected Europeans' long-held ideas about race and social evolution (Tcherkézoff 2003). In mapping Oceania, Melanesia was the only sub-region named after the skin colour of its inhabitants: islands of the 'black-skinned people' or 'black islands'.

Polynesia and Micronesia are geographical descriptions.[3] It is obvious that Dumont d'Urville's use of the term 'Melanesia' was loaded with more meanings than simply a description of the skin pigmentation of the islands' inhabitants. It reflected sixteenth- to nineteenth-century discourses about race in Europe that categorized human beings worldwide into a racial hierarchy that placed 'white' or 'Caucasian' people at the top and 'black' people at the bottom. Serge Tcherkézoff traces how the tripartite division of Oceania 'was not a simple matter of geography and map-making, but of race … long before Dumont d'Urville's invention, the "Black" races were already labelled in the most disparaging terms… The history of the contrast between Polynesia and Melanesia is not the story of a nineteenth-century French navigator, but the history of European ideas about "skin colours", between the sixteenth and the nineteenth centuries' (Tcherkézoff 2003:175, 195, 196). Dumont d'Urville discusses how Melanesians were different from and inferior to Polynesians because of their comparatively darker skins:

> Among the many varieties of the human species that live on the various islands of Oceania, all travellers, without exception, have reported two that differ very markedly from one another. Their many peculiar moral and physical features no doubt require us to regard them as two separate races. One of those races comprises people of average height, with relatively pale olive-yellow complexions, sleek hair usually brown or black, a fairly regular build and well-proportioned limbs. They are often organised into nations and sometimes powerful monarchies. Moreover, this race displays almost as much variety as the white race of Europe, that Duméril called Caucasian and Bory de Saint-Vincent, Japhetic. The other race comprises people with very dark, often sooty, skins, sometimes almost as black as that of the Kaffirs, and

curly, fuzzy, fluffy but seldom woolly hair. Their features are disagreeable, their build is uneven and their limbs are often frail and deformed. They are organised into tribes or clans of varying size, but very seldom into nations, and their institutions are far from attaining the degree of refinement that can sometimes be found among people of the copper-skinned race. Nevertheless, there is as much variety in skin colour, build and features among the black people of Oceania as among the numerous nations who live on the African continent and make up the race that most authors have referred to as Ethiopian.

(Dumont d'Urville 1832:164)

Note that Dumont d'Urville draws parallels in physical features, morality and social organizations between Melanesians and Africans, a continent that was, by then, extensively colonized by Europeans. This seems to imply that the dark-skinned people of Oceania are similar to, and therefore should be treated in the same way as, Africans and other dark-skinned people. As discussed below, this was a view that was not uncommon at that time and was expressed in other arenas of European society (see Reynolds 2008; Rochette 2003). Note also that the descriptions of Melanesian social organizations focused largely on how they were different from those of Europeans and those of eastern Oceania, rather than on what they had achieved, and that helped them to survive on these islands for thousands of years. The absence of 'nations' and institutions that have attained a 'degree of refinement' – along with their dark skin (and therefore low moral values) – implies deficiencies and therefore inferiority. European depictions of race and social organization were the bases for the division of Oceania into the sub-regions that persists today.

The use of racial variations to divide Oceania reflected ideas about human social evolution and racial hierarchy that Europeans developed as they interacted with and colonized peoples from other parts of the world, and justified colonialism (Douglas and Ballard 2008; Rochette 2003). By the sixteenth century, Europeans had been engaged in the creation of the inferior 'Other', or the Oriental to use Edward Said's term (1978). This is a discourse about biological and social evolution that places Europeans at the top, and therefore explains and justified Europe's colonial and economic domination of the rest of the world.

To illustrate this point, let me turn to our neighbour Australia, a place where race relations were magnified by the mid-seventeenth century. Writing about people of mixed descent in Australia, historian Henry Reynolds (2008) argues that racial categories that had already taken root in Europe and North America were transmitted to Australia and helped define race relations in this emerging white colony. Reynolds describes how at the first Commonwealth

Parliament meeting in 1901, 'Members and Senators agreed about the centrality of race. They agreed that there was a demonstrable hierarchy of races with the northwest Europeans, the Nordics or Caucasians at the top and the Africans, Melanesians and Aborigines at the bottom.' (Reynolds 2008:85). In this racial categorization, Aborigines and Melanesians were referred to as 'Oceanic Negroes' and placed in the same category as 'black-skinned people' from Africa who had by then long been subjected to European-perpetrated slavery in the New World (Ballard 2008). This reflected over three centuries of racial discourse that influenced European interactions with the rest of the world. Notions of racial hierarchy and references to 'black-skinned people' as the most primitive of human races were, its proponents argued, supported by science. At the centre of this was phrenology, which involved the measuring of human skulls and brains to determine the place of their owners in the racial hierarchy. In these studies, the Oceanic Negroes – like their African 'relatives' – were placed low in the hierarchy (Rochette 2003). In a lecture in 1819 the British biologist Sir William Lawrence asserted that the distinction of colour between white and black was not more striking:

> than the pre-eminence of the former in moral feelings and mental
> endowments... The later ... indulge, almost universally, in disgusting
> debauchery and sensuality, and display gross selfishness, indifference to
> the pains and pleasures of others, insensibility to beauty of form, order and
> harmony, and an almost entire want of what we comprehend altogether
> under the expression of elevated sentiments, manly virtues and moral
> feeling. The hideous savages of Van Damien's Land [Tasmania], of New
> Holland [Australia], New Guinea, and some neighbouring islands, the
> Negroes of Congo and some other parts exhibit the most disgusting moral
> as well as physical portrait of men.
>
> (quoted Reynolds 2008:86)

Reynolds quotes French aristocrat and novelist Joseph Arthur De Gobineau as saying that the Oceanic Negroes 'had the special privilege of providing the most ugly, and degraded and repulsive specimens of the race that seemed to have been created to provide a link between man and the brute' (Reynolds 2008:68). Similarly, in dividing Oceania into Polynesia, Melanesia and Micronesia, Dumont d'Urville, like his predecessors, emphasized skin colour. He identified Melanesians – which included New Holland (Australia) and Van Diemen Island (Tasmania) – as:

> more or less black in colour, with curly, fuzzy or sometimes nearly woolly
> hair, flat noses, wide mouths and unpleasant features, and their limbs are

often very frail and seldom well shaped. The women are even more hideous than the men, especially those who have suckled children, as their breasts immediately become flaccid and droopy, and the little freshness that they owed to youth vanishes at once.

(Dumont d'Urville 1832:169)

These discourses were influenced largely by the work of European explorers and scholars, especially botanists and zoologists (Tcherkézoff 2003). Consequently, the mapping and naming of the south-west Pacific Islands along racial lines reflected prevalent ideas of social evolution and racial hierarchy in Europe at that time. It was no surprise that the 'darkest' of the Pacific Islanders were identified by the colour of their skin, rather than by the geographical characteristics of the places where they lived. Right from the beginning, the term 'Melanesia' was impregnated with racial overtones and superiority-inferiority complexes. This type of racial discourse – of Melanesia as a place and Melanesians as peoples – justified the colonization of the region, as it did other parts of Oceania. Papua New Guinean scholar Regis Tove Stella (2007) discusses in detail how race was used in European colonial discourses to describe and represent Papua New Guineans as inferior to Europeans and other Pacific Islanders, partly because of their darker skin. Stella (2007:21) states that, 'Colonial discourse produced and circulated knowledge and imagery that regularly depicted Papua New Guineans as inferior and subordinate, portraying them in positions of subjection, savagery, and powerlessness in accordance with the widespread operation of the discourse.' This is true of depiction of the rest of Melanesia, as discussed above. This essentialist view of Melanesia, which started in the seventeenth century, set the tone for the way the peoples and cultures from that part of Oceania were represented in the centuries that followed, even up to the present day.[4]

Long-established European images of Oceania were vividly expressed and perpetuated through the work of romanticists like Jean Jacques Rousseau. For him, Pacific Islanders were not just 'savages', but 'noble' ones at that. Rousseau's representation of Pacific Islanders was largely influenced by the accounts of two prominent European explorers: James Cook and Louis Antoine de Bougainville, each of whom had described their encounters with South Seas peoples and places in great detail. To Rousseau and other romanticists, the people of the South Seas lived in a 'Golden Age' (Smith 1960:25) where the '"natural man" was healthy, happy and free' from the wraths of civilization (Barnard 2000:21). But, much of this imagery was based on Bougainville's accounts of his encounters with Polynesians, more specifically Tahitians and Marquesian landscapes and women, who were often sexualized and portrayed as submissive, willing and ready to be taken, especially by European men

(Bougainville 1967).[5] Consequently, with the stroke of Europeans' pen and the swipe of their brushes, the 'noble savage' of the South Seas was established and dominated European (and other) imaginations for centuries thereafter.

Islands of ignoble savages

I have often wondered how Rousseau's idea of the 'noble savage' would have developed if he had encountered my ancestors from the Solomon Islands. Perhaps the 'savage' would have shifted from being 'noble' to 'ignoble'. I have also wondered how the early European contact discourses and racial mapping of Oceania have fuelled contemporary conversations about, perceptions of and relationships to Melanesia and Melanesians. I am also interested in how it has influenced Melanesian perceptions of themselves and their relationships with others.

As discussed above, the Melanesian identity – like the Polynesian and Micronesian identities – was a European construction, built from scholarly and popular writings, arts and oral storytelling (Stella 2007). It was the academy that popularized the works of people like Dumont d'Urville and Rousseau and contributed to essentialist representations of Melanesian societies (Knauft 1999; Thomas 1994). It is interesting that the mapping of Oceania and the descriptions of Melanesian social organizations in the twentieth century were often similar to, and seemed to follow the same rationale as, that of Dumont d'Urville in the previous century (Sahlins 1963). Central to understandings of Melanesia and Melanesians was anthropology, a discipline that pioneered scholarly descriptions of these places and peoples. But, while anthropology has contributed enormously to our knowledge about Melanesia, it has also contributed to distortions and misunderstandings and perpetuated early Eurocentric and racist views. Epeli Hau'ofa, writing in 1975, commented on the role of anthropology in perpetuating what he called 'distorted' images of Melanesia:

> after decades of anthropological field research in Melanesia we have come up only with pictures of people who fight, compete, trade, pay bride-prices, engage in rituals, invent cargo cults, copulate, and sorcerise each other. There is hardly anything in our literature to indicate whether these people have any such sentiments as love, kindness, consideration, altruism, and so on. We cannot tell from our ethnographic writings whether they have a sense of humour. We know little about their systems of morality, specifically their ideas of the good and the bad, and their philosophies...
>
> (Hau'ofa 1975:286)

Anthropology as a discipline has evolved quite a bit since Hau'ofa made these observations. Other disciplines, including political science – the one that I was trained in – are equally responsible for the 'ignoble savage' representations of Melanesia. There is a tendency among political scientists to understand and explain contemporary issues and developments in Melanesia almost entirely with reference to Western ideas and models of governance. They measure the failures and successes of Melanesian societies by using Western criteria, often in the guise of universalizing theories of governance. This is often done without reference to the ways that Melanesians organize themselves in their own terms, which have kept their societies stable throughout the turbulent times of the twentieth and twenty-first centuries. Terence Wesley-Smith (2008) discusses how the concept of the state is exported and promoted as if it is the most natural and appropriate institution for organizing all human societies, including those in Melanesia. The state is presented as unproblematic, or at least 'given' in ways that ignore the violent history of the development of the Western state.

The negative representation of Melanesians – and hence the construction of the 'ignoble savage' – is found not only in academic research and writings, but in physical academic spaces as well. I am often troubled by images of Melanesians that are framed and hung on the walls of university offices. They look uncomfortable, as if they have been trapped in time, for the sole purpose of the entertainment, amusement and curiosity of those who walk the corridors. When I first went to the Australian National University I found that the only picture of bare-breasted women on the walls of the Coombs Building was one of Solomon Islanders. I wrote about that elsewhere (Kabutaulaka 1997). When I joined the East-West Center in Honolulu, I noticed that the only half-naked pictures found in the entire John Burns Hall were those of people from Tanna in Vanutau. They were on the third floor, where the Pacific Islands Development Program (PIDP) – where I once worked – is located. The pictures were hung at the corner of the PIDP corridor. As you walk along that corridor, you will pass the half-naked Tanna people and then come to pictures of Micronesians, who are dressed, and represented in studio poses – as though they had been liberated from savagery, unlike the Melanesians at the other end of the corridor. I often wondered what those people in the pictures were thinking as they stared at me from their framed existence. They probably wondered why I was walking along the corridor and why I was not up there, framed with the rest of them.

This is what Bhabha, in his discussion of representation in colonial discourses, refers to as the 'dependence on the concept of "fixity" in the ideological construction of otherness' (1994:66). This presents colonial subjects, or 'others', as naturally and permanently and fixed in a particular time and state-of-being, which in turn naturalizes their domination (see Hall 1997; Spurr 1993). In this case, the constant representation of Melanesians as naked or half naked, posing in jungles or villages, portrays them as naturally trapped in a particular state-of-being and unchanging, and therefore 'backward' compared to the West, which is constantly changing and 'progressing'. Melanesians are therefore suitable subjects to be displayed in Western spaces – books, paintings, buildings, museums etc. – as ignoble savages, to feed Western curiosity and fetishism for savagery.

The negative representations of Melanesians are not restricted to academia. Public media and popular writings, such as those by travel writers, have also contributed. For example, in writing about his travels through Solomon Islands in 1911 and the diseases that the crew contracted, Jack London states, 'If I were a king, the worst punishment I could inflict on my enemies would be to banish them to the Solomons. On second thought, king or no king, I don't think I'd have the heart to do it.' (London 2003:178). Travel writer Paul Theroux, writing in the 1990s, said that he found the Solomons to be 'the most savage islands in the Pacific' (1992:155). In his book, *The Happy Isles of Oceania*, Theroux had a go at nearly all the Pacific Islands, but he reserved his most horrendous comments for Melanesians, describing Solomon Islanders in Honiara as 'among the scariest-looking people I had ever seen in my life' (Theroux 1992:155). For Fiji, Theroux made a distinction between the people of eastern Fiji and those that he referred to as 'Melanesian Fijians'. He wrote, 'the Lau Group is one of the pretty little star clusters in the universe of Oceania. Melanesian Fiji is another story. Fiji is like the world you thought you left behind – full of political perversity, racial fear, economic woes, and Australian tourists looking for inexpensive salad bowls...' (Theroux 1992:219). While such descriptions may raise eyebrows, they also appeal to European curiosity about the savage Melanesians. It is no surprise that Theroux's book became a *New York Times* bestseller – it fed the Western imagination of Melanesian 'backwardness' and savagery that had existed since the seventeenth century (Farber 1993).

The media has also contributed to the 'ignoble savage' representation of Melanesia. In 2007 a British television company produced a three-part programme entitled *Meet the Natives*. The producers promoted this as 'reverse anthropology', in which 'natives' would be taken to metropolitan cities and their interactions with the peoples and cultures of the West would be filmed. The first task was to find the 'native'. And of course, where did they look? – Melanesia. In the first part of the series five men from Tanna in Vanuatu were taken to London and filmed as they interacted with 'English peoples and cultures'. I find the idea of 'reverse anthropology' troubling. On 8 September 2007, the British newspaper, *The Independent*, carried a story entitled, 'Strange Island: Pacific Tribesmen Come to Study Britain'. In this article the five men from Tanna had no voice at all. They were merely objects of media commentary, and the article was obviously written to feed the British imaginary of native savages in faraway islands.

After that London episode of *Meet the Natives*, I received an email from the producers asking me to facilitate the production of a sequel. This time they wanted to take men from the Weather Coast of Guadalcanal in Solomon Islands, where I come from, particularly followers of the Moro Movement, to New York. I seriously considered their request, knowing that many of my village folks would love to go to New York, even if they had no clue where it was, or what they were required to do. After careful consideration, however, I refused to facilitate the project, and emailed the producers saying that I was unable to help. I saw the project not as 'reverse anthropology', but simply as a relocation of the 'native', or the 'ignoble savage', who continues to be the subject of Western curiosity. This time the 'native' was to be placed in an unfamiliar environment and gazed at through television camera and screen. On second thoughts, the mischievous side of me – quite a bit of me – was tempted to facilitate the project. I even thought it would be fun if I could fly home, dress up in *kabilato* (barkcloth) like the native that they wanted to see, and get myself recruited as part of the delegation to New York, as they didn't know what I looked like. I thought that it would be amusing if, in the middle of filming the documentary, I would begin to debate with the filmmakers about issues of representation. I could even demand to be taken to Broadway, to the United Nations headquarters, and ask to be wined and dined at the most expensive restaurants. In this scenario I would suddenly break out of the native binary, and run amok in New York. The sensible side of me, however, won the day, and I dropped the idea.

Re/presenting Oceania

The tripartite division of Oceania into Polynesia, Melanesia and Micronesia has been widely discussed, especially amongst scholars concerned that the divisions serve the agendas of its European architecture and perpetuates colonialism and neo-colonialism, rather than reflecting actual divisions among Islanders. Some view it as an essentialist and racist representation of Oceania (Ballard 2008; Douglas 1998:5; Hau'ofa 2008).

Some propose, therefore, that there is a need to shift beyond these geographical and racial categories and emphasize the interconnections between Islanders, encouraging pan-Oceania connections and identities. Such interconnections and Oceanic identities, it is argued, existed prior to European contact, or if they did not exist, needed to be established because 'we belong to the same ocean' or '*wan solwara*'.[6] The former Prime Minister and President of

Fiji, the late Ratu Sir Kamisese Mara, for example, was credited for coining and first articulating the term 'Pacific Way' at a United Nations General Assembly meeting in October 1970. In that address, Ratu Mara used the term to refer specifically to Fiji's smooth transition from colonial rule to independence, as reflecting a 'Pacific Way' that was consensual and peaceful (Mara 1997:238). However, the term has since been used broadly in an anti-colonial sense, and as a representation of Oceania, as a region with similar cultures, as politically united, and so to address issues through collective diplomacy, invoking a Pan-Oceania identity (Crocombe 1976; Lawson 2010).

Epeli Hau'ofa, in his essay 'Our Sea of Islands', highlights how pan-Oceanic connections transcend national and sub-regional boundaries, arguing that the ocean connects, rather than divides the Pacific Islands. He describes Oceania prior to European contact as:

> a large world in which peoples and cultures moved and mingled, unhindered by boundaries of the kind erected much later by imperial powers. From one island to another they sailed to trade and to marry, thereby expanding social networks for greater flows of wealth. They travelled to visit relatives in a wide variety of natural and cultural surroundings, to quench their thirst for adventure, and even to fight and dominate.
>
> (Hau'ofa 2008:33)[7]

While I agree with Hau'ofa about the trans-Oceanic connections and identities, it must be noted that the national and sub-regional boundaries persist, and have become the 'realities' for most Islanders today. In fact, while there have been critical discussions about the tripartite divisions among scholars – which are important and must be encouraged – there is relatively less discussion about how the terms Polynesia, Micronesia and Melanesia have taken on 'lives' of their own, adopted by Pacific Islanders and used to frame their identities, and influence relationships between them, and with non-Islanders.[8] Consequently, in order for the discussions – especially among Pacific Islanders – to transcend the colonial categories and establish and reinforce the trans-Oceanic identities that Hau'ofa talks about, it is important that Pacific Islanders acknowledge how these colonial discourses have influenced how they perceive and relate to each other. This is a discussion that might be uncomfortable, but one that is important and we must not shy away from. Hau'ofa himself has raised some of these issues in his works over the years (Hau'ofa 2008).

Let me begin this conversation by noting that the 'ignoble savage' representations of Melanesia have shifted beyond the European imagination and become entrenched among non-Europeans as well. To illustrate this, let me recount an event that occurred in Canberra in the late 1990s, when I was a Ph.D. student at the Australian National University (ANU). One afternoon, I was in a bus with John Naitoro[9] – another Solomon Islander who was also doing his Ph.D. at the ANU – on our way to ANU housing. We sat at the back of the bus chattering away in Solomon Islands Pijin. Next to us was a black man, whom we later learned was from Somalia. After listening to us to for a while he asked:

'Are you from Papua New Guinea?'

'Yes, we are from Papua New Guinea,' John quickly responded before I could say anything.

The man was quiet for a while and then asked, 'Do you eat people in Papua New Guinea?' I was shocked.

'Yes, we eat people,' John quickly responded.

'But that was long time ago, right?' the man asked after moments of silence.

'No, we still eat people,' John quickly answered with a serious expression on his face. I looked at him and then at the man, wondering where this conversation was going.

After a while and as though to assure himself of his safety, the man asked, 'But, you only eat white people, right?'

'No, we eat black people as well,' John said looking straight at him and more serious than before. The man immediately stood up and went to the front of the bus.

That incident set me thinking about where and how this African man got the image that Papua New Guineans in Canberra in the late 1990s could be cannibals. Perhaps he thought that you could take the man out of cannibal land, but not cannibalism out of the man. I also wondered what he might have asked if we had told him that we were from Tahiti. Perhaps he would have asked if in Tahiti we danced *tamure* all day, ate from abundant breadfruit trees, and made love under coconut trees. I also wondered why John responded to him in the way he did. John said to me afterwards, '*Hem na wat fo talem long pipol karage olsem.*' (That's what you say to people who are as ignorant as that.)

I had long suspected that the savage Melanesian exists, not only in European and African minds, but also in Pacific Islander minds. The perception of Melanesians or black people as 'ignoble savages' has, to a certain extent, been internalized by Pacific Islanders, including Melanesians. This is reflected in the languages, perceptions and relationships among Pacific Islanders, and is often not openly discussed because it is sensitive. In Samoa, black people (including Melanesians) are commonly referred to as *mea uli*. *Uli* is the word for 'black' and *mea* literally means 'thing'. Hence, one could argue that the use of the term *mea uli* (either consciously or unconsciously) strips the black person of his/her humanity and reduces him/her to a 'thing' – *mea uli*. In March 2009 there was a debate in the *Samoa Observer* following the use of the term *mea uli* to refer to the then newly elected first black President of the United States of America, Barack Obama. One of the contributors suggested the use of the term *tagata uli*, which literally means 'black man', and *taine uli* as appropriate for 'black woman' (*Samoa Observer*, March 2009).[10] In Tonga, the term used to refer to black people is *uli'uli*. The Tongan word for 'dirty' is also *uli'uli*, making one wonder whether a black person is equated to dirty.

In June 2010, I presented a version of this chapter at the University of the South Pacific (USP) as a way of starting a conversation about the perceptions associated with the divisions of Oceania and the way Melanesians are represented. The USP Student newspaper, *Wan Solwara*, published a story about my presentation and comments from USP students and faculty. This was later reprinted by the Auckland University of Technology (AUT) Pacific Media Centre's online publication, *Pacific Scoop*. The comments by two prominent Pacific Islander scholars were insightful and important in this conversation. Education Professor Konai Helu Thaman was reported as saying that 'referring to black-skinned people as *uli* or *uli'uli* is purely for descriptive purposes and not meant to be offensive'. She said that, 'When Tongans say *uli'uli* it does not mean that they are superior, being a Tongan. They are just describing the person, but if there is a feeling that whoever is *uli'uli* is black and is compared to white, then that is problematic'. Historian Morgan Tuimaleali'ifano was reported as saying that '*mea uli* [in Samoan] means black people without negative connotations'. But, he added that there were people who put 'value behind the word' (*Pacific Scoop*, 24 June 2010).

Epeli Hau'ofa, who was born of Tongan missionary parents in PNG and spent his early years in that country, provides a slightly different perspective. In an interview with Nicholas Thomas in 2006, Hau'ofa stated:

> My upbringing in Melanesia was very important. I am extremely sensitive
> to Polynesian cultures and the contemporary situation and modernization,
> but they are rather dominant. Always, when I went to Tonga, I found that
> the way Polynesians feel and think about Melanesians rather appalling. It's
> racist. There is a feeling of superiority. Because part of me is Melanesian,
> I'm always trying to go beyond that divide.
>
> (Thomas 2012:126)

I raise this, not to accuse Tongans and Samoans (or other Pacific Islanders) of being racist towards Melanesians. Rather, it is to highlight, and begin considerations and discussions of, the way we, Pacific Islanders, have internalized the divisions of Oceania and the perceptions and prejudices associated with their European construction. This could be a factor in preventing us from achieving the Oceanic identity that Hau'ofa envisions in his essay (Hau'ofa 2008).

Perhaps it was such language and the perceptions and prejudices associated with it that contributed to the establishments of the Melanesian Spearhead Group (MSG) in 1983. The reasons that were often given for the establishment of the MSG were political, especially in relation to Melanesian leaders' frustrations over what they saw as the region's indecisiveness on issues such as the decolonization of New Caledonia (MacQueen 1989). Ron May asserts that 'The MSG had its origins in a broad sense of Melanesian cultural solidarity and a desire to assert a Melanesian voice among the members of the Pacific Islands Forum, which some island countries perceived to be dominated by Australia and New Zealand.' (May 2011:6). The MSG later developed economic goals (Grynberg and Kabutaulaka 1995) and continues to explore economic potentials through trade agreements etc. It could be a formidable economic block in the Oceania region because of the size of the Melanesian countries and their relatively richer natural resource endowment. I have long felt, however, that underlying these publicly expressed views, another reason for the establishment of the MSG was Melanesian leaders' irritation about the sense of superiority and domination that Polynesian leaders exert at the regional level; there was a feeling that Melanesians were looked down upon. At that time, the perceived superiority included Fiji under Ratu Sir Kamisese Mara, who came from Lau and had close connections with Tonga and its royal family. The establishment of the MSG triggered further sub-regional divisions with the establishment of the Micronesian Chief Executives in 2004 and the Polynesian Leaders Group (PLG) in 2011.

But, the prejudices and racism towards darker skin people also exists amongst Melanesians. Relatively lighter skin Melanesians sometimes speak in disparaging ways about darker skin Melanesians and associate them with more 'savagery' because of their skin colour. For example, in Solomon Islands, a month prior to independence in July 1978, the government newspaper published a poem titled 'Ode to the West Wind' written by a man from Malaita, in which he described those from the Western Solomons, who are generally darker than other Solomon Islanders, as 'Black and ugly, proud and lazy' (*News Drum*, 9 June 1978).[11] The poem incited debates (*News Drum*, 23 June 1978) and fuelled sentiments for the Western Solomons to secede from the rest of the country (Premdas, Steeves and Larmour 1984; see also Hviding, this volume). The issue was deemed so serious that the author of the poem was charged with sedition (*News Drum*, 8 September 1978).

Apart from race, there is also a tendency to represent Melanesian traditional social organizations as 'undeveloped' in comparison to the nation-states of Europe and the hierarchical chiefly systems of Polynesia (Sahlins 1963). This is because traditional Melanesian polities are comparatively smaller and their societies are ethno-linguistically diverse with no 'centralized' state that resembles the Weberian bureaucracy and sovereignty associated with the Westphalian model of the nation-state that were established in Europe and exported to the rest of the world through colonialism.

Polynesian societies, on the other hand, have hierarchical chiefly systems, which in some ways resembled the feudal systems that existed in Europe. Furthermore, by the 1800s centralized 'governments' had been established in parts of Polynesia. The rise and establishment of monarchs in Hawai'i, Tahiti and Tonga (Howe 1984) were often pointed to as signs of 'development' in Polynesian social organizations because they resemble Western feudal societies or modern states. In Fiji, the rise and establishment of Bau as the central power was never complete, because Ratu Seru Epenisa Cakobau did not have control over all of Fiji (Lal 1992).

It was the perception that large centralized institutions were the best way of organizing societies that contributed to the denigration of traditional Melanesian social organization, and to a push for reforms that proposed the wholesale adoption of the Western form of the state and the values that come with it. Hau'ofa took issue with the ways in which Melanesian social organizations were often described, especially in academia. He argues that anthropological descriptions 'deny that traditional Melanesian leaders have any genuine interest in the welfare of their people and insists that their public actions are all motivated purely by selfishness'. He goes on to say that this kind of ethnographic work is 'erroneous' and described it as 'an invidious pseudo-evolutionary comparison between the "developed" Polynesian polities and the "underdeveloped" Melanesian ones'. He decried the fact that Europeans have long romanticized Polynesians and denigrated Melanesians and that this kind of anthropology 'has the potential of bolstering the long-standing Polynesian racism against Melanesians' (Hauofa 2008:6).

I think that the description of Melanesian traditional social organizations as 'undeveloped' were due largely to Europeans' inability to relate to and understand their complexities. These are reflected, for example, in the Kula Ring in PNG (Malinowski 1920; Ziegler 1990), a complex interaction between peoples of different language groups, which weaves together trade, politics, ceremonial exchanges and social relationships that hold these societies together and make them function and survive despite their ethno-linguistic diversities. They have not survived in isolation, but are synergistic and co-dependent. Another example is the shell-money trade between the people of Langalanga Lagoon on Malaita in Solomon Islands and Bougainville, as well as other parts of island PNG. This continues today, outside of the purview of the state, and despite the trade and immigration regulations that the governments of Solomon Islands and Papua New Guinea impose. Melanesia baffled and perhaps also frightened Europeans because it was unlike anything they were familiar with. They therefore employed pseudo-evolutionary ideas that placed European social organizations at the top along with those that resembled them, and 'others' – those unfamiliar and dissimilar – at the bottom.

In the last three decades, the predominant image of Melanesia has been that of a place of conflicts and coups, where there is always trouble. The diversity of cultures and languages is often presented as a problem, rather than as a rich cultural heritage. Ethno-linguistic diversity, it seems, does not fit into the idea of a homogenizing world, where collective 'imagined communities', to reference Benedict Anderson (1991), and identities at the level of nation-states are normative and regarded as more 'civilized'. As stated above, political scientists have played an important role in representing Melanesia as a region of 'weak' and 'failing' states. Melanesian countries have been described as part of an 'arc of instability' that stretches from Indonesia to Fiji (Duncan and Chand 2002; May 2003). Furthermore, Melanesian countries were often referenced as the primary contributors to the 'Africanisation of the Pacific' (Reilly 2000). Reilly's 'Africanisation of the Pacific' thesis invokes the connection between Oceania, especially Melanesian, and Africa that was frequently made in early European writings about Oceania, as discussed above. It implies that these connections were 'natural' and that the same challenges were to be expected of black people, whether they are in Africa or Oceania. Other scholars of Oceania have challenged Reilly's 'Africanisation of the Pacific' thesis, arguing that it made broad and erroneous generalizations and did not fully consider the colonial histories and experiences that contributed to Oceania's contemporary challenges (Chappell 2005; Fraenkel 2004b).

One could indeed argue that Melanesia has enormous economic, political and social challenges. The major violent conflicts of Oceania in the last three decades were in Melanesia. These include the violent demands for decolonization in New Caledonia in the 1980s (Chappell 2013), the continuing violent struggles for independence in West Papua (King 2004), the coups in Fiji (Fraenkel *et.al.* 2009), the Bougainville Crisis (Regan 2010), the Solomon Island civil unrests (Bennett 2002; Fraenkel 2004a; Moore 2004), and the ongoing law and order challenges in Papua New Guinea (May 2003). The governments of PNG, Solomon Islands, Vanuatu and Fiji also face challenges such as political instability, corruption and economic mismanagement. Furthermore, in the last decade there has been an increase in investments by foreign companies in large-scale natural-resource extraction industries, especially mining and forestry. These will contribute to improvements in the economies of Melanesian countries, but could also engender environmental, social and economic problems. Local conflicts associated with mining and logging are common, especially in PNG and Solomon Islands.

These political, economic and social challenges that Melanesian countries face are real and must not be ignored. But, representations of Melanesia framed largely through conflicts, crises and economic and governance problems prevent us from fully understanding and appreciating Melanesia and the aspirations and innovations of its peoples. We should not only view these places and societies through the frame of conflict and crisis, but instead also appreciate the complexities and rich cultures of this part of Oceania, and the way they continue to be resilient in the face of almost four centuries of negative representations. To continue to view Melanesia in predominantly negative ways is to use the old frame of Europeans in the seventeenth century – the 'ignoble savage' frame, bordered with centuries of racism and prejudice – to attempt to understand modern day Melanesia. If Pacific Islanders are not intellectually vigilant, we could – if we have not already done so – internalize these negative representations. Such framings ignore the resilience, dynamism and innovation of the largest population of Oceania, whose under-appreciated cultures are both rich and amongst the oldest of our region.

Melanesian alter-natives

In light of the above, one could propose that because the term 'Melanesia' has origins in the colonial projects of mapping and boundary formation, and is associated with racial prejudices, it would be empowering and decolonizing to reject it altogether in favour of locally meaningful names and categories. Similarly, one could also recommend that the sub-regional divisions of Melanesia, Polynesia and Micronesia be erased in favour of a pan-Oceania identity.

While such a proposal would be desirable as a way to decolonize, it is also important to note that the term 'Melanesia' has been adopted and used in powerful and empowering ways by Melanesians in popular and official discourses. For example, the Solomon Islands prime minister's call for Melanesian countries to carve their 'place in the sun in Oceania' does not suggest discarding their Melanesian identities. Rather, it advocates an embracing of those identities as they 'rise up to the challenges facing their region and find their place amongst the nations of the world' (Lilo 2013). Even in the 1970s, we saw the embracing of the term 'Melanesia' through the concept of the 'Melanesian Way', of which Bernard Narokobi from PNG became the greatest advocator. According to Narokobi, the 'Melanesian Way' does not necessarily imply a single Melanesian identity. Rather, it is a celebration of Melanesia's diversity, and the fact that such diversity is a source of strength rather than of problems and weakness. He also advocates the harnessing and celebration of commonalities that weave through the ethno-linguistic diversities of Melanesia (Narokobi 1980). Furthermore, in the 1980s the prime minister of the then newly independent state of Vanuatu, Fr. Walter Lini, proposed the establishment of 'Melanesian socialism' as an alternative governance system that embraces communalism (Howard 1983).

A common pidgin language reinforces the weaving of this Melanesian mat. The Melanesian sub-region has a high 'language density',[12] and there are about 1,319 languages in the region (Landweer and Unseth 2012). But Melanesia also constitutes the largest population in Oceania – about 7.9 million people – who speak a common language other than English. Although there are slight difference between PNG *tok pisin*, Vanuatu *bislama* and Solomon Islands *pijin*, the people of these countries can carry out mutually intelligible conversations entirely in pidgin. This is empowering and marks the pidgin-speaking Melanesian countries – PNG, Solomon Islands and Vanuatu – as *wantok* countries. Although Fijians do not speak pidgin, their interactions with other Melanesian countries through the Melanesian Spearhead Group (MSG) have caused them to be increasingly seen as part of the *wantok* community. New Caledonia has also long been viewed as part of the *wantok* community, though the Kanaks speak French rather than pidgin.

This raises the importance of the *wantok* system or *wantokism*.[13] Western scholars have often identified this as a factor contributing to poor governance and economic mismanagement. Francis Fukuyama (2008), writing about post-conflict and development challenges facing Solomon Islands, argues that *wantokism* is one of the major obstacles to post-conflict development in Solomon Islands. Morgan Brigg, however, argues in favour of 'the innovative possibility of drawing on *wantokism* as a culturally recognised and valuable resource for addressing the current challenges faced by Solomon Islands' (Brigg 2009:148). Brigg suggests that *wantokism* could be used to mobilize locally emerging national identities, that it does not necessarily drive corruption, and could be utilized to facilitated governance at the local level. Gordon Nanau (2011) also discusses how the *wantok system* could potentially be an important network that enhances relationships both within and between countries. I think that *wantokism* or the *wantok* system could be the foundation on which Melanesia 'alter-natives' emerge and re/present themselves.

Melanesia is also a potential political and economic power in Oceania. The establishment of the Melanesian Spearhead Group (MSG) plays an important role in this. As Ron May states, '[i]n terms of population, land and resources, the Melanesian countries – particularly Papua New Guinea – are the dominant forces in Pacific island politics and economics, and have been largely responsible over recent years for the growing Chinese and European interest in the Pacific' (May 2011:1). Since its establishment, the MSG has become a powerful voice in the region, especially in countering Australia and New Zealand. Economically, Melanesian countries are relatively well endowed with natural resources and therefore have enormous potential. That is often hindered by poor management, though in the past decade we have seen the expansion of PNG businesses investing in other Pacific islands. Bank South Pacific (BSP) has expanded to Solomon Islands, Fiji and Niue, buying up major banks in those countries. It has as its vision 'To be the Leading Bank in the South Pacific.' Several other PNG companies, including Lamana Development Company Ltd and Mineral Resources Development Company Ltd (MRDC) have bought large hotel properties in Fiji. This trend is likely to increase, as PNG experiences an economic boom with new mining developments.

Apart from politics and economics, music and popular culture often affirm Melanesian identities and celebrate the place and its cultures. For example, the PNG band Haos Boi has a song titled 'Melanesia' in which they sing about 'living in paradise on this land I'll never give away' and about going to other places and realizing that there is no place like PNG in Melanesia. They also affirm the values of Melanesian cultures and *tubuna pasin* (ways of the elders).[14] Popular US-based musician, O-Shen, in his song also titled 'Melanesia', sings about 'Melanesia my Pacific Islands paradise' using PNG *tok pisin* and English.[15] In that song, O-Shen reflects on growing up in PNG and valuing his connections with Melanesia. Fijian musician, Jale Maraeau also celebrates his Melanesian connections.[16] A popular Solomon Islands band is called Onetox, which is a play on the term *wantok* and the concept of *wantokism*, which – as will be discussed below – connects the Melanesian countries in a pan-Melanesian identity. Melanesian musicians have popularized pidgin – PNG *tok pisin*, Solomon Islands *pijin* and Vanuatu *bislama* – through their music, creating awareness about Melanesia in ways that transcend the negative representations. They also reach out to younger people who probably never read academic papers about representations. Nowadays, Melanesian musicians have also used audio-visual technology and the internet – especially YouTube and websites such as PNG's www. CHMSupersound.com – to promote their music and positive images of Melanesia as a place and Melanesians as peoples.

Consequently, rather than attempting to erase the term 'Melanesia', it would be useful to examine how Melanesians have adopted and altered the meanings associated with it. In the process, they have created 'alter-natives' who are clawing their way out of the 'ignoble savage' cocoon in which they have been encased for centuries. Melanesians, armed with diverse and rich cultures that are strongly rooted to place, have captured the 'ignoble savage', turned it on its head, and used the term 'Melanesia' to grace the pages of books, canvas, stages and the airwaves.

As Steven Winduo (2000) asserts, the colonial process never completely erased what existed prior to colonization. Rather, it simply wrote over it. I think it not only 'wrote' over it, but it also spoke, danced, sung, painted and chanted over what existed prior to colonization. Winduo, in writing about Oceania in general, suggests the need to 'unwrite' the colonial text. Melanesians, along with other Pacific Islanders, are writing, dancing, singing, chanting and painting over the remnants of colonialism. Many do this by using what were previously colonial tools, such as the English language and the written text, Western musical instruments, the canvas and paintbrush, and now the internet, a powerful instrument of globalization. They have captured the colonizers weapon and used it for self-empowerment, creating a new breed of natives who are neither noble nor ignoble; they are the 'alter-natives' are scratching away the colonial texts, dances, songs, chants and paintings, and draw strength from what lies beneath, empowering Melanesians and freeing them from the 'ignoble savage' image.

This empowerment and freedom could be found in valuing indigenous epistemologies and utilizing them to transform inherently colonial concepts and processes like 'development', putting an indigenous twist to them. David Welchman Gegeo (1998) discusses how the Kwara'ae people of Malaita in Solomon Islands have infused Kwara'ae worldviews and epistemologies into development. I imagine this to be what Bernard Narokobi envisaged when he coined and advocated the 'Melanesian Way'. It is not only about the past and 'traditional' values. It is also about new, creative and empowering futures that draw from the past and from indigenous epistemologies and uses Western ideas and technologies to weave a uniquely Melanesian mat.

We Melanesians are searching for 'our place in the sun'.

Notes

1   I am conscious that by saying that I contribute a Melanesian perspective, I am appropriating the term 'Melanesia' and representing myself as a Melanesian as well as a Pacific Islander. I will discuss this further below.

2   Epeli Hau'ofa (2008), however, proposes an Oceanian identity that expands beyond across these tripartite divisions and across the entire Oceania region, but also to places where Pacific Islanders have migrated and settled.

3   The terms 'Polynesia', 'Micronesia' and 'Melanesia' were derivatives of the Greek words *'poly'* which means 'many', *'micro'* which means 'tiny' or 'small' and *'mela'*

which means 'black'; '-nesia' comes from the Green word *'nesi'* or *'nesia'* (in plural) which means 'islands'. So, Polynesia means 'many islands', Micronesia mean 'tiny' or 'small islands', and Melanesia means 'black islands' or by implication the 'islands of the black-skinned people'.

4   Racial discourse as a justification for colonialism is not restricted to Melanesia and Oceania. It is found elsewhere and widely discussed by scholars (see, for example, Ashcroft *et.al.* 1995; Bhabba 1994; Fanon 1967).

5   Contemporary scholars are rewriting and reimagining these European depictions of Oceanian places and peoples. For example, Marata Tamaira (2010) discusses how the European construction – especially in visual arts – of the Polynesian 'dusky maiden' conceals the power of women, and how contemporary Polynesian women artists are reimagining and re-establishing that power.

6   *Wan solwara* is Papua New Guinean *tok pisin* (pidgin), meaning 'one salt water' or 'one ocean'. It is also the name of the student newspaper at the University of the South Pacific, Suva, Fiji, published there by the Journalism Department. The name is an attempt to create that sense of Oceanic identity among students.

7   Hau'ofa's essay was first published in *A New Oceania: Rediscovering Our Sea of Islands* (1993), eds V. Naidu, E. Waddell and E. Hau'ofa, Suva: School of Social and Economic Development, University of the South Pacific. A version was later published in 1994, *The Contemporary Pacific* 6(1):147–61. It was then republished in Hau'ofa 2008, the version I refer to here.

8   Many institutions in the region have adopted these names, perhaps indicating that Pacific Islanders have taken on these categories and used them for their own purposes and in empowering ways. The establishment of the Melanesian Spearhead Group (MSG) and its increasing influence in the region, for example, is an indication of the use of the term 'Melanesia' in an empowering manner. Other examples include the Polynesian Cultural Centre at Brigham Young University (BYU) in Hawai'i, which has not only helped create a pan-Polynesian cultural identity in Hawai'i, but used the term Polynesia to present and market a particular image and product to the tourism industry. The categories have also framed organizations as well as political and social relationships between Pacific Islanders. Classic examples of these include the Melanesian Spearhead Group (MSG), the Polynesia Leaders Group (PLG) and the Micronesian Chief Executives Summit.

9   John Naitoro passed away not long after completing his Ph.D.

10   Meleisea (1980) uses the term *tama uli* to refer to the descendants of Melanesians who were taken to work in the plantations in Samoa in the late 1800s and early 1900s. This is seen as a more respectable Samoan term for 'black people'.

11   The 'West Wind' poem was written to ridicule the Western Solomon's demands for greater autonomy, which they believed could be achieved through a federal system of government, or state government, as it was commonly known at that time. The poem was, therefore, not primarily about race.

12 Language density is used here to refer to languages in relation to land mass. Lynn
    Landweer and Peter Unseth say that there is a proportion of about 716 sq. km per
    language in Melanesia, giving it the greatest density of languages on earth. This is
    almost three times as dense as Nigeria, a country famous for its high number of
    languages per land area.

13 This is derived from the term *wantok*, which is a pidgin for 'one talk', meaning
    people who speak the same language. It is also about relationships and looking
    after each other as people who are related through kin, with the same language,
    island and region.

14 www.youtube.com/watch?v=zqyk7t2LvJA (accessed 23 July 2013).

15 www.youtube.com/watch?v=lYdUMPYiFSM (accessed 23 July 2013). O-Shen is a
    US-based musician who was born and grew up in Papua New Guinea of American
    missionary parents. He regularly visits Papua New Guinea and other Melanesian
    countries to seek inspiration for his music. He writes, performs and records songs
    in *tok pisin*.

16 www.youtube.com/watch?v=LLaEIcYT8is (accessed 23 July 2013).

References

Anderson, B. 1991 *Imagined Communities: Reflections on the Origin and Spread of
    Nationalism*. New York: Verso.

Ashcroft, B., G. Griffiths, and H. Tiffin. 1995. *The Post-Colonial Studies Reader*.
    London and New York: Routledge,

Ballard, C. 2008 'Oceanic Negroes': British anthropology of Papuans, 1820–1869. In
    Foreign Bodies: Oceania and the Science of Race 1750–1940, B. Douglas and
    C. Ballard (eds), 157–201. Canberra: ANU E-Press.

Barnard, A. 2000 *History and Theory in Anthropology*. Cambridge: Cambridge
    University Press.

Bhabha, H. 1994. *The Location of Culture*. London: Routledge.

Bennett, J. 2002 Roots of conflict in Solomon Islands – though much is taken, much
    abides: legacies of tradition and colonialism. state, society and governance
    in Melanesia *Discussion Paper* 2002/5. Canberra: Australian National
    University.

Bougainville, L.A. de 1967 *A Voyage Round the World* (trans. J.R. Forster). New York:
    Da Capo Press.

Brigg, M. 2009 Wantokism and state building in the Solomon Islands: a response to
    Fukuyama. *Pacific Economic Bulletin* 24(3):148–61.

Chappell, D. 2005 'Africanization' of the Pacific: blaming 'others' for disorder in the
    periphery? *Comparative Studies in Society and History* 47(2):286–317.

——— 2013 *The Kanak Awakening: the Rise of Nationalism in New Caledonia*.
    Honolulu: University of Hawai'i Press.

Clark, G. 2003. Dumont d'Urville's Oceanic provinces: fundamental precepts or arbitrary constructs? *The Journal of Pacific History* 38(2):155–61.

Crocombe, R. 1976. *The Pacific Way: An Emerging Identity*. California: Lotu Pasifika.

Douglas, B. 1998 *Across the Great Divide: Journeys in History and Anthropology*. Amsterdam: Harwood Academic Publishers.

Douglas, B and C. Ballard, eds. 2008. *Foreign Bodies: Oceania and the Science of Race 1750–1940*. Canberra: ANU ePress.

Dumont d'Urville, J.-S.-C. 2003. On the islands of the great ocean (trans. I. Ollivier, A. de Biran and G. Clark). *Journal of Pacific History* 38(2):163–74.

Duncan, R. and S. Chand 2002. The economics of the 'arc of instability'. *Asia-Pacific Economic Literature* 16(1):1–9.

Fanon, F. 1967. *The Wretched of the Earth*. Harmondsworth: Penguin.

Farber, T. 1993. Unhappy in the Isles of Oceania. *The Contemporary Pacific* 5(2):383–5.

Fraenkel, J. 2004a. *The Manipulation of Custom: From Uprising to Intervention in the Solomon Islands*. Wellington: Victoria University Press.

——— 2004b. The coming anarchy in Oceania? A critique of the 'Africanisation of the South Pacific' thesis. *Commonwealth and Comparative Politics* 42(1):1–34.

Fraenkel, J., S. Firth and B.V. Lal (eds) 2009. *2006 Military Takeover in Fiji: a Coup to End all Coups?* Canberra: ANU E-Press.

Fukuyama, F. 2008. State building in the Solomon Islands. *Pacific Economic Bulletin* 23(3):1–17.

Gegeo, D.W. 1998. Indigenous knowledge and empowerment: rural development examined from within. *The Contemporary Pacific* 10(2):289–315.

Grynberg, R. and T. Kabutaulaka 1995. The political economy of Melanesian trade integration. *Pacific Economic Bulletin* 10(2):48–60.

Hall, S. 1997. The spectacle of the 'other'. In *Representation: Cultural Representations and Signifying Practices*, S. Hall (ed.), 223–79. London: The Open University.

Hau'ofa, E. 1975 Anthropology and Pacific Islanders. *Oceania* 45: 283-89.

——— 2008. *We Are the Ocean: Selected Works*. Honolulu: University of Hawai'i Press.

Howard, M.C. 1983. Vanuatu: the myth of Melanesian socialism. *Labour, Capital and Society* 16:176–203.

Howe, K. 1984. *Where the Waves Fall: a South Seas Islands History from Settlement to Colonial Rule*. Pacific Islands Monograph Series 2. Honolulu: University of Hawai'i Press.

Kabutaulaka, T. 1997. I am not a Stupid Native: decolonising images and imagination in Solomon Islands. In *Emerging from Empire? Decolonisation in the Pacific*, D. Denoon (ed.), 165–71. Canberra: Division of Pacific and Asian History, Research School of Pacific and Asian Studies, Australian National University.

King, P. 2004. *West Papua & Indonesia Since Suharto: Independence, Autonomy or Chaos?* Sydney: University of New South Wales Press Ltd.

Knauft, B.M. 1999 *From Primitive to Postcolonial in Melanesia and Anthropology*. Ann Arbor: University of Michigan Press.

Lal, B.V. 1992. *Broken Waves: A History of the Fiji Islands in the Twentieth Century*. Honolulu: University of Hawai'i Press.

Landweer, L.M. and P. Unseth 2012. An introduction to language use in Melanesia. *International Journal of the Sociology of Language* 214:1–3.

Lawson, S. 2010. 'The Pacific Way' as postcolonial discourse: towards a reassessment. *The Journal of Pacific History* 45(3):297–314.

Lilo, G.D. 2013 MSG: our place in the sun in Oceania. Statement by the Prime Minister, Honourable Gordon Darcy Lilo, for the 19th MSG Leaders' Summit, 21 June 2013, Plenary Session, Leaders Retreat, SPC, Noumea, New Caledonia: http://goo.gl/K8m88y (accessed 27 July 2013).

London, J. 2003. *The Cruise of the Snark* (introd. A. Brandt). Washington DC: National Geographic Society.

MacQueen, N. 1989. Sharpening the spearhead: subregionalism in Melanesia. *Pacific Studies* 12(2):33–52.

Malinowski, B. 1920. Kula: the circulating exchange of valuable in archipelagoes of Eastern New Guinea. *Man* 20:97–105.

Mara, R.S.K. 1997. *The Pacific Way: A Memoir*. Honolulu: University of Hawai'i Press.

May, R.J. 2003 'Arc of instability'? Melanesia in the early 2000s. State, Society and Governance in Melanesia Project, Australian National University / Macmillan Brown Centre for Pacific Studies, University of Canterbury, *Occasional Paper* 4.

——— 2011. The Melanesian Spearhead Group: testing Pacific islands solidarity. *Australia Strategic Policy Institute (ASPI), Policy Analysis* 74.

Meleisea, M. 1980 *O Tama Uli: Melanesians in Western Samoa*. Suva: Institute of Pacific Studies, University of the South Pacific.

Moore, C. 2005 *Happy Isles in Crisis: The Historical Causes for a Failing State in Solomon Islands*. Canberra: Asia Pacific Press.

Nanau, G.L. 2011 The wantok system as a socioeconomic and political network in Melanesia. *OMNES: The Journal of Multicultural Society* 2(1):31–5.

Narokobi, B. 1980. *The Melanesian Way* (ed. H. Olela). Port Moresby: Institute of Papua New Guinea Studies.

Pacific Scoop, Auckland University of Technology, Pacific Media Centre. pacific.
    scoop.co.nz/2010/06/wansolwara-academic-rues-islander-racism-against-
    melanesians (accessed 27 July 2013).

Premdas, R., J. Steeves and P. Larmour 1984. The western breakaway movement in
    the Solomon Islands. *Pacific Studies* 7(2):34–67.

Reilly, B. 2000. The Africanisation of the South Pacific. *Australian Journal of
    International Affairs* 54(3):261–8.

Reynolds, H. 2008. *Nowhere People*. Sydney: Penguin Books.

Regan, A. 2010. *Light Intervention: Lessons from Bougainville*. Washington DC:
    United States Institute of Peace Press.

Rochette, M. 2003. Dumont d'Urville's phrenologist: Dumoutier and the aesthetics of
    races (trans. I. Ollivier). *Journal of Pacific History* 38(2):251–68.

Sahlins, M. 1963. Poor man, rich man, big-man, chief: political types in Melanesia and
    Polynesia. *Comparative Studies in Societies and History* 5: 285–303.

Said, E. 1978. *Orientalism*. New York: Vintage Books.

Samoa Observer, March 2009.

Smith, B. 1960. *European Vision and the South Pacific 1768–1850: A Study in the
    History of Art and Ideas*. London: Oxford University Press.

Spurr, D. 1993. *The Rhetoric of Empire: Colonial Discourse in Journalism, Travel
    Writing and Imperial Administration*. Durham, NC: Duke University Press.

Stella, R.T. 2007. *Imagining the Other: The Representation of the Papua New Guinea
    Subject*. Pacific Islands Monograph Series 20. Honolulu: University of
    Hawai'i Press.

Tamaira, M. 2010. From full dusk to full tusk: reimagining the 'dusky maiden' through
    the visual arts. *The Contemporary Pacific* 22(1):1–35.

Tcherkézoff, S. 2003. A long and unfortunate voyage toward the invention of the
    Melanesia/Polynesia opposition (1595–1832). In 'Dumont d'Urville's Oceanic
    Provinces: Fundamental Precepts or Arbitrary Constructs?', G.Clark (ed.),
    175–96. Special Issue, *Journal of Pacific History* 38(2).

The Independent 2007. Strange island: Pacific tribesmen come to study Britain. www.
    independent.co.uk/news/uk/this-britain/strange-island-pacific-tribesmen-
    come-to-study-britain-401461.html (accessed 22 March, 2009).

Theroux, P. 1992. *The Happy Isles of Oceania: Paddling the Pacific*. New York:
    Ballantine Books.

Thomas, N. 1994. *Colonialism's Culture: Anthropology, Travel and Government*.
    Princeton, NJ: Princeton University Press.

——— 1997. Melanesians and Polynesians: typifications inside and outside
    anthropology. In *In Oceania: Visions, Artefacts, Histories*, 133–55. Durham:
    Duke University Press.

——— 2012. 'We are still Papuans': A 2006 interview with Epeli Hau'ofa. *The
    Contemporary Pacific* 24(1):120–32.

Wesley-Smith, T. 2008. Altered state: regional intervention and the politics of state failure in Oceania. In *Intervention and State-Building in the Pacific: The Political Legitimacy of 'Co-operative Intervention'*, G. Fry and T. Kabutaulaka (eds), 37–53. Manchester: Manchester University Press.

Winduo, S. 2000. Unwriting Oceania: the repositioning of Pacific writers scholars within a folk narrative space. *New Literature History* 31(3):599–613.

Ziegler, R. 1990. The kula: social order, barter and ceremonial exchange. In *Social Institutions: their Emergence, Maintenance and Effects*, M. Hechter, K.-D. Opp and R. Wippler (eds), 141–70. New York: Gruyter, Inc.

Tarcisius Kabutaulaka is Associate Professor at the Center for Pacific Islands Studies, University of Hawai'i at Mānoa.

Imagining the state as a vehicle for cultural survival in Oceania

✳

RALPH REGENVANU

As a former Director of the Vanuatu Cultural Centre (1995–2006), and since 2008 a Member of Parliament, I have been engaged for some years in trying to have culture 'mainstreamed' into national development on a policy level. This chapter provides an account of this engagement as a background to my entry into politics. This is a story that has a much longer history than my personal involvement and is essentially a tale of decolonization – a process that is still continuing for many countries like Vanuatu that have gained recent political independence. More fundamentally, however, it is a story of cultural heritage as an important tool in this decolonization process, of cultural heritage as a source for an alternative vision for the development of the country. This is not really a new vision, but one rooted in a concern about the alienation of land from communities and, hence, their cultural survival. Hopefully, with the benefit of hindsight, what will emerge is a better-informed vision built by a broader range of groups than was involved before. This, then, is also the story of the building of a coalition for change in Vanuatu.

The Vanuatu Cultural Centre

It starts with the Vanuatu Cultural Centre (the 'VKS'[1]), the country's national heritage institution, which consists of the National Museum, the National Library, the National Archives, the National Film and Sound Archive, the National Cultural and Historic Sites Register, the Women's Culture Programme and the Young Peoples Programme. An important aspect of the programmes at VKS is the focus on the living cultures of Vanuatu, comprising the majority of the population who live in the traditional economy. A tool that has proved particularly effective in implementing this focus is the

Fieldworkers Programme, which has been going on for over 30 years, and involves rural ni-Vanuatu in audio and audiovisual documentation of aspects of their cultures.

The fieldworkers programme, which started in the 1970s, was designed to assist participating communities to become managers of their own cultural heritage. People are selected by their own communities to become, in effect, liaison officers with the VKS. They receive training in basic ethnographic documentation techniques to enable them to conduct basic research, documenting sites and oral traditions, and to promote culture by organizing festivals and revitalizing ceremonies that have been lost from practised (but not living) memory. Documenting languages, working on language revival and promoting the inclusion of indigenous languages in schools are another important focus of the VKS fieldworkers. While undertaking this varied work, the fieldworkers are at the same time important entry points for the VKS, as the national institution, into the more than 100 language/cultural communities throughout Vanuatu. They have become, in effect, extensions of the VKS – like our family in the islands, allowing us to enter a community using a family relationship that already exists. Currently, there are over 60 men and 50 women fieldworkers. The aim of the VKS is to recruit one man and one woman for each of the language/cultural groups in the country, which is seen as the best solution for a single national institution dealing with Vanuatu's cultural diversity. The goal is to encourage groups to determine their own priorities for the management of their cultures through genuine community participation.

The Traditional Money Banks Project
An exciting new idea which came from the work of one particular fieldworker, James Teslo from the island of Malekula, has led the VKS in a direction that could never have been expected. As part of his effort to organize revitalization of certain activities of his traditional culture, Teslo found that he was frustrated because of a lack of pigs. In Malekula and throughout Vanuatu (and, indeed, in most areas of Oceania) pigs are very important for use in traditional ceremonies; for example, marriages, achieving chiefly titles, reconciliation ceremonies etc. What Teslo found was that when trying to revitalize ceremonies, there were simply not enough pigs available to perform them. According to him, this has historical reasons. In the past, missionaries encouraged their converts to resettle from the interior of the larger islands down to coastal areas, where they had established their mission stations. This led to many changes in local ways of life. The importance of traditional ceremonies declined, and people have become involved in planting and

harvesting cash crops rather than engaging in production in the traditional economy, which includes pigs.

Dealing with this problem became a priority for Teslo, as pigs are essential to cultural revitalization. The VKS, therefore, started what was initially called the 'pig bank' project, which involved setting up a 'stock' of pigs that fieldworkers could access to do their ceremonies. The idea was that it would operate in the same way as was used to deal with a shortage of pigs traditionally – pigs would be loaned out and eventually given back to the lender when required for their own ceremonies, but with interest. This 'interest' would take the form of bigger pigs and/or longer tusks.[2]

In my time as the VKS Director, my team and I began to think about how we might develop a project to provide more pigs. We soon realized that for other areas of the country, and for women as well as men, there were other items also needed in traditional ceremonies, so we widened the focus to include all traditional wealth items – among other things, shell money, mats, yams and kava. We also realized that it was necessary to deal with the way people today use cash to meet some of their basic needs, that is, to purchase certain items for daily use and to pay for government services, primarily charges for health and education. We therefore partnered with the Vanuatu Credit Union League to provide advice on how individuals and communities could be assisted in managing their cash. Another key strategic partner was the Malvatumauri (National Council of Chiefs), which has the constitutional mandate for the preservation of culture. Tim Curtis, an anthropologist who had just finished working in this area of Malekula with Teslo, assisted us in applying for UNESCO funding for the project that came to be called the Traditional Money Banks Project.

The project commenced in June 2004 and had as its primary objective the maintenance and revitalization of living traditional and cultural practices. At the same time, the project hoped to be able to stimulate the generation of cash incomes for the rural populations that produced traditional wealth items. The Traditional Money Banks Project, therefore, reflected the current context in which we are living, where ni-Vanuatu require cash to meet needs in their daily lives and at the same time want to preserve, revitalize and transmit our living culture to future generations. The idea was to encourage people who were already involved in the production of various forms of traditional wealth to continue to produce such items. Production was dropping off, and it was hoped that this trend could be reversed by encouraging people primarily involved in the cash economy, like myself living in town on a salary, to access traditional valuables and use them for ceremonial activities – to facilitate the exchange of traditional wealth items for cash. By linking the formal and informal sectors in this way, it was hoped that people involved in traditional spheres of life would be able to increase their cash income, while at the same time encouraging the revival of traditional practices among those primarily involved in the cash economy.

The first activity of the Traditional Money Banks Project was to find out what the actual situation was with regard to the production of traditional wealth items. A survey, which was completed at the end of 2004, found that in some areas the production was robust and ongoing; the skills involved were alive and being transmitted and people were using traditional wealth items in their ceremonies. In other areas, the know-how was still there but the skills had begun to go out of practice. The main reason for this change appears to have been the need for people to pay for state health and educational services, which required more focus on the production of cash crops as a source of income. Nevertheless, even in these areas, the survey found that there was a strong interest in revitalizing the production of traditional wealth items and their use in traditional ceremonies.

The issue of 'development'

At this stage we started to see that this was more than just a cultural-heritage issue. There was a need to address broader policies on development. Why was the rural population being forced to use cash that they did not have to pay for school fees? They were being told that they had to send the kids to school, but not being provided with the means to earn the necessary cash required. My awareness of this problem had been growing for some time. I was working at the VKS, which was a part of the state system – a very small unit within the government with a miniscule budget, trying to preserve and revitalize traditional practices. At the same time, the majority of the government's efforts were concerned with making cash and – most significantly from our perspective – educating our kids in Western cultural forms, which were eroding the very traditional cultural systems and perspectives we were trying to promote in our work. So the obvious question I began to ask myself was, why is this happening? Why is the government giving us money to do something that the rest of the government is trying to get rid of? This was especially puzzling as we found that most ni-Vanuatu were very interested in and concerned about our revitalization work, and saw that it was something they wanted to teach their children – to stop the erosion of their traditional culture and values. This led me to ask, why was the development model being promoted for the county not reflective of community values and concerns? What, indeed, was this development agenda that our government had embraced?

The development agenda is, of course, very familiar and widely promoted around the world. According to the United Nations, Vanuatu is a Least

Developed Country (LDC), which is based on the calculation of the Gross
Domestic Product (GDP), that is, the amount of cash produced per person
per day. This designation is due to the fact that the vast majority of ni-Vanuatu
(nearly 80 per cent of the population) live in rural areas and produce most of
what they require in their lives through subsistence agriculture. The production
of cash crops is only a minor activity and, therefore, they have very low cash
incomes. The recent development agenda for Vanuatu includes private-sector
growth, downsizing of the public services, and integration of the country into
the regional and world economy, with an emphasis on 'free trade' and the goal
of joining the World Trade Organisation.[3] The primary target, above all others,
is increased economic growth defined in monetary terms. The government
of Vanuatu has, therefore, adopted the all-too-familiar, standard, orthodox
form of development, which measures success in terms of monetary growth
of the economy. What is not allowed for in this model is recognition of the
values and the cultural heritage of the great majority of the people, which they
continue to live every day. This is deemed unimportant, despite the amazing
cultural diversity and strength of traditional culture of our country. Vanuatu is
seen instead as in need – lacking or wanting 'development'.

We saw, therefore, two conflicting policy directions emerging in the
country. One was government-sponsored economic growth – a response to
the propaganda of the inevitability of globalization and a small but emerging
educated middle class with Western tastes; the other was the promotion
of the existing traditional society and economy in which the vast majority
of the population were participating. The discussion in this chapter of
'cultural survival' is about an agenda which recognizes that our indigenous
cultural values, knowledge systems, economy and practices have provided
a sustainable livelihood for our people for thousands of years. Likewise, it
promotes the idea that these systems and values will continue to provide a
better basis and framework for maintaining a sustainable livelihood for our
people in the future than many of the introduced European-derived capital-
oriented systems that we have experienced over the past 150 years.

This cultural-survival agenda also recognizes that despite indigenous
people taking over political power at independence in 1980, the introduced
governance system (the state) continues to erode and displace our indigenous
systems – a process that is happening faster and deeper in Vanuatu as
globalization accelerates. This does not mean the wholesale rejection of
change, but we now need to ensure that the introduced system engages
appropriately with our indigenous systems so that the transmission of our own
cultural values, knowledge and economic and traditional practices continues
and is rejuvenated in the future. This is absolutely necessary if cultural survival
is to be possible. A hypothesis began to form in my mind: if it is the introduced

governance system that is the prime facilitator of this process of erosion and displacement, does it not follow that it may be possible to use the same governance system as a vehicle for cultural survival in Vanuatu? This was one of the principal rationales that led to my involvement in politics.

Expanding goals

The progressive implementation of the Traditional Money Banks Project, therefore, inevitably made us think in broader terms. One of the first things we did was to organize what we called the 'Workshop to recognize and promote the traditional economy as the basis for achieving national self-reliance'. The title of the workshop was deliberately chosen; it was the first time we were talking about 'traditional economy' and about the goal of national self-reliance. The Malvatumauri (the National Council of Chiefs) hosted the workshop, which involved a wide range of participants, including chiefs and community leaders from throughout Vanuatu, provincial government officers, people from different government departments, and representatives from NGOs. The President of the Malvatumauri officially opened the workshop, and the Deputy Prime Minister closed it. The Minister of Education also gave a talk at the closing ceremony. Our aim was to bring these key policy-makers and the state into the programme to try and encourage a stronger feeling by them of responsibility for the issues at hand.

The workshop produced a set of recommendations – an action plan for recognizing and promoting the traditional economy. Included among them was a call for the National Council Of Chiefs to stop the use of cash in all traditional ceremonies; for example, in marriage and death ceremonies and, in particular, with regard to bride price. Many people were using cash and cash crops in these traditional ceremonies, and the aim was to try to stop that from happening as the practice degraded the traditional cultural value of the ceremonies. The workshop also agreed the necessity of identifying the traditional wealth items used in these exchanges, and of using them again. It was encouraging to see the National Council Of Chiefs declare a ban on the use of cash in the payment of bride price the following month.

A further meeting, at the national level, followed-up on the initial workshop and was entitled the 'National Summit for Self Reliance and Sustainability'. This was a deliberate move away from talking about cultural heritage to talking solely about development. We were, in a sense, creating a Trojan horse within the state system by using the terminology of development to introduce cultural-heritage and cultural-survival agendas at the highest state policy level. The 'National Summit on Self-reliance and Sustainability' meeting produced a further set of recommendations for policy and other initiatives to support the broad objectives of the project. This set of recommendations was

called 'The Vanuatu National Self-Reliance Strategy 2020' – '2020' referring
both to 20/20 vision and the date by which these goals should be achieved.
The recommendations included:

* that research be done on a national model for a traditional governance
  system that could be introduced to compliment the Western parliamentary
  system currently being used;
* that the National Self-Reliance Strategy to be adopted as one of the main
  policy platforms for national development, alongside 'The Priorities and
  Actions Agenda' (PAA);
* that there be a national land summit to address and resolve issues relating to
  the increasing alienation of land from customary tenure;
* that alternative indicators of well-being be developed, to reflect the reality
  of people's lives not measured by GDP, and to look to Bhutan with its gross
  national happiness index as a model;
* that measures be taken to improve food security; limiting the importation
  of processed foods and boosting consumption of local foods, with a focus
  on feeding urban areas;
* that traditional resource management be reinforced as the basis of national
  environmental management; to use traditional systems of resource
  management including restricting access to certain biological resources as
  opposed to Western models of national parks and protected areas;
* that it be made possible to pay school fees and medical consultation fees
  in traditional wealth items (which are readily accessible to rural people)
  as opposed to cash, and for this policy to be implemented nation-wide by
  government;
* that the year 2007 be declared the 'Year of the Traditional Economy' to
  raise awareness of the importance of the traditional economy to national
  development.

Positive developments

Following the Summit, many of these recommendations began to be acted
upon – things started to happen at a policy level, or at least the 'right'
statements began to be made by government. The National Lands Summit
happened in the following year, September 2006 – a major event, preceded by
consultations throughout the islands to talk about what people wanted from
land policies. People came to Port Vila from every island, and were involved
in serious debate for a whole week. They discussed issues like the weaknesses
of the current leasing system – particularly, the abuse of ministerial powers to
lease customary land. The summit produced twenty recommendations that
were later endorsed by the nation's executive arm, the Council of Ministers.

In 2006, the government also declared the following year to be 'The Year of the Traditional Economy' and a working group was set up, including representatives of the Malvatumauri, government departments, NGOs, women's groups, youth groups and the VKS, to develop an activity and policy matrix to set the objectives of the 'Year' and plot the expected progress.[4] The matrix incorporated recommendations from all of the preceding forums that had taken place, and included additional ideas, such as using physical planning as a tool to assist cultural survival. We felt it was important for communities themselves to be involved in deciding, for example, what resources were needed for cultural activities, what land should be made available to people from outside the community, and for what purposes leases of customary land should be entered into. Likewise, we wanted to encourage communities to start engaging with issues such as population growth and planning.

Activities, therefore, began to proceed on two fronts: on a national policy level, to get the activities of the matrix implemented as much as possible, and on a community level, to raise awareness about these recommendations. A priority of the awareness campaign was to promote the recommendations derived from the first action plan: to recognize and emphasize the traditional economy with the aim of encouraging the expanded production of traditional wealth items and their use. The aim was to popularize the concept of traditional economy by promoting the production of traditional foods, traditional exchanges and the replacement of cash transactions by traditional wealth items.

The concept of the traditional economy came to be the focus of our effort to re-set the country's development strategy. In its broadest definition, an 'economy' means the way a society organizes and sustains its members, manages and shares resources between them, and feeds, clothes and accommodates them. The 'economy' instils in its members the values required to keep society going – values related to governance. The 80 per cent of ni-Vanuatu who live in rural villages with other members of their traditional extended families on land that has been theirs under traditional tenure systems for centuries (their ancestral land) are able to satisfy most of their food requirements using traditional methods of production, and distribute rights to land and sea resources as they see fit. They speak their traditional languages and are governed by traditional leaders to a far greater extent than by institutions of the state. It is clear that traditional values and institutions underpin the operation of the 'economy', and that while the cash economy does exist, it is the traditional economy that is dominant in Vanuatu. Its benefits are enormous: we have no homelessness, there is no problem with hunger and there is a general level of peace and social harmony throughout the country that would be the envy of many in the so-called 'developed world'.

After we began to promote the concept of the traditional economy, it did not take long to see a response. In 2006, the report of an 'economic opportunities fact finding mission' sponsored by NZAID and AUSAID – the aid arms of the Australian and New Zealand governments respectively – stated, that

> [Vanuatu's] most understated productive sector is the massive response
> within its traditional (island) economy to a rapidly growing population....
> Although growth of Vanuatu's GDP has not been spectacular, it's traditional,
> largely non-monetarised, rural economy has successfully supported a 90%
> increase in the rural population in the 26 years since independence (from
> about 95,000 in 1980 to an estimated 180,000 now).
>
> (Bazeley and Mullen 2006:7)

We were greatly encouraged to see the aid donors and others beginning to adopt the terminology and take on board our perception of the economic reality in Vanuatu.

However, although the Vanuatu government had declared its support for this new vision by declaring 2007 as the Year of the Traditional Economy, the level of actual implementation was disappointing. We worked on this project to establish frameworks within the state to support the objectives of cultural survival, and had been able to convince the government to declare the Year of the Traditional Economy for which we also developed the policy matrix to support it. Nevertheless, this seemed to happen on the sidelines of the macro-economic policy debate. The concept of the traditional economy remained barely a footnote in the discussion and data related to the country's economic growth.

Politics

By 2008, it had become clear that we were banging our heads against a wall by pursuing conventional policy advocacy through the bureaucracy. I decided that the only way forward – to get our objectives realized – was to go to the next level and become actively involved myself in the political process. That is what led to my decision to stand in the elections that year. It was clear the executive and central agencies of the government were unable to take on board this agenda, despite the fact that we had done everything necessary to work within the bureaucratic process to affect policy change, and that their earlier pronouncements of support had no substance.

The question was, however, whether or not it would be possible via national politics to achieve policies for cultural survival. Would it be possible for the state to be concerned with something other than generating money to sustain itself? When I decided to go into politics, I consulted with all the partners we had been working with, and everyone agreed that this was what I should do. They felt that we had 'hit the ceiling' in our advocacy work and the only option was, therefore, to attempt direct political action to achieve our agenda. It was, in fact, the President and the CEO of the National Council of Women who finally convinced me to stand for election in Port Vila, saying that women would support me. They did, indeed, give me their support, but the campaign was actually launched at the VKS. While the issue of cultural heritage was a key element in my campaign platform, the campaign team also emphasized the issues of anti-corruption and transparency in government. We realized that it was also necessary to promote these (as well as the strengthening of our cultural heritage) in order to bring about the introduction of policies to safeguard the traditional economy. Many of the recommendations from our earlier cultural-heritage work were contained in the campaign platform, but we felt we needed more; we needed to promote an alternative model for leadership, in contrast to that displayed by many of the Members of Parliament we had got used to. Our main campaign slogan therefore became, 'To demonstrate a new way of providing leadership as an MP and national leader'. The key policies listed in my campaign materials were: increased participation by ni-Vanuatu in the cash economy, devolved governance to communities, increased participation of chiefs, women, churches and youth in decision making, greater enforcement of the law and enhanced transparency and accountability in state spending.

During the campaign all the independent candidates formed a block, though unfortunately none of them were elected except me. However, our efforts to create a block of like-minded politicians did have the effect of forcing us to agree on a set of policies that we said would guide us in our efforts to form a coalition in government, once the election was over. That was my first lesson in coalition-building within national politics, an activity which unfortunately has come to occupy way too much of my time, but which is a reality of politics in Vanuatu.

Despite our high hopes, the result of the election was a great disappointment. We had campaigned against the existing parties, saying that they were incompetent and had failed to deliver, but all the major parties had gained seats. The election turned out to be a great vote against change, except in Port Vila, where I got the highest number of votes among the six winning candidates.

In my very first Parliament session I tabled a private members bill to remove the power of the Minister of Lands to sign leases on behalf of customary landowners when there was a dispute over land ownership – a long-standing grievance among customary landowners that was a key recommendation of the National Land Summit. Despite the government being comprised of the same parties that less than 48-months prior to the election had endorsed the recommendations of the National Land Summit, this bill failed to win support in Parliament, simply because I was in opposition. It was a rude awakening for me to realize the blatant oppositional nature of parliamentary politics in Vanuatu.

In the various parliamentary sessions after the 2008 election, I regularly raised questions about the 'economic growth' and 'development' agenda being pursued by the government, particularly in the context of what effect such policies have on issues such as ni-Vanuatu alienation from their land and conditions of employment. I renewed the critique within parliament of the government's seemingly inexorable tendency to spend on itself – to give its functionaries more allowances and cars and perks. In order to meet an ever-increasing budget for services to an ever increasing population, the government has continued to promote policies that have the effect of incorporating more people into the cash economy in order to generate more tax revenues. In addition, seldom did a month go by that some new story of corruption and mismanagement was not revealed. At the same time, requests for support of important policies affecting the cultural survival of the grassroots population were regularly ignored. For example, there was widespread support among ni-Vanuatu for vernacular education – for our children to learn their own languages in schools. We want them to learn their culture, and yet the government refused to fund the implementation of policies to achieve this goal. Proposals to hire language experts at the village level to teach traditions, and the development of spelling systems for vernacular languages and related teaching materials were ignored. Moreover, funding for the VKS and Malvatumauri's efforts to protect and promote traditional knowledge remained weak.

Postscript: reflections and progress

I resigned from my directorship of the Vanuatu Cultural Centre at the end of 2006 not primarily to enter politics, but to be able to fully focus on my law degree. I did already then have the idea of entering politics, but the definite decision to do so was only made in 2008. My motivation for becoming a parliamentarian was founded in the efforts described above to advocate for more broad-based development policies for the country. We – the VKS and in particular its community-grounded fieldworkers – knew there were better development strategies that could be pursued that would ensure the maintenance and promotion of the cultures of Vanuatu while creating sustainable and inclusive development for the country's rural-based majority. We felt strongly that the policies so far pursued by the government were having the opposite effect. From our involvement in larger networks that included chiefs (in particular the National Council of Chiefs), VKS fieldworkers, women (in particular the National Council of Women), NGOs and many other stakeholders, we had, since around 2003, come up with a number of policy proposals to the government, including:

* ✳ 'Recommendations of the Workshop to Recognise and Promote the Traditional Economy as the Basis for Achieving National Self Reliance' (2005)
* ✳ 'The Vanuatu National Self-Reliance Strategy 2020' (2005)
* ✳ 'The Resolutions of the Land Summit' (2006)
* ✳ 'The Year of the Traditional Economy Matrix' (2007)

All these proposals instituted through the VKS network included recommendations to the government on what policies should be implemented and which laws needed to be changed. The proposals were forwarded to the government with the specific request that the government consider implementing them.

By the start of 2008 the government was still not implementing our proposals – that is, the government was not doing what, as we saw it, the majority of the Vanuatu population had asked it to do. So I thought, 'Well, if the existing political parties and leaders are not going to implement our proposals for development, then we ourselves have to get into parliament and into government for implementation to be possible.' That is why I got into politics, to seek the implementation of the policies and legislative changes that we had for so long requested of the government without result.

In 2008 I had been elected to parliament as an independent candidate for the Vanuatu capital Port Vila. Immediately we were faced with the question of how to build the necessary numbers to affect change in parliament when we did not have a political party, and we quickly realized that it was impossible. The next challenge was to build a party that could avoid the pitfalls experienced by other parties. In November 2010, in preparation for the 2012 general election, we launched our own political party, with the Bislama name of the *Graon mo Jastis Pati* (GJP) (The Land and Justice Party).

In the 2012 elections the GJP won four seats, including my own. This was an amazingly good result for a brand new political party, and made us the fourth largest party in the highly fragmented 52-seat parliament (as a result of the subsequent defection of a number of MPs from the parties they were elected under, and the defection of one MP to the GJP, one year after the election we had become the second largest party in Parliament). Although we initially were in the opposition, within six months of the election a successful vote of no confidence put us into government. The GJP's principal demand for supporting the new government was that I was to be given the Lands Ministry portfolio. Within one year of becoming Lands Minister, we had changed the

Constitution to give the power to determine ownership of customary land to local-level traditional customary institutions called *nakamals*, stripping this power from the common-law courts, and had changed the land legislation to implement all of the resolutions of the Land Summit. Our 2005 recommendation to create alternative indicators of well-being to recognize the traditional economy has also been achieved, with new indicators that define well-being in terms of what is important to ni-Vanuatu now included in the national accounts. The government is also now working on its development strategy for the post-2015 (post-Millennium Development Goals) era and has decided that the new National Sustainable Development Plan will have culture as its foundation, underpinning and directing the three conventional pillars of economy, society and environment. The new culture-based indicators will be pivotal to measuring the success of the Plan.

Now we are preparing for the 2016 elections, to continue to push this agenda of cultural survival at the highest policy level within the state. It may yet be possible to prove that, for Vanuatu at least, the state can be a vehicle for cultural survival.

Notes

1   In Vanuatu's national language Bislama, a form of pidgin English, the Vanuatu Cultural Centre translates as 'Vanuatu Kaljoral Senta'. The acronym 'VKS' is how the Centre is commonly known in the country, and is how I will be referring to the Centre in this chapter.

2   Tusked pigs are unique to Vanuatu and are the most valuable wealth item in parts of the country.

3   As a point of interest, I was the first Minister of State in Vanuatu to ever vote against my own government, and it was on the issue of Vanuatu's accession to the WTO in 2011 (I opposed the bill and was duly sacked for my action).

4   A detailed discussion of the Year of the Traditional Economy and its wider context and subsequent developments is given in Regenvanu and Geismar 2011.

References

Bazeley, P. and B. Mullen 2006. *Vanuatu: Economic Opportunities Fact-Finding Mission*. Canberra: Department of Foreign Affairs and Trade.

Regenvanu, R. and H. Geismar 2011. Re-imagining the economy in Vanuatu. An interview with Ralph Regenvanu. In *Made in Oceania: Social Movements, Cultural Heritage and the State in the Pacific*, E. Hviding and K.M. Rio (eds), 31–50. Wantage: Sean Kingston Publishing.

Ralph Regenvanu is a Member of the Vanuatu National Parliament.

Index

www.ingramcontent.com/pod-product-compliance
Lightning Source LLC
Chambersburg PA
CBHW070842300326

41935CB00039B/1367